Planting Churches in Muslim Cities

Planting Churches in Muslim Cities

A Team Approach

Greg Livingstone

BAKER BOOK HOUSE
Grand Rapids, Michigan 49516

Published by Baker Book House
P.O. Box 6287, Grand Rapids, Michigan 49516–6287

Printed in the United States of America

Library of Congress Cataloging-in-Publication Data

Livingstone, Greg.
    Planting churches in Muslim cities : a team approach / Greg Livingstone.
        p.   cm.
    Includes bibliographical references and index.
    ISBN 0-8010-5682-9
    1. Missions to Muslims. 2. Converts from Islam—Religious life.
I. Title
BV2625.L585 1993   93-6623
266'.08'82971—dc20

To
George Verwer, Jr.,
my mentor and friend of 34 years
who was used by God to get me to
"give up my small ambitions,"
and gave me in their place
a magnificent obsession:
to change church history in the Muslim world!

and

the pioneers of the 1990s
who are, or soon will be,
harvesting on the last frontier for the Great Commission.
Also, with deep gratitude
for past pioneers who have struggled
to see Muslims rescued from the Kingdom of Darkness
since Henry Martyn laid down his life
in Turkey one hundred years ago!

Contents

Preface   9
Introduction   11

Part 1   *The Challenge of Planting Churches in Muslim Cities*

1. One Billion Muslims: What Does God Have in Mind?   25
2. Past Failure and Future Prospects   35
3. Instances of Church Growth among Muslims   55

Part 2   *The Prerequisites for Planting Churches in Muslim Cities*

4. The Change Agent's Role   65
5. Making Critical Choices   87
6. Establishing Significant Relationships   117
7. Proclaiming the Message   139

Part 3   *The Task of Planting Churches in Muslim Cities*

8. Characteristics of a Church Planted   169
9. Two Case Studies   189
10. A Proposed Urban Church Planting Strategy   205
11. Finishing the Task   225

Appendix A: *Interview Questions Put to Church Planters in Muslim Cities*   233
Appendix B: *Steps to Conversion*   235
Bibliography   239
Index   267

Preface

Among many societies of the Muslim world the church of Jesus Christ has become extinct. Or it is a tiny group in isolation. Among many Muslim peoples, it has been prevented from ever getting rooted! Hostile governments and influential Islamic leaders blockade Muslim peoples and cities from learning about or taking the claims of Christ seriously. Wherever a commitment to Islam is more than a veneer, congregations of former Muslims are extremely few.

Why is this so? Why are the Muslims the exception to the success the church of Jesus Christ is experiencing worldwide? What is the God of the Bible intending to do about it? How is it possible to establish the first congregations of redeemed Muslims where today they do not exist?

This book seeks to answer these questions. It will explain how several Muslims, as part of a personal network, can be baptized at the same time, creating an immediate support group for such a radically unpopular behavior. It stipulates how Muslim seekers will become followers of Jesus as Messiah when they become acquainted with an already ongoing fellowship of former Muslims whom they respect and who whet their appetite.

You will learn what it takes to develop, nurture, and be a catalyst for such voluntary associations. Also, the requirements for church forming, demands placing, and the supervision of a team of appropriately gifted adults in the same area of a Muslim city, for probably at least a ten-year period. This book may help you find your part in this God-glorifying endeavor.

In my own mission work I have absorbed information from over one hundred missionaries who work in the cities of Africa, the Arab World, Turkey, Iran, Afghanistan, the Indian subcontinent, China, and Central and Southeast Asia. Based in Uttar Pradesh, India, Beirut, Lebanon, and

Brussels, my wife Sally and I have been associated with nearly everyone directly identified with church planting among Muslims in North Africa and the Middle East since 1963, and in Asia since 1983. I have a wide awareness and sense of partnership with Muslim church planting efforts. We spent years among Muslims in cities as diverse as Brussels and London in Europe, Beirut and Cairo in the Middle East, and Allahabad, Bombay, and Hyderabad in the Indian subcontinent. From those bases, we advised work in Pakistan, Iran, Turkey, Israel, and Afghanistan.

As the General Director of Frontiers, I continue to "coach" (as field advisor) missionaries in North Africa, the Middle East, the Arab Gulf, the Muslim republics of the former Soviet Union, China, the Indian subcontinent, and Southeast Asia. Since 1977 I have been a participant-observer of over 400 missionaries, tent-makers, and nationals seeking to plant churches among Muslims in the dominantly Muslim cities of the world.

Both on site and in their sending countries, I have focused on solving the problems described in this book with God's servants: missionaries, tent-makers, and nationals. Through my Islamic studies at the Near East School of Theology in Beirut, Lebanon, and doctoral studies at the School of Intercultural Studies at Biola University, I have sought to integrate theological, sociological, historical, and anthropological insights with the church planting task.

I have sought to illustrate my theories with the work of practitioners who have been working in 30 Muslim cities over the last 25 years. As I continue to receive reports from these church planting efforts every month, I realize this study can have only tentative conclusions. Hopefully it will, however, amplify and accelerate exploration until vital congregations of transformed Muslims become a reality in every city of the world with a significant Muslim population.

This book has taken over five years to produce. During that span, Mrs. Ginny Williamson and Mrs. Betty Ann Stevenson were incredibly patient and persevering to squeeze in the typing of bits and pieces from dictation, as I sought to put it together while serving as General Director of Frontiers.

I must also express gratitude to Drs. Judy Lingenfelter, Marguerite Kraft, and Phil Parshall who as my doctoral committee were a constant "reality check"!

Introduction

The church of Jesus Christ has been triumphant in the sense that it is at least the nominal faith of 1.7 billion men and women worldwide (Barrett 1988). Tragically, we have until recently failed to detect that, in fact, the church of Jesus Christ among large segments of the world's population has become nearly extinct, a tiny group in hiding, or has been prevented from ever getting rooted.

Commonly known as one of the world's great religions, Islam blockades many hundreds of people groups from ever taking the claims of Christ seriously. Where a commitment to Islam is more than a veneer, congregations of former Muslims are extremely few.

Some congregations constituted by former Muslims do exist among rural peoples in East and Central Java, Bangladesh, Burkino Faso, Malawi, and some other sub-Saharan African states. Closer observation, however, would likely reveal that these former Muslims were 90 percent animistic and very nominally Muslim before becoming "Christians."

Yet it is a foundational premise of Christianity that its adherents are to establish communities of believers among every *ethnos* (people group, cultural grouping) on earth (Matt. 28:19–20). In recent years, missiologists have identified major ethnic groupings, such as the Kurds, the Malays, the Berbers of Morocco, Albanian Muslims of Yugoslavia, and even entire Muslim countries including Mauritania, Egypt, Syria, Malaysia, and Iraq where established congregations of former Muslims with their own national leadership still do not exist! Nor are there significant numbers of former Muslims in existing churches of minority people with a non-Muslim background.

This study focuses especially on the approximately 400 million Muslims who are living in Muslim dominated cities across North Africa, the Middle East, and Central, South, and Southeast Asia, whose people are still without their first church, and how we can change all that!

Assuming Jesus Christ's prognosis as recorded in Matthew 28:19 (i.e., that his disciples in turn will "make disciples of all nations") infers these would-be disciples should be gathered in congregations with their own national leadership, then it is fully within the purposes of God to see such congregations come into existence also among Muslims in the cities where Islam is the dominant worldview.

Why are churches still extremely few among Muslims, especially in the urban areas of Muslim countries? What is preventing it from happening? What variables are relevant to seeing congregations of Christ-loyal Muslims become reality?

These critical issues demand relevant research by missiologists and field workers who will identify the human factors. God's wisdom will lead to the conversion and congregating of urban Muslim people into the church of Jesus Christ. Since 1975, there has been an encouraging rise of interest among Christians to establish new indigenous congregations in the growing dominantly Muslim cities from Agadir, Morocco, to Agra, Uttar Pradesh. But whether mission-minded volunteers become effective change agents among Muslim people—who historically have been resistant to conversion—may well depend on them having access to information that will guide them through the process of church growth.

This textbook proposes to help fill that information gap. In any given, dominantly Muslim city there exists a large number of Muslims who deeply desire to be acceptable to God and who are not satisfied with the status quo.

This book, then, is to help you think through the team approach to urban church planting among Muslims. Drawing on earlier studies in urban anthropology and missiology, we will look at specific methods that have potential to produce viable congregations of former Muslims. These congregations will in turn plant more new churches.

There is, thankfully, an increasing amount being written describing various Muslim peoples and the religion of Islam. Books on generic church planting and case studies among non-Muslims are also available. Urban studies by Christians concerned with "reaching the city" have been emerging in the last decade. Books and manuals on "How to witness to a Muslim" are more readily available. But who will tell us what it will take to see vital congregations of Muslims who love and worship the Lord Jesus become a reality in the great cities of northern Africa, the Middle East, Central and South Asia, China, and Southeast Asia?

It could be argued that Muslim converts do not "think church," because the few missionaries among them tend to believe that it is nearly impossible to establish Muslim churches in hostile environments. There is a tendency among western change agents to think linearly. There is no point, many would argue, in planning to establish a congregation with its own national leadership if we are in fact finding it very difficult even to find one or two Muslims who will make a sustained and clear stance of allegiance to Christ!

Churches will not become a reality, however, until the change agents plan on it. Church planting is not necessarily a sequential operation. Even before Muslims confess Christ as their Savior, they must be instilled with the notion that commitment to Christ (the Head) must include and involve commitment to Christ's body, the community of fellow believers. Without this conscious shift, adopting the other believers as brothers and sisters for whom they have responsibility, conversion is not complete. Conversion includes an internalizing of allegiances, not only from whatever has been the highest authority in the Muslim's life to the lordship of Christ, but also from blood relatives being first community to the new notion of Christ's community (1 Pet. 2:9–10).

This does not mean that new believers should be taught to disobey the fifth commandment. Their conversion should lead to an increase in their "honoring of mother and father." Both these seemingly contradictory goals can be accomplished because they are both the will of God.

To what degree are the issues of understanding Muslims and their sociocultural context, understanding appropriate procedures for church planting, and understanding and working within the felt needs of city dwellers key issues or variables for church growth in Muslim cities? It seems that the main reasons Muslims in Muslim cities are not switch-

ing their loyalty to the Lord Jesus Christ and gathering as his people in
those cities are:

- They do not see any relevant reasons to change from the status quo.
- They have no models, "significant others" in their cultural milieu becoming and meeting together as Christians.
- The vast majority have a bias or predisposition against Christianity as a viable worldview.
- Most Muslim urban populations are still shame-societies, which greatly discourage independent reflection or action that would be seen as a detriment to the status and goals of that society or their extended families.
- An immeasurably tiny number of persons in these Muslim cities have ever known an evangelical Christian well enough to be aware that Jesus Christ is a living personage who is adhered to, followed, and obeyed to a person's betterment.

I have focused on mission work among Muslims since 1960. I am convinced that in any given, dominantly Muslim city there exists a large number of Muslims who deeply desire to be acceptable to God and who are not satisfied with the status quo.

Empowered, trusted, gifted articulators (in a particular Muslim's language) could assist significant numbers to embrace the Person and work of Christ and his community of believers if these Muslims were personally acquainted with, and respected, a voluntary association (*ekklē-sia*) of converts like themselves who would take personal responsibility for each other's welfare. In other words, if Muslims could trust that a living Messiah and his followers would indeed meet their needs on this earth and after, they would be willing to embrace and identify with Christ despite opposition. This calls for several members of a personal network to be baptized at the same time, thus creating an immediate support group for such a radically unpopular behavior. This could be described as the principle of critical mass. Muslim seekers will become followers of Jesus as Messiah when they become acquainted with an already on-going fellowship of former Muslims whom they respect, and who whet their appetite for following the Lord Jesus.

To identify, nurture, and be a catalyst to such a voluntary association, church, or congregation, demands placing and supervising a team of at least six appropriately gifted adults in the same area of a Muslim city for at least a ten-year period.

Why Work Carefully Through This Book?

This is a book for the hungry and ambitious man, woman, team, or sending church who realizes that becoming effective in the task of pioneer church planting will demand as much concentrated study and effort as an aspiring medical student puts into getting into med school; getting through med school, internship, and residency; and staying current with the latest research. Why is it that most are so superficial and unwilling to put that kind of work into the most important task on earth?

This book will assist you to review the contributions of various missionaries and scholars in the area of church growth among Muslims, identifying both concepts and methods that have shown evidence of being helpful in actual church planting efforts; to integrate relevant insights by urban anthropologists and missiologists that may be applicable to our goal of planting the first churches among Muslims in pioneer areas; to build upon what has been discussed, written, and attempted among Muslims with the goal of helping you to envision what steps could be taken to upgrade current efforts; to learn from case studies the principles and behaviors advocated or disavowed by this study; to develop practical procedures to use as missionaries, bivocational disciple-makers, or citizen Christians involved in church growth among Muslims in Muslim cities. (An example of a "citizen Christian" would be a Batak believer in Indonesia, or a Copt in Egypt, who are not of Muslim background or culture.)

Many dedicated Christian workers who love God "with all their heart" have too often failed to utilize their critical faculties and also "love God with their minds." For example, some years ago a critical study was proposed to discover why a flourishing church of perhaps 100 Muslim converts exists in Algiers, when in Casablanca the largest regular gathering of Muslim converts is seven! Each city had roughly the same number of missionaries for the same length of time. The proposal was quickly rejected on the grounds that "fruit is in the hands of the Lord." The purpose here is not to criticize God's servants—especially not those who have spent 20 to 25 years seeking to win the Muslims. But if we are truly Kingdom minded, we will want all the help we can get. To love a co-worker is to be unwilling to allow him to fail.

It may be that the Muslim world has drawn workers with a strong Calvinistic bent who have emphasized the sovereignty of God to the extent that, on the positive side, they were enabled to persevere, even if often it was without expectant faith. But an attitude that says, with a spirit of resignation, "Well, God will work when he chooses; there is little we can do," results in a tendency to not hold ourselves responsible for improving our understanding of either God or man. The cliche, "When God chooses to open eyes, he will" is only a half truth.

This book assumes that God is doing his part. Therefore, we must examine our methods. We must go beyond evangelism or cross-cultural communication among Muslims. The goal is to develop methodology aimed at not merely changing the worldview of Muslims, but at seeing their allegiance switch to Jesus Christ as their final authority, and that adoption into God's family would manifest itself by adoption into the local expression of that family: a house church.

There exists little guidance for change agents on what steps to take in order to become a catalyst, forming voluntary associations of converted Muslims. For example, in Morocco more than 200 Muslims have been identified as baptized Christians, yet only 5 percent choose to gather as a congregation or community of believers. What is wrong? How can network theory become procedure that will minimize barriers to the congregating of believers in Christ from Muslim backgrounds?

If those of us working with Muslims have any consensus, it is this: There are no easy answers. The specific science of church planting among Muslims is, unfortunately, only in the embryonic stage. How many books or even articles have you seen? Perhaps it has been assumed that Muslims, if they would be converted, would naturally seek to meet with and be supportive of other Muslim converts. In any case, the literature that exists emphasizes "reaching Muslims," but not gathering the believers into a community that demonstrates the reality of the Lord Jesus Christ in that area (Matt. 5:16).

However, 100 years of missionary work among Muslims has shown that it is not the inclination of Muslim converts to "think church." Even today in Casablanca, Morocco, the most mature believers in Christ from Muslim background choose to meet sporadically in groups of no more than five other believers, on a hospitality basis, for mutual encouragement. That the majority of western converts to Christ meet together may be a reflection of our history and culture rather than evidence of an innate, or even Spirit-led, behavioral pattern.

It may not be realistic to attempt to identify procedures that will be equally helpful to those working among Muslims in cities as diverse as those in Northwest Africa, Northwest China, Malaysia, Bangladesh, or Kuwait. The Muslim world is hardly monolithic. Islam takes as many different forms across the world as Christendom. Islam has as many denominations, cults, and sects as those who call themselves Christian. Evangelical Christians complain about the indigenous churches of Africa that have become syncretistic with African religious practices, and orthodox Muslims make the same complaint about the practice of Islam in many parts of the world. Social, economic, urban, and rural factors, plus pre-Islamic culture and religion, all affect the worldview and practice of any particular Muslim.

What Will and Will Not Be Covered

Much more must be written to integrate biblical, Koranic, historical, and social science data. To what degree is an issue relevant mainly to its time and place, versus relevant to establishing networks of committed Christians of Muslim background in a particular Muslim city today? What weight and significance are we giving to church planting if after establishing a group of converts it is short-lived? Should "planting" be considered one task, but establishing or maintaining a group so significantly another task that it calls for different people or methods?

In this ongoing survey of several years, what most would call a functioning church—a congregation of baptized believers from Islam, gathering regularly for worship and the study of Scriptures (with their own national leadership)—has only been identified in a few cities of the world (excluding sub-Sahara Africa): Casablanca, Algiers, Tunis, Istanbul, Ankara, Ismir, Dhaka, and in the cities of East and Central Java.

A closer look would indicate that, both among the Javanese and in Bangladesh, Muslims have primarily come to Christ in rural areas, then afterward have become part of the ruralized segments of the primary cities because of a need for work.

Hence, a good portion of church planting effort in urban cities has been spent conserving adherents to Christ who were converted in rural areas. There is, therefore, a need for a study that would aim at conversion growth (versus transfer growth) to provide guidance for establishing churches directly in the urban context of the Muslim world, where missionary visas are not available.

This book also delineates between the supernatural and human factors—although these two areas obviously overlap. The need for further exploration in methodology that utilizes those gifted in the working of miracles, healing, a word of knowledge, exorcism, and so forth is recognized. It is not the purpose of this book to minimize or devalue the place for such intervention of God's Holy Spirit through human instruments. If this study seems to have a bias toward the human factors, it is because the purpose is to examine the nonsupernatural variables and discern their relative importance. There is no intent to insinuate, however, that this study covers all the factors or components involved in bringing urban Muslims into fellowship with God and other believers.

It is of concern, however, to balance a popular but mostly unexamined hypothesis that "there won't be any breakthrough in the Muslim world except through signs and wonders," the notion that there is no point in attempting to establish new churches in Muslim cities apart from the working of the miraculous in the physical sphere. One assumption of this work is that a primary reason why more churches do not exist in Muslim cities today is a quantitative, not a qualitative one. Where there is "little sowing, there is little reaping" (2 Cor. 9:6).

Starting Point: 1960

Following a historical review will be a deductive study drawing directly and indirectly from the experience of 300 missionaries and nationals working in the 44 dominantly Muslim countries since 1960. This is because there is so little record of either theorists or practitioners advocating the establishment of separate Muslim convert churches before 1960. Work among Muslims has been singularly difficult and ineffective over the last century. It appears that very few missionaries involved with Muslims thought it realistic to hold the establishment of a congregation as their aim. "One convert per lifetime" was often the price expected to be paid. The emphasis has been on perseverance, as faithfulness to God. With "realism" dictating, one would not expect Muslims to form into congregations of Christians, nor even join the existing Christian churches (composed of peoples from a non-Muslim background). It is hoped that this work will be upgraded quickly by more actual case studies of fully established, former Muslim congregations. At this writing, such a dream is only "a tiny cloud on the horizon" of the Muslim world's cities. Because this subject tends to instigate a certain segment of Muslim fundamentalists to hostility and the persecution of Christians, and to protect many co-workers living among Muslims, certain names and places have been altered.

This book builds on a foundation commonly called the "church growth school of missions" and its extensive literature. The premises of Donald McGavran and his disciples, (early) Peter Wagner and Ralph Winter, and—particularly in the Muslim context—Phil Parshall form the foundation on which this study builds. The term "foundation" is used because, while there is a quantity of material in the areas of evangelizing Muslims and generic church planting, there exists no comparable work that describes and verifies the methodology that will lead to the completed task of established Christian congregations among Muslims—especially those living in cities. Most of the relevant literature deals with understanding Muslims, their history, culture, and politics; the difficulties incurred in approaching Muslims with the claims of Christ; and methodology for improving communication and relationships with Muslims.

Parshall has sought to conceptualize what a Muslim convert church might look like theoretically. He has outlined characteristics of new churches recently established in rural Bangladesh, and admits that he has seen almost no successful church planting efforts among Muslims in an urban context. His works tend to focus on failures or shortcomings. "It is frustrating to have a good perspective on the obstacles but to lack clear guidance on how to overcome them" (1985:180).

Parshall's works also tend to focus on the pre- or post-church planting issues. He sobers the would-be church planter by his vivid and extensive descriptions of the failures and present-day obstacles that confront those committed to the task. He focuses prophetically on what prevents effective church planting from occurring. He is embarrassed by the ethics and values of the so-called Christian countries, and the lifestyles and methodologies of many missionaries in Muslim countries. He contrasts these failures with what he considers biblical ideals. His works must be studied as a prophetic call to go beyond past effort. The status quo will not do. God must enable us to find his answers on how to actually see vital congregations of former Muslims spring up in Muslim cities like Tripoli, Alexandria, Baghdad, or Banda Aceh, Sumatra.

Although current examples are taken mostly from the interdenominational efforts of International Missions, Arab World Ministries, Frontiers, SIM, and other church planting agencies among Muslims, they have been "backlit" with the views of denominational pioneers of yesteryear, such as Jens Christiansen of Denmark. Bishop Christiansen spent a lifetime working among Muslim Pathans in the northwest frontier province of Pakistan. The Bishop of Karachi, Rev. Arne Rudvin, had this to say about Christiansen:

> As few others, he was committed to the church of Christ and to the apostolate to Islam. His own scholarly study of Islam was profound. Nevertheless, he trusted his experience of the living Islam rather than the academic presentation of it by western scholars. He is one of the very few original thinkers in missiology since the Second World War. His excellent Pushto translation of the New Testament is among the best in any language of the Indian subcontinent (Christiansen 1977:Preface).

Christiansen's challenge to those working among Muslims in 1949 was: "What is your aim in approaching the Muslim? To try to get him converted? To try to influence him so a mass movement might get started? To try to sow the seed and leave it at that?" (p. 119). Christiansen complained that missionaries from the West inadvertently brought with them a mentality of individualism that has led to the extraction of Muslim converts from their people. This practice annihilates any hope of leaving behind groups of mutually supportive believers.

Christiansen traces this modern evangelical mentality to the pietist movement of Europe, which he sees as a reaction to the Roman Catholic Church's misuse of the doctrine of Corpus Christi (the body of Christ). The biblical doctrine of the "priesthood of the believer" was swung too far, creating individualistic Christian workers in understandable reaction to the controlling domination of the Roman Catholic Church (1977). The *Zeitgeist* of the times, bred by the Reformation and the Renaissance, proclaimed men free to think as they like. This, unfortunately, led to individuals who got their instructions solely "from the Lord," opting out of accountability to his church. Such individualistic missionaries produced individualistic Muslim converts (if any at all) who have had little model of commitment to other believers in the body of Christ.

Christiansen and other denominational missionaries may have stressed churchmanship more than today's independent worker. But new brothers and sisters in Christ must see themselves under the authority of the Word of God, submitted to Christ's prophets and apostles, and under the lordship of Christ himself through the governing of local church elders. This study, then—in Christiansen's vein—holds to a local church with authority, if not the authoritative, Episcopalian model of control from the outside.

Because the western missionary has historically come out of a democratic society, we have been blind to our error of trying to plant a church with Muslim inquirers who are marginal—unsubmissive to the elders of their own society. Christiansen points out that commonly the missionary has the erroneous idea that Christianity is going to make something very good out of a misfit. It seldom works out that way. "In over a quarter of a century of observation, I have yet to see the misfit (in his own society) who turns out to be a strong, self-supporting, self-respecting, and witnessing disciple-maker" (p. 126).

Wendell Evans of Arab World Ministries concurs. "One of the key reasons why repeated attempts to establish an independently functioning church in one of the main cities of Morocco has failed was the repeated missionary recognition of leaders who did not have the confidence and support of their own people" (1982:3).

Thus Christiansen anticipated today's concerns that missionaries are extracting converts from their own people. "It is a sin against any individual to coach him to break away from the natural body, of which he is a cell, and try to get him to live alone in the 'spiritual' environment of the foreign missionary" (1977:126).

Missionaries do not normally minister with bad motives, but they sometimes make bad decisions with good motives. Often the problem is an inability to truly understand the church planting process—not unlike helping a butterfly out of a cocoon and unknowingly consigning it to death.

Christiansen maintained that the majority of missionaries simply do not know what to do. Some insist that a seeker should at least bring his wife and family with him before he can be baptized. Others insist on his bringing with him a certain number of fellow seekers. All of these efforts to manipulate converts are absolutely arbitrary. The Holy Spirit does not convict a group because some missionary thinks it is a good idea (1977). The Holy Spirit may desire to convict a group or an extended family, but the missionary may not be sensitively working with the Spirit within cultural boundaries and dynamics to bring an entire extended family, neighborhood, or clan to God.

Part 1

The Challenge
of Planting Churches
in Muslim Cities

One Billion Muslims:
What Does God Have in Mind?

Is God active in a process of bringing tens of thousands of Muslims under the lordship of Christ? We assume that God is effectively carrying out his role. The would-be missionary must be aware of what the Bible teaches about the divine factors involved in apostolic church planting.

Clearly, we cannot come to Christ unless God draws us to himself (John 6:44). Unless the Spirit of God is at work bringing conviction of sin—where true righteousness comes from, and awareness of the judgment to come—and if one does not attain the righteousness that only Christ can provide, then regeneration cannot be effected by human change agents.

Building on the theological base described by Alan Tippett in *Church Growth and the Word of God* (1970), in the area of church planting methodology, this study assumes these premises.

Premise One

Church planters among Muslims can count on God's presence alongside them. "Surely, I am with you always" (Matt. 28:20).

Premise Two

The human factor will be the variable between effective and ineffective church planting efforts.

Premise Three

God has at his disposal followers who are appropriately gifted to carry out the methodology effectively.

Premise Four

Sufficient motivation and commitment exist among aspiring change agents.

Premise Five

Efforts to establish congregations of former Muslims, as opposed to efforts to bring Muslims into existing churches of dominantly non-Muslim believers, is not counter to the biblical principle of the unity and equality of all believers in Christ.

Premise Six

Expatriate change agents will most easily gain residence in the over 100,000 cities of the Muslim world where they can obtain work permits. The exception will be those allowed to do relief and development projects in rural areas.

Premise Seven

Power evangelism is not necessarily normative. Earlier, the increasingly popular notion that "nothing is going to happen in the Muslim world without signs and wonders" was introduced. The intention of proponents of this view is to motivate Christians to go beyond merely presenting the propositions of Christ's message by demonstrating the reality of God's presence and power in everyday life.

Even Dudley Woodbury, a Presbyterian Islamicist at Fuller Seminary, is relating that, where conversions from Islam are reported, so are supernatural manifestations (1989). Clearly, relying on God to authenticate the name of Christ and the authority of his ambassador is basic.

However, we see no scriptural evidence to support some proponents of "signs and wonders" who insist that what God did through Elijah to the prophets of Baal (1 Kings 18) is necessarily normative, or even always helpful.

Understandably, since Muslims have historically been unresponsive to Christianity, those missionaries (especially from the Pentecostal/charismatic traditions) who are only now considering the challenge of Islam, tend to assume that Muslim reticence can only be overcome by "signs following"—a supernatural confirmation that the messenger has indeed been sent by Allah to the Muslim.

Who can disagree that a revival, a heightened level of obedience and godly lifestyle among God's people, or a supernatural manifestation of God's power would be pertinent to effective church planting? But is there evidence in church history that either revival among believers, or miraculous signs and wonders performed at a sustained level, have been preconditions to Muslims, Buddhists, Hindus, or Tribals turning to Christ in significant numbers? Those who assume that what John Wimber (1985) calls "power evangelism" is normative, tend also to assume that until God enables the change agents to powerfully heal the sick, raise the dead, eat poisonous things, speak a "word of knowledge," or supernaturally walk out of prison, there is no hope for effective church planting among Muslims. Interestingly, because the Pentecostal-charismatic oriented denominations have by and large avoided Muslim work in restricted access countries until recently, neither they nor an opposing view have much with which to illustrate their presuppositions.

This study, then, would seek to avoid two extreme positions: that God does not intend to ever again accompany his servants with supernatural manifestations, and that the change agent's work is futile if not accompanied by signs and wonders.

Hiebert (1982) is most known for his premise that, until recently, most western Christians tended to live without an awareness of what he calls the "excluded middle." Hiebert would maintain that the "middle" world of supernatural beings and activity, which lies between the transcendent supreme God and the natural world, is a part of everyday life in most nonwestern cultures. Thus, if change agents are not willing to deal with the unseen, they will not, according to Hiebert, be dealing with felt needs, or entering into the worldview and experience of the target people.

Premise Eight

Suffering is normative for the Christian life. It is not something to be avoided at all costs. An avoidance mentality is antithetical to following him who said, "Anyone who does not take his cross and follow me is not worthy of me" (Matt. 10:38) and "A student is not above his teacher, nor a servant above his master" (Matt. 10:24). Is not the New Testament an agreement between God and his disciples to follow the Lord Jesus, assuming that it will include suffering for his Kingdom's sake (Mark 10:30)?

What is the difference between necessary and unnecessary suffering? That which comes as a result of obedience, despite every effort to practice the fruits of the Spirit in the midst of our incarnational witness, is what the Lord would have us accept with "exceeding gladness" (Matt. 5:12, KJV). Until the change agents seeking to do pioneer church planting in Muslim countries thoroughly understand that fear, persecution, and suffering are normative, they will not be able to sufficiently demonstrate to the Muslim convert how God enables us to stand for Christ in the midst of a fearful, difficult situation.

In fact, the suffering that is likely to come to most expatriate change agents in a Muslim city, is usually little more than rebuff, social ostracism, and possibly expulsion. And since the subject here is establishing viable congregations of Muslim converts, the more relevant issue is: How can new Muslim believers be encouraged to gather and serve the Lord Jesus as a church in the face of hostile reaction from their fellow citizens?

Premise Nine

Church growth is inevitable. In prophetic passages such as Isaiah 19 there is indication that the nations of the Middle East will eventually encounter the one true God. Indeed, both Revelation 5:9 and 7:9 indicate that there will, in the end, be Christ-devoted worshippers from every tribe, tongue, kindred, and people group worshipping the Lamb. Obviously that must include all Muslim groups. Thus, we conclude that

Abe Wiebe of Arab World Ministries is correct when he says, "Church planting among Muslims is not an exercise in futility" (1978:2).

There is no indication in Scripture of any geographical areas or peoples being exceptions among whom we should not expect fruit. The majority may always be unresponsive or resistant, but would it not be reasonable to look at any given Muslim city through the window of Acts 18? Paul was opposed by abusive Jewish religious leaders in Corinth (Acts 18:6). We next learn that Crispus, the synagogue ruler, and his entire household believed in the Lord. "And many of the Corinthians who heard him believed and were baptized" (Acts 18:8). It would seem, however, that Paul still was not able to shake his fear of being harmed or rejected. God was apparently concerned that Paul see the city as he did. Thus God privileged Paul with a visit, telling him in a vision, "Do not be afraid; keep on speaking, do not be silent. For I am with you, and no one is going to attack and harm you, because I have many people in this city" (Acts 18:10).

Can we deduce that if Corinth was approximately 100,000 people, and God was planning to draw "many people" to himself from that population, that the same is likely to be true today in any given Muslim city? If so, church planters can labor in the confidence that God has many "elect" in their adopted Muslim city. The task is to find them.

Premise Ten

Historically, there is little precedent for attempting to establish churches of mainly Muslim converts. Since the beginning of the nineteenth century, mission to Muslims has been theoretically on the Church's agenda. There have been heroic efforts attempted by Henry Martyn (India and Iran), and Carl Gottlieb Pfander (Turkey and India), but for most of what church growth historian Latourette calls "the Great Century" (1790–1900) missionaries sailed past the Arab world, Turkey, and Persia. Before and after the Reformation, the Church has also mostly avoided the Muslim populations of India, China, Russia, and Southeast Asia. From 1890 to 1940 a number of valiant penetrations into Muslim territory were attempted by the American Congregationalists (Turkey), American Presbyterians (Syria, Egypt, Iraq, and Iran), some British (Morocco, Algeria, Tunisia), and the Dutch Reformed (Java, Indonesia). Yet at no time in history have we seen anywhere near the quantity of missionaries focusing on Muslims as have gone to non-Muslim peoples in sub-Sahara Africa, China, India, Japan, the Philippines, and Latin America.

Indonesia, for example, has more Muslims than any other country. Many denominations of Europe and North America eventually sent missionaries to Indonesia. However, the estimated 3,000 missionaries resident in Indonesia since World War II almost totally by-passed the majority Muslim peoples until the abortive Communist coup in 1965 (Cooley 1968). Roger Dixon (1984) claims, for example, that the vast majority of missionary work in West Java was either with the Chinese, or to service animistic tribal people who had become Christians and moved to West Java for employment. Those who did approach Muslim peoples usually took an approach through a medical or educational institution, with little attempt to persuade Muslims to follow Christ. Dixon insists that never at any one time were more than 14 missionaries attempting to make disciples of the 30 million Sundanese Muslims in West Java. Apparently, missionaries in Java followed the same pattern as those who originally went to Egypt, Turkey, and Malaysia to work among Muslims; they turned from the Muslim population to more receptive non-Muslim peoples. Therefore, outside of the heroic efforts of a few individuals, there were almost no early sustained efforts to plant Muslim convert churches on which research can be done.

Premise Eleven

Muslims have not historically heard "good news," even when in contact with Christians. Until recently, professors of missions have been reticent to utilize the social sciences, partly because ideas of the secular universities were considered "worldly thinking," and partly because most social scientists overtly devalued the aim and practice of missionaries. Yet many missionaries have confessed that they wished they had been trained in sociology and anthropology. Many who hurried to a Muslim country to bring the good news soon became aware that the gospel presentation was not being heard as good news, but rather as bad news. They would preach of the marvels of Christ's redemption and find people angry. Listeners filtered the message down, thinking it advocated the breaking of the fifth commandment, "honor your father and mother."

Alan Tippett warns us that even a sound biblical theology has to be communicated effectively across cultural barriers. There is the problem of meaning. When Muslims "accept the gospel," what do they take it to mean? Does it mean the same thing to the foreign advocate as to the indigenous acceptor? How does one express biblical concepts using Muslim terminology? By inventing a new vocabulary?

If the hope is to establish a church, how will it fit with the existing social structures? What are the patterns of relationship in the family? Who marries whom and why? Does a Muslim polygamist divorce his wives before being baptized? These and hundreds of other questions are what anthropology is about, and they are also the burden of the missionary (1987).

Premise Twelve

Donald McGavran is the most relevant missiologist to address our task. He starts (1955) with God's purpose in history, concluding that Christ's command to "make disciples of all nations" must lead to a mentality that aims to establish a community of disciples loyal to Christ among every *ethnoi*. If people normally become Christians only when they receive truth from a trusted significant other, someone must cross over a cultural boundary to establish that prior question of trust (cf. Mayers 1974).

McGavran (1980) teaches that Christian workers must concentrate not merely on outreach or "the work" of doing evangelism, but on forming churches—a task that is definable and measurable. He also advocates a theology of harvest as opposed to a search theology. He sees biblical mission as not merely proclaiming the good news, but also effectively persuading people to become Christ's disciples, assembling as a local gathering of his church. He sees philosophical relativism as the greatest enemy of a theology of harvest. People will not be persuaded to wholly follow Christ if the change agents are not persuaded that Jesus is the only bridge to God.

McGavran maintains that since God has created mankind as peoples, kindred, and tribes, missionaries need a *people group* mentality. Throughout the Bible, God makes covenants with families and people groups, villages, and even cities. The task then is to establish new communities of disciples among every people. India may have as many as 3,000 separate people groups who see all others as "them"—in other words, as outsiders. McGavran (1979) could identify Protestants or Catholics within only 71 of those people groups. One hundred million Muslims in India make up some of those groups that are still without their first church.

McGavran (1980) believes that it is biblically valid for a group or household to come to Christ together through what he calls "multi-individual," mutually interdependent decision and consensus. His appeal to history would claim that most of Europe was converted through people movements, not individual decisions. Western Christians have easily missed Acts 9:35, "All those who lived in Lydda and Sharon saw him and turned to the Lord." How did the church in Philippi get established in a few weeks? The Philippian jailer and Lydia brought in their entire households (Acts 16:15, 33–34, 40).

McGavran (1984) considers the comparison between quality and quantity of conversions to be an unnecessary dichotomy. There must be very few mature Christians if church growth is not taking place; and if it is, there will be many immature Christians who will need nurturing. A healthy church will always have immature, weak, new believers in its midst.

McGavran has been misunderstood in his emphasis on the responsive. He does not say to avoid the places or people groups where there is little response, but that the change agent must learn to find the responsive families among each people group or homogeneous segment of a city. Concentrate the ministry among the most open while continuing to sow among those less responsive.

Missionaries need to be diagnosticians. They are to utilize their critical faculties to better understand what is and what is not happening. Then plans for greater progress can be made, based on reality.

McGavran (1980) argues for using measurement in church planting efforts. He differentiates among biological growth, transfer growth, and conversion growth. For example, churches do exist in northern Sumatra, but a close look reveals that they are transfer growth congregations of Dyaks and Bataks who have migrated there for work. He also believes that social uplift ministries should be subservient to establishing churches, which will in turn attract more new people to Christ. These congregations must be networks with their own national leadership where the targeted Muslims will "feel at home."

Unfortunately, McGavran does not focus specifically on Muslim countries that do not issue missionary visas. His case studies come from areas where relatively little government opposition exists. McGavran, like Parshall, advocates people movements, but is generally unhelpful in instructing how to trigger one, or even how to assist an extended family in coming to Christ.

J. Robertson McQuilken (1974) summarizes the four presuppositions of McGavran's church growth teaching that are foundational to the analysis of the task before us.

1. Numerical church growth is a most crucial task of the pioneer missionary.
2. The church planting team should identify and concentrate on the responsive elements of a society.
3. Multi-individual, interdependent decisions should be promoted.
4. Anthropological factors affecting a people's responsiveness should be analyzed and utilized.

McQuilken agrees that the first two seem to flow directly from biblical mandate. The second two are derived from biblical principle. Obviously, the God who "is not willing that any should perish" is interested in seeing large numbers of people come to know him and live eternally with him.

The Lord Jesus Christ expressly commanded those involved in his worldwide program to "make disciples of all nations" (Matt. 28:19). Did he mean all nations except Muslim nations? In order to be justified in expecting little fruit among Muslims, should there not be scriptural evidence for such a pessimistic stance? Our experience must submit to biblical eschatology as reviewed above.

The apostle Paul looked at circumstances of seeming defeat and cried out, "Let God be true and every man a liar" (Rom. 3:4). Experience that falls short of Christ's promises is not biblical reality; it is merely experience. Biblical Christians cannot set their agenda first on the basis of their own experience, but must constantly come back to the premises and promises of the God of Scripture.

Premise Thirteen

A covert methodology is neither biblical nor missiologically practical. There is no biblical justification for a covert operation, and it is possibly the greatest hindrance to progress in church planting among Muslims. Would not such a mentality be foreign to the Christians of the first three centuries? Is it not the opposite strategy of those who spread Islam? Muslims respect change agents more if, as soon as it is culturally sensitive, they make it clear that they are in that city because God sent them. They may be English teachers, but the central focus of their life is to obey God and be Christ's ambassadors.

2

Past Failure and Future Prospects

Although Christians universally admit that evangelism and especially church planting among Muslims has been singularly ineffective, very little exists to document the reasons. Until recently, the church worldwide has assumed that (1) Muslims simply are not open to seriously consider Christianity, or, (2) God has not opened their eyes.

It has been considered cruel to place or insinuate blame on the few Christian missionaries who have attempted to make and gather disciples among Muslims. Is it not the work of the Holy Spirit to bring fruit? So why are there so few congregations of former Muslims?

Common Hypotheses

It Is God's Fault

The cliche "We should go where the Lord is working" indicates that many hold to a mission theology of geographical grace. God simply chooses to open up the eyes of some peoples and not others. God has given grace to the Latin Americans, the Filipinos, the Koreans, and Africans south of the equator that he has not given to Muslims. God loves the Sawi of Indonesia but not the Buginese, as in "Jacob have I loved. Esau have I hated" (Rom. 9:13).

Few theologians or other Christians hold this view consistently. It is often used as a fallback position when no other explanations are satisfactory. A Christian worker would be foolish to evangelize where God is choosing not to work, or among a people from which God does not intend to bring any to himself.

However, based on the hermeneutic principle of understanding Scripture at face value in its most natural mode, we assume that the early Christians understood "make disciples of all *ethnos*" to mean it would indeed occur—no exceptions. Therefore, they did not need to discern where God was not working. It is unlikely that early Christians interpreted lack of response to God's abandonment of a people. Possibly some of their undaunted optimism was due to John's Revelation (5:9; 7:9) that there would indeed be persons reconciled to God from every kindred, tribe, *ethnos*, or people group. This would include every Muslim people group. Therefore, unresponsiveness among Muslims in any given city is not God's fault.

Satan Is the Problem

In missionary rhetoric, some speak of "strongholds of Satan," perhaps alluding to Pergamum "where Satan has his throne" (Rev. 2:13). The implication is that there are peoples who, perhaps due to their wooing of demons, are more solidly locked into the kingdom of darkness than other peoples, and therefore more resistant. Islam has been called by Francis Steele "Satan's masterpiece" (1981). Has Satan, after much practice, become so skilled that he could design a religion that could resist almost all attempts of the Christian church?

Peter Wagner's *Territorial Spirits* (1991) and George Otis Jr.'s *Last of the Giants* (1991) articulate the latest version of a recycled idea—note Oswald J. Smith's *Passion for Souls* and Art Mathew's *Born for Battle* (1978)—namely, that Satan as the Prince of this world has designated demonic forces in each geographical area of the world, even on the village level. Unless in each place, the "strong man" is bound, God's ambassadors will not be able to see the people respond to Christ (Matt. 12:29). The implication is that the Muslim world is "the last of the Giants" to be conquered by God's people, and unless we are specially trained in appropriate "exorcism," or in nullifying demonic influence and power, there will be no fruit.

The problem with laying the final blame at Satan's feet is that such a position inadvertently makes Satan stronger than Christ. Christ is "bound" until his servants get precisely equipped to release a people or place from Satan's chains. But the Lord Jesus, in saying, "All authority in heaven and earth has been given to me" (Matt. 28:18), clearly implies that spiritual authority and power are tilted in the disciples' favor, not toward the agents of the wicked one. If, indeed, Christ through his ordinary saints cannot "make disciples" in certain demonically held kingdoms, Jesus Christ is not who the Scriptures make him out to be. This is not to minimize the complicating deterrent of the demonic. The increasing consensus among missionaries is the need for more skill in power encounter. There is no biblical evidence, however, for the simplistic view that as soon as the missionary finds out how to defuse the power of territorial spirits, multitudes will flock into the Kingdom.

It Is the Muslims' Own Fault

Perhaps Muslims do not want truth. This view sees Muslims as a mindless monolithic block of especially wicked people. Yet, it is difficult to reason why the Dani cannibals of Indonesia wanted truth more than the citizens of Casablanca, Morocco. Have not God's grace and his messengers redeemed some of the most hardened, evil, cruel peoples on the earth? At the turn of the century, it seemed impossible to find Koreans who would give the gospel a hearing. Today Korea is considered potentially Asia's first Christian country. Did the Koreans suddenly decide to be good and seek the Lord? What made the difference?

Actually, those who have worked among Muslims find the majority to be monotheists desirous to honor the Creator, sometimes with a reverence not often seen among Christians. Like Saul of Tarsus, before his conversion, large numbers of Muslims seem sincerely concerned about God's reputation, showing at least external deference to Allah. Parshall (1989) gives evidence that many Muslim people seem to be searching for God more than other groups who now have a multitude of Christians among them.

It Is the Missionaries' Own Fault

They are not spiritual enough. Historically, missionaries have tended to blame themselves when fruit was not forthcoming. Was the problem a lack of prayer and fasting? Was it a lack of righteousness? "The prayer of a righteous man is powerful and effective" (James 5:16). Commonly, unresolved conflict with co-workers is blamed for fruitlessness. Art Glasser concluded at the 1978 North American Conference on Muslim Evangelism that missionaries have not loved the Muslims sufficiently. Several missionary couples left North Africa recently, deciding that they were working in the "flesh." They had come to the Muslim world in their own strength, not waiting on God to get "endued from on high."

But are the missionaries in the Muslim world less "spiritual," less loving, or less sacrificial than those in Latin America, Korea, the Philippines, or sub-Saharan Africa? Has not God been pleased to use inconsistent, struggling sinners with blind spots throughout history? Where there has been a "turning to the Lord" it is commonly assumed that there was concentrated prayer beforehand. But there has probably been an equal amount of prayer (or equal lack thereof) in the direction of the Muslim world as toward other countries (at least by the participating missionaries and their friends, if not by the church as a whole).

Have missionaries used the wrong methods? Methods is a broad category. It could be subdivided into (1) interpersonal relationships with target people; (2) ability to understand, communicate, and function within the adopted culture; (3) levels of preparedness and maturity in the messengers; (4) use or neglect of appropriate ministry gifts; and (5) degree of time investment with appropriate people in the culture.

It is precisely these, and related issues, that are addressed in this book. If this included the mobilization of God's church worldwide to focus their resources on Muslim cities, then methodology may indeed be the variable that will enable Christ's ambassadors to enact a new chapter of church history in the Muslim world's cities.

But the people who live there are powerful and the cities are fortified and very large. Then Caleb silenced the people and said "we should go up and take possession of the land, for we can certainly do it." But the men who had gone up with him said, "we can't attack those people; they are stronger than we are . . . we seemed like grasshoppers in our own eyes and we looked the same to them" (Numbers 13:28–33).

Is it realistic to be optimistic, or pessimistic? Is there historical evidence that God is in process, or at least planning, to open the eyes of significant numbers of Muslims if our methodology improves? Is faith for a breakthrough among Muslims anything more than wishful thinking?

A review of Christian magazines, including *Moody Monthly, Eternity, Christian Life, Christianity Today,* and even mission-oriented periodicals like *Evangelical Missions Quarterly, Missiology,* and the *Church Growth Bulletin* indicate that, until 1977, the Muslim world was not for the most part on the agenda of the Christian church worldwide.

Most North American Christians in the 1950s and 1960s seldom thought about the existence of Muslims. Some were aware of Islam as one of the world's great religions, of Mohammed as their prophet, and of a pilgrimage that Muslims make to Mecca. Few could recall knowing of a missionary trying to establish a church among Muslims. Although a number of churches supported missionary work in dominantly Muslim countries (Indonesia, Lebanon, Egypt, and Pakistan), seldom did one read of Muslim converts joining existing churches or forming new ones.

A sober and chastened mood meets the visitor in the Middle East who tries to sense the mood of missions and churches in relation to the real encounter between Christianity and Islam. Norman Goodall wrote in 1957, "The visible conquests have been few . . . almost everywhere I met either bewilderment in face of frustration, admissions of failure to build up a Christian community in which converts from Islam can find a natural place, or eager questioning as to the right missionary policy towards Islam." In 1966, speaking of the rising tide of Islam in West Africa, Clyde Molla regretted, "for the last twenty years Islam has been on the move again. Its progress goes on and cannot simply be put down to the upward curve of the African population graphs. In Senegal, half of the more than 200,000 Diolas have become Muslims. Eighty percent of the 45,000 Falis in North Cameroun have gone over to Islam. One city in 1952 was 40 percent Muslim and ten years later it is 70 percent" (1966:261).

Because of their defensive, survival mentality, Christians in countries overrun by Islam have made little effort to evangelize their Muslim neighbors. The first Protestant missions were established in the Middle East early in the nineteenth century. It was their hope that the Christian Armenians, Assyrians, Copts, and Greeks—members of the ancient churches—when instructed in the Bible and given new life by the Holy Spirit would become God's instrument for evangelizing all the Muslim peoples of the Middle East and Asia. Accordingly, they devoted themselves to the task of reviving the Christian minorities.

It was not their purpose to divide the ancient Christian communities and create Protestant churches, but this is what happened. Those who accepted the evangelical teaching were often pushed out of the ancient churches, which resisted Protestant renewal. The new biblically oriented believers had to form "evangelical" churches of Christian minorities, which still exist in Turkey, Lebanon, Syria, Iraq, Egypt, and elsewhere today.

Foreign missionaries became almost totally occupied serving these new churches they produced. Occasionally, one of these Protestant nationals became a zealous and courageous evangelist to the surrounding Muslims; but, for the vast majority of believers, the walls of dialect, custom, prejudice, and fear—which have existed between Christians and Muslims for more than a thousand years—were too high to scale and too ponderous to move. The "evangelical" churches have done little more than the Catholic or Orthodox churches to confront Muslims with the claims of Christ.

Could a new trickle of post-World War II missionaries do better? The mood has been pessimistic. The mainstream denominations did not see any need for missionaries, since the Protestant churches were established. Muslims did not need to become Christians, they felt. "It is possible that in the providence of God the role of the Western Christians in the evangelization of the Middle East will in the future be a decreasing one" (Miller 1971:235).

In January 1974, Bill Bell of the North Africa Mission was still writing pessimistically. In an article entitled "Muslim World Still Looks Like Impregnable Fortress," Bell writes of the number of black athletes who have become Muslims, taking a Muslim name. He referred to orthodox Muslims emigrating to America and making their influence felt. "This expansion of Islam in North America is an illustration of the challenge which this great religious system represents to Christians around the world today" (p. 75).

Bell held out some hope, mentioning "new techniques" such as Bible correspondence courses, radio, and book exhibitions on Operation Mobilization's ships. Then he wrote about reaching Muslims in Europe, without admitting that this was a strategy of retreat from the countries of Morocco, Algeria, Tunisia, and Libya.

Bell saw little to indicate any significant change in response to the gospel among Muslims in the near future. With what he called "realism," Bell pointed out that Muslims still take a very hard line against Christian activity inside their countries (p. 77).

He wrote about the destruction of the only Protestant church building in Kabul, Afghanistan, despite the missionaries' care in their contacts with Afghans. Even of radio ministry, he says, "So long as the government-controlled local stations remain closed to Gospel broadcasts, missions will be touching only a small percentage of the Muslim population through radio" (p. 78).

Missionaries from western countries, Bell predicted, can expect a cold reception in most of the Muslim world, especially the Arab countries. He mentions how governments were moving effectively to censor the mails and stop the flow of correspondence courses. Thus, he warned that those aspiring to serve in the Muslim world should note the refrain from the missionary hymn, *So Send I You* "to serve unrewarded, unpaid, unsought, unknown."

Most important, Bell notes one basic reason why the gospel has made so little impact on the Muslim world. The church as a whole has never been particularly concerned about Islam. Considering Muslims too difficult, it has turned away. There is really no hope for a greater impact on Islam until the church as a whole begins to concentrate prayer on that part of the world, softening it up, and then pouring forth more of its choicest young people who know how to live a self-sacrificing, committed life for Christ (1974).

A Historical Perspective

Missing from these pessimistic views, however, is historical perspective. How many hours of evangelism were logged in China, Japan, or India before believing communities became a reality?

It is important to remember that Korea had only a few tiny groups of Christian believers at the turn of the century. Everett Hunt (1980) writes that the pioneers in Korea were all young. The Board in New York informed them that no senior missionary waited to welcome them. No precedents had been established. "We cannot give you much information. You will have to feel your way" (p. 34). The first missionary doctors to arrive reported to New York: "You can't enter Korea with regular missionaries. The way is by no means open for missionary work. You should be exceedingly cautious . . . " (p. 44).

The government's stance was, "In order to preserve the honor and dignity of the Orient, we must destroy the trespassing foreigners" (p. 48). The Royal court felt threatened by foreigners who, in the name of a foreign religion, encouraged Koreans to ignore centuries old tradition (1980). Yet those early missionaries were convinced that they were called by God to establish his church in Korea. There was a sense of urgency. They were not reticent about planning strategy like a military commander. They were going to "take Korea for Christ. . . . We will be satisfied with nothing less" (p. 90).

Colombia is another example too soon forgotten. As recently as the 1950s missionaries had their homes burned and national pastors were being assassinated. For two decades the evangelical church in North Colombia felt like Job. The wrong people died at the wrong time. Dismal failure greeted well intentioned efforts. Confusion and hypocrisy beset what had started as a genuine visitation from God. Anger, retaliation, and sexual immorality muddied the water, but God gave the increase (Howard 1969). Advocates of going only to countries that are friendly would have instructed missionaries to avoid Colombia. Yet churches sent more missionaries to help believers persevere and today there are tens of thousands of evangelicals throughout Colombia.

The Turning Point

A New Awareness of the Muslim World

While North America and Europe focused on their own turbulent 1960s, and as the greatest response in the history of Muslims becoming Christians was going on in Java, the Middle East exploded with the Arab-Israeli War in 1967. Amidst talk of possible confrontation between the superpowers in the Middle East, Christians began to ask questions about the one of every five persons in the world called a Muslim.

Continuous terrorism, the oil crisis, and the emergence of Moammar Khaddafi and Ayatollah Khoumeni brought Arabs, Iranians, and other Muslims into the news and thereby into the consciousness of western Christians.

During the 1960s, as Bell noted, Americans became aware that Cassius Clay changed his name to Mohammed Ali. Soon other black basketball, football, and baseball superstars took Muslim names. Christians began to recognize that thousands of black Americans in the inner cities of the United States were leaving the Baptist churches, covering their heads, and identifying with the worldwide "colored community" of Islam. Was the first wave of black leaders converting to Islam a civil rights protest against perceived white domination of the Christian churches or truly religious conversion? Then waves of immigrants and foreign students from Muslim Africa, the Middle East, Pakistan, Bangladesh, and Indonesia brought Christians face to face with orthodox Muslims in colleges and the workplace. In America and Europe, Muslims were no longer exotic people "over there" someplace. They were becoming neighbors.

The need for laborers to do jobs Europeans would not do opened the door for over three million Muslims from Morocco, Algeria, Tunisia, and Turkey who took up residence in Western Europe. Government-sponsored Saudi, Libyan, Iranian, and Pakistani students began to be noticed on university campuses across North America and Britain. Thousands of Yemeni took places at the auto assembly lines in Detroit. Then, the 1974 oil crisis was used to cause a face-off between the "Christian West" and the "Muslim Middle East." Ralph Winter (1978) believes that it was equivalent to the later Ethiopian drought in its impact on America and Europe. Not since Europe fought off Muslim armies in Vienna and Tours, France, have western Christians been so aware of Muslims!

A phenomenon began to occur in the second half of the 1970s. American and northern European evangelicals (after they recovered from the shock and paranoia of the new "Muslim invasion") began to see the migrated Muslims as an opportunity. Could God have actually engi-

neered these Muslims to our countries to learn of Christ and his forgiveness? Thus, Great Commission Christians began to think and talk
about how Muslims could be reached for Christ.

The Muslims' New Awareness of the Christian World

A Saudi Arabian was once asked on a plane what he knew about Christianity. "Everything," was his reply. "I watch a Christian movie on my
VCR every night." He was obviously equating Christianity with modern western cultures. Many Muslims have come to understand "Christian doctrine" as the worldview propagated by the TV programs "Dallas" and "Dynasty," and by Hollywood movies. The colonial merchants,
government officials, and military from Holland, Germany, England,
France, and Spain, who were normally irreligious, were for decades the
Christian majority among Muslims. In Morocco today, the colloquial
Arabic word for Frenchman (or foreigner) *Franjiyeh,* is the same word
the Moroccans use for Christian. Traditionally, the Moroccan Muslim
has understood a Christian to be someone who does not believe in God,
does not pray, does not read a holy book, does not honor his mother
and father, drinks whiskey, and conquers women.

Yet in recent years, due to the mass media, radio, magazines, and television, more Muslims are becoming aware of "religious Christians."
Some realize that missionary-type Christians exist who are committed
to establishing the church of Christ among Muslim peoples. The Muslim periodical *Impact International* published an article entitled "Enter
the Tentmaker" in 1981.

To the Muslim press, even traditional strongholds such as Malay seem
vulnerable to missionary encroachment. A newspaper in Kuala Lumpur
in 1986 reported that in Temerloh, Malaysia, "almost 50,000 Malay
Muslims have become apostate because they have stepped outside of
Islam. The representative of the PAS [a political party] of the State of
Pahang, Haji Muhamed Rushi bin Arief, stressed that 40,000 of them
have become Christian, 400 have become Hindu, and some have entered
other religions." According to the Haji (high religious official), the Malay
public have become interested in Christianity because they feel too
restrained by the teaching of Islam. He warned that certain groups have
arisen, such as the Persaiuan Melaya-Kristian Singapura (the Fellow-

ship of Singapore Christian Malays), who constitute a challenge to the Malay society.

Investigation revealed no evidence that 40,000 Malays had become Christian. Perhaps some tribal conversions in north Malaysia provoked the article. Warren Chastain of the Zwemer Institute regarded the article as fiction aimed at embarrassing the ruling political party.

A New Era of Hope

In 1976 the tide began to turn. Vivienne Stacey (1976) of Interserve, and John Wilder (1977) of the Presbyterians (USA), both in Pakistan, wrote slightly optimistically in *Missiology* a year apart. Stacey says, "We read in 1 Chronicles 12:32 that the children of Issachar were men who 'had understanding of the times, to know what Israel ought to do.'" This implies an effort to discover what God is doing in this world. Surely God has a time program. In the fullness of time Christ was born (Gal. 4:4). In due time he died for the ungodly (Rom. 5:6).

Apart from the movement into the church in Spain in the thirteenth century and large movements in Indonesia (East and Central Java), in our time there have been no large responses to the Christian message in the Muslim world. It would seem logical that many Muslims should find Christ before history reaches its consummation in him. "Let us therefore try to see what God is permitting in the Muslim world and what he is actively doing through his church" (pp. 363–64).

Stacey concludes that there is a Muslim counterreaction occurring, with definite plans coming out of Islamic conferences to eliminate missionary work from Muslim countries. "Christians in the financially troubled western world will find intensified sacrifice is needed if their efforts in world evangelization are not to be outdone by a well-heeled, resurgent Muslim missionary movement." But if God is permitting Islam to be on the rise, then maintains Stacey, we must assume that our sovereign Lord of history is accomplishing his own strategy—not retreating. She is convinced that God is presently working through migrations and dispersions, such as Indian and Pakistani Muslims in the United Kingdom and the Persian/Arab Gulf. Besides Third World Christians penetrating Muslim areas with secular jobs, Stacey recognizes that western Christians abroad can be "field partners" to increase the effectiveness of missionaries. She is, however, overly optimistic about potential revival in the ancient churches of the Middle East and the younger churches of South Asia (1976).

Other articles followed, generating a new "can do" spirit until almost imperceptibly a new optimism began to arise, even among veteran field missionaries. The North Africa Mission (AWM) in 1978 set a goal to establish 25 indigenous churches in Morocco, Algeria, and Tunisia in the following 10 years—no small goal when they had established only one congregation in the previous century! Parshall wrote *New Paths in Muslim Evangelism* (1980) and provoked optimism that contextualization, similar to the messianic synagogue paradigm among Jews in the United States, might be a key to "Jesus mosques" and a "Muslims for Jesus" movement. World Vision (1980) produced a film, *Unlocking the Door,* optimistically proposing that a sociological key can be found that will lead to a breakthrough among each Muslim people group.

By 1980, missionaries in Morocco, Algeria, Turkey, and Pakistan had reported more conversions among Muslims in one four-year term than they had seen in the previous 15 or 20 years! On their own initiative, Algerian believers declared a resolve to establish sister Muslim convert churches in every province of Algeria.

Evangelical Missions Quarterly (*EMQ*) increased the number of articles on Islam, reflecting this new hope for a breakthrough in the Muslim world. The January 1978 *EMQ* was given to the contextualization debate coming out of McGavran's "harvest theology" at Fuller Seminary's School of World Mission, and Ralph Winter's U.S. Center for World Mission. Harvest theology teaches that it is the church's failure that harvest has not come in the Muslim world, not God's decision to leave Muslims in blindness.

Don Rickards, then at Liberty Baptist College, made another of his series of protests about the Muslim world being neglected in the April 1978 *EMQ.* The difference this time was the hope that was missing in his earlier articles.

> God is moving among North Africans today. He brought the attention of the world to focus on these countries as each successfully experienced its revolution for independence. With several million Muslim Arabs emigrating to Europe, can we hear the cry of the Spirit of God to Christians in Europe to share the Gospel with them? Personnel and money are

needed in large doses. Muslim North Africa is a frontier that must be penetrated by the Church of Jesus Christ. In spite of the enemy's opposition, the number of converts today is ten times greater than any time previously (1978:91–92).

"Obstacles in the Way of Winning Muslims," an article by an anonymous author in the July 1978 *EMQ*, claimed that Muslims are being converted to Christ, being baptized, and joining the Orthodox Coptic church in Egypt through the ministry of a Coptic priest whose eastern look, sound, and style is much closer to Islam than the westernized Protestant churches there. This should motivate missionaries to examine how they may be hindering church growth by their western approaches, lifestyles, and church customs. The implication is that, if the hindrances can be removed, church growth will occur. Merle Inniger (1979), of International Christian Fellowship (now merged with SIM International), wrote about a key to reaching Muslims, as did Phil Parshall, in several articles from 1978 to 1988.

In the October 1980 edition of *EMQ*, Gerald Otis claimed that power encounter is the way to a Muslim breakthrough (1980). His idea is illustrated by a case study in the Philippines. In January 1983, John Haines wrote that worship is the neglected key to reaching Muslims. In an October 1984 article, Haines claimed that he had found a successful methodology for cities in France. In July 1985, Parshall wrote about restructuring medical missions among Muslims to be more effective (1985b). In the July 1986 edition of *EMQ*, a plea was made for cooperation among missions working with Muslims, reflecting the same hope that a breakthrough was on the horizon (Livingstone 1986a).

New Leadership

Comparing articles before and after 1976, it is startling to discover the shift toward optimism. As if suddenly the Muslim world had become "open" or responsive. Did this shift reflect a turnover of church and mission leadership focusing on the Muslim world, or a penetration of the new church growth ideas?

Around 1977, thanks to opinion-makers like Winter and Wagner, Great Commission evangelicals began to be conscious of the people groups of the world who still did not have a viable community of believers capable of evangelizing their own people (*ethnos*). It was suddenly obvious that the Muslim bloc was the least penetrated by apostolic disciple-makers. The church's spotlight turned to the Muslim world.

In 1978, leaders connected with World Vision and the Lausanne Committee for World Evangelization invited mission executives and churchmen from Muslim dominated countries to Colorado Springs, for a historic conference aimed at moving work among Muslims significantly forward. Out of that week came the mandate to establish the Zwemer Institute for Muslim Studies (the only training school in North America dedicated solely to the task of disciple-making and church planting among Muslims).

The Zwemer Institute was both a cause and effect of what was happening. Its classes grew overnight. Bible colleges and seminaries came under pressure by students to offer courses in ministry to Muslims. Muslim awareness seminars have been in increasing demand among churches and colleges in North America and Britain ever since. Even though the new emphasis on unreached peoples has included Hindus, Buddhists, and Chinese, it is noteworthy that efforts to establish institutions equivalent to the Zwemer Institute for Hindus or Buddhists have not had the same significant results.

Christians accustomed to the notion of "lost people" began to think about lost "peoples." This caused concerned Christians to reexamine the progress of the Gospel around the world. A fresh look revealed that political boundaries drawn up by colonial governments tend to obscure the existence of many people groups (*ethnos*) who still do not have their first community of believers. Now, instead of thinking *Pakistanis*, mission-minded believers think about the Punjabis, who have churches, versus the Pathans, Bhils, Baluch, and Bihari in Pakistan who still do not have their first Christian church. Long neglected social and political issues tended to be the focus of evangelicals from 1965 to 1975. Suddenly, many western evangelicals returned to a conviction that every person's first need is a saving knowledge of Christ. The church growth people (with Winter's 16,750 unreached "nations") were waiting for them.

New Mobilization Efforts

Most mission agencies suffered a significant drop in new appointees from 1965 to 1975. An examination of the ages of missionaries in the societies of the Interdenominational Foreign Missions Association (IFMA), and the Evangelical Fellowship of Mission Agencies (EFMA) will, for the most part, reveal this ten-year gap. The North Africa Mission (AWM), for example, was averaging 1.5 new missionaries a year during that decade, and losing far more than that from its fields.

But the 1976 Urbana Missionary Convention in Illinois was attended by students in a new mood. As Dave Howard wrote in *EMQ*, there was an upsurge of interest among university students to get involved in evangelism, especially among people groups who were beyond the range of existing ministries. Howard excitedly wrote, "This is a new day. It's different from 6 or 7 years ago. The student today is asking, 'What can I do? I'm ready to move.' He wants to be in on what God is doing" (1977:144).

One reason for the new readiness of students to sign up to serve among unreached peoples was the rise of the "tent-maker" emphasis. Ruth Siemens, of Overseas Counseling Service, and Christy Wilson, a veteran facilitator of missionaries with secular jobs in Afghanistan, were instrumental in spreading the vision of new possibilities for entering countries previously considered "closed" (because those governments did not extend residence visas to missionaries). 1976 to 1986 was the first decade since the peak of the Student Volunteer Movement at the turn of the century when evangelical students in secular universities were able to envision themselves serving under mission agencies without going to seminary. Suddenly, committed Christians from Inter-Varsity, Campus Crusade, Navigators, and other Christian university groups were dreaming of how they could be disciple-makers in a closed country, as engineers, computer programmers, or English teachers.

This new thinking, combined with a focus on the Muslim world, resulted in an increase at the Urbana convention of its workshops on mission to Islam—from four in 1979, to eight in 1981, to 21 in 1984. Mission agencies that concentrate on Muslims (for example, Arab World Ministries, Frontiers, and International Missions) were surrounded with inquiries eight deep at their exhibit booths. Apparently, the Muslim world was becoming known as the place where one can serve Christ without going to Bible school or seminary, and taking on the identity of the professional clergy. Up until that time, mission agencies had mainly welcomed Bible school and seminary graduates who wanted to serve as full-time ecclesiastical professionals. It is still difficult for ordained mission agency leaders to visualize how workers with only secular degrees can do church planting.

Ralph Winter, to keep "the people groups without a church" as the priority on the church's agenda, convinced some students and missionary leaders to attend a conference on frontier missions in Edinburgh in 1980. Winter rationalized that few mission executives attended because mission agencies historically do not initiate new ventures, but typically follow the lead of incoming missionary candidates. True to his thesis, out of Edinburgh '80 came the Caleb Project, the National Student Mobilization Coalition, and Theological Students for Frontier Missions. Later, a like-minded student mobilization organization, Student Missionary Advance, was chartered in Canada. Although some were short-lived or absorbed into other organizations, all of these "student-run" organizations were significant in imparting vision and mobilizing evangelical university students to the unreached peoples of the earth. Yet again, as these students were presented with the challenge of the "hidden people blocs" of Chinese, Buddhists, Hindus, and Muslims, by far the majority of response was toward the Muslims.

New Plans by Mission Agencies

This groundswell of interest to serve in the Muslim world as a "tent-maker missionary" was either unnoticed, or subtly opposed by mission agencies. Older leaders conceived of a tent-maker as a threat to their structures. The agencies would be rejecting qualified candidates merely because they did not fit inflexible organizational structures. Some mission agencies are in danger of going the way of the defunct passenger railroad companies, who forgot that their business was not trains, but transportation.

Most agencies were slow to remember how the Jesus people movements of the 1960s led to the establishment of entire denominations (for example, the Calvary Chapel movement, the Vineyard movement, and People of Destiny). New dynamic outreach organizations like Campus Crusade for Christ, Operation Mobilization, Youth With a Mission, Agape Force, and Keith Green's ministries sprang up because existing organizations or churches did not find a way to harness the vision of young people who wanted to try a different way.

In 1959, few students considered or had the possibility of a summer missionary experience. When the first summer charter flight of Operation Mobilization was organized to take students to Europe, agencies and mission committees in churches complained about wasting a great deal of "mission money" that could have been given to career missionaries. Today, over 30 years later, it is difficult to imagine a mission agency or missions-minded church that does not have a summer program.

When Operation Mobilization took mostly untrained young people from eight different nations into Spain from 1961 to 1963, it resulted in daily arrests and literature confiscation. Few could have imagined that such refusal to accept Spain as a closed country would lead to Spain legalizing Protestant missionary endeavor as it did. And was it not also "young people" who founded the once radical/now traditional faith missions (Overseas Missionary Fellowship, CIM, WEC International, RBMU International, SIM International, Africa Inland Mission, and others)? They refused to accept the seasoned wisdom of older missionaries who adamantly told them it was impossible to have fruitful ministries in the interiors of India, China, or Africa.

Is God planning to bring thousands of Muslims to himself? The increasing number of people across North America, northern Europe, sub-Sahara Africa (and now even Latin America, Singapore, and Korea), who are determined to find a way to get in, stay in, and minister among Muslim peoples in so-called closed Muslim countries, is a clear indication that God is making his move!

Institutions either catch up with student "demands" or go out of business. Most mission agencies were not prepared for a new influx of candidates wanting to do church planting in the Muslim world. Applications began to multiply in 1977 to agencies that encouraged work among Muslims. Allan Thompson, then of Worldteam, tells of inquirers to his mission who quickly turned away when they discovered that Worldteam, at that time, had no ministry among Muslims. A female student at Columbia Bible College was confused as to whether she had a call to the Muslim world, or whether it was simply peer pressure. When in the history of Christianity has there ever been peer pressure to go to the Muslim world?

Those working among Muslims are increasingly sought out to speak at student and church meetings. Worldteam opened up a Muslim ministry in England. So did International Teams and Gospel Missionary Union. The Evangelical Free Church followed suit in Brussels. SIM International announced its intention to go to new Muslim people groups in Africa, and to expand efforts of its newly absorbed agency, International Christian Fellowship, in Pakistan and Bangladesh. World Evangelical Outreach changed its name to "Pioneers" to highlight its intent to "blaze new paths" to unreached peoples, including Muslims. People International, focusing exclusively on Muslims, was founded in England in 1982. North Africa Mission grew so quickly between 1977 and 1982 that it had to establish a new experimental wing in order to find room for the number of candidates. Then, because "NAM Associates" grew so quickly, NAM (now Arab World Ministries) decided that NAM Associates should become a separate sister mission: Frontiers. Frontiers is well along toward its goal of overseeing 200 church planting teams in the unchurched Muslim cities and people groups of Muslim countries as well as among Muslims in China, India, Sri Lanka, Singapore, and the Muslim republics of the former Soviet Union.

New Programs in Training Institutions

Bible schools and seminaries must be sensitive to new trends if they are to enroll new students. The remarkable growth of Fuller's School of World Mission has apparently provoked other seminaries and colleges to establish similar programs. Wheaton Graduate School, Trinity (Chicago), Asbury (Kentucky), Denver, Western (Portland), and Gordon Conwell seminaries, plus Biola University now have schools of missiology, joining Fuller and Columbia (South Carolina) Graduate School of Missions. Since 1975 other seminaries have added mission professors and increased their courses and degree programs in missions.

What does it mean? To what is it leading? Several IFMA/EFMA mission agencies that had no net growth in their total number of missionaries during the 1980s are planning on significant increases in the 1990s. As mentioned, Frontiers hopes to facilitate 2,000 new missionaries to serve on 200 new church planting teams among Muslims, and SIM plans to double its co-workers to Muslims. Wycliffe Bible Translators, the Southern Baptist Foreign Mission Board, and the Assemblies of God have unprecedented goals for ministry in Muslim countries. Would God be putting Muslim peoples on the agenda of his Church if he was not intending to bring unprecedented numbers of Muslims to himself?

Until recently, American Christians did not realize that Christians in Egypt, Lebanon, Jordan, Pakistan, and Indonesia were almost totally culturally isolated from the Muslims of their cities. By word, and by placing personnel in their midst, western Christians are now challenging Middle East, Pakistani, and Indonesian Christians to renounce their segregation from their Muslim neighbors and reach out in compassion. Western Christians are becoming less supportive of existing churches in Muslim countries who ignore the Muslim majority in their midst. Whispers around the Amsterdam '86 international conference for itinerant evangelists indicated that Christians in Egypt are quietly establishing cell groups determined to find ways to share the gospel with Muslims. Servants Fellowship International, a coalition of Asian, Middle Eastern, and African leaders, is already being used to foster an attitude of change among the churches they represent, toward evangelizing the Muslims.

New Results among Muslim Peoples

Interviews with African evangelists attending Amsterdam '86 indicate that new efforts are taking place to establish churches among Muslims in Mali, Sierra Leone, Ivory Coast, Liberia, Nigeria, Chad, Burkino Faso, and Malawi. Several indigenous mission societies aimed at Muslims seem to be organizing annually in Africa. Luis Bush, George Patterson, Federico Bertuzzi, and Carlos Caldron join others from Latin America who believe that the numbers going from South and Central America to Muslim countries as tent-maker missionaries will soon increase from a trickle to a full stream. Since 1985 Pablo Carillo's Project Maghgreb has been training and supervising couples from Mexico who have taken up residence in Morocco.

A few Christian leaders in India are beginning to make conscious efforts to establish church planting efforts among Muslims. The recent news of unprecedented numbers of baptisms in Bangladesh has lifted faith. Three Punjabi Christians in Karachi are leading efforts to the

Baluch and Mahajirs in Pakistan. YWAM has placed Indonesian workers among the totally unreached Buginese of Sulawesi. The vast majority of so-called third world missionaries are not working cross-culturally with unreached peoples (especially not Muslims), but Africans, Asians, and Latins are doing genuine church planting among Muslims in greater numbers every year!

So What Does It Mean?

All of the above is circumstantial evidence that God is indeed gathering his forces for harvest in the Muslim world. History shows that God's people, once aware of a need, eventually begin to pray. Prayer results in leadership being raised up, which in turn mobilizes more laborers. Englishman Martin Goldsmith says that in this particular era the American church seems to be gifted in innovation. This innovation is in finding ways to place cross-cultural disciple-makers among Muslim peoples where there has not been a significant witness before. In the last five years at least 400 new missionaries have spurned the unavailability of missionary visas and have managed to get residency among Muslims in North Africa, Turkey, Egypt, the Balkans, Albania, the Arab Gulf, Afghanistan, Kazakhstan, Uzbekistan, Kyrghzistan, the Indian subcontinent, and among Muslim people groups in China, Malaysia, and Indonesia. There is no indication that this momentum toward Muslim peoples will lessen. Hopefully, the constant new blood will keep the level of expectancy high, and new methodologies being proposed will eventually result in the most effective evangelism and church planting ever accomplished among Muslim peoples.

3

Instances of Church Growth among Muslims

Why do any Muslim convert churches exist? Why has church planting in rural areas been more effective than urban efforts? A review of the history of evangelism among Muslims maintains that very few missionaries before 1970 envisioned and therefore sought to actually establish Muslim convert churches. A review of the entire index of the journal *The Muslim World* from its beginning to the present reveals only three articles that deal with incorporating Muslim converts into the existing non-Muslim background churches. Only one article, by Henry Riggs, "Shall We Try Unbeaten Paths in Working For Moslems?" in 1941 approached the subject of a separate Muslim convert church.

Thirty-four years later, in 1975, Phil Parshall—challenged by Riggs' article—called for a paradigm shift toward experimental "new paths," moving away from models of evangelistic technique that had proven barren. Parshall builds on Samuel Zwemer's advocacy of synthesizing orthodox Islam with how Muslims actually practice their religion. Parshall goes beyond Zwemer, however, in that he claims Zwemer "engaged in little actual experimentation or innovation in areas of methodology" (1980:19).

Bangladesh

Although Parshall's mission agency began in what is now Bangladesh in 1958, by 1975 there were still very few Muslim followers of Christ there. They decided to take a new direction, following McGavran's church growth theory of contextualization, including the homogeneous unit principle. In recent years, several churches of Muslim converts have been planted. Focusing mainly on male heads of families, the numbers of Muslims baptized is reported by three leading change agents to be from 5,000 to 35,000—absolutely unprecedented! These barely literate but landowning farmers are reading the New Testament, which was especially translated into the Muslim Bengali dialect of Bangladesh. Most meetings take place without the presence of a foreigner and without a church building.

In evangelistic witness, they stress Old Testament stories that are found in the Koran; the universality and culpability of sin; the biblical teaching of atonement with Isa Messiah (Arabic-Koranic title for Jesus) as the mediator between man and God; and the second coming of Christ in judgment as the Last Day intercessor for bad Muslims who are not good enough to qualify for Mohammed's intercession (1980:222–23).

Most of the believers reside outside of the larger towns where the missionaries live. Most have suffered ridicule for their faith, but none have been killed and few have left their village or asked for asylum. Increasingly, wives and children are also baptized in the name of Christ, although the typical Muslim convert husband seems slow to believe that his wife could grasp the meaning of faith in Jesus.

Physical amenities were not offered to believers nor were schools or hospitals started among them. Converts were not taken out of their area for training, especially in the beginning, although now some village leaders have discovered the existence of the larger body of Christ in Bangladesh and have gone to Dhaka for instruction. In fact, the existing Baptist denomination of Bangladesh has received at least six of the new Muslim convert congregations into its fold, while not insisting that the churches receive pastors of non-Muslim background.

Parshall claims that cultural contextualization, or sensitivity, what some would call being a "Muslim to the Muslims" is a basic reason why these Bangladeshi Muslims have been able to embrace Christ. For several years a male missionary traveled to the most important villages where he rented a room in which to serve tea and "dialogue" with the more curious men of that town. Concentrating on male heads of families, they avoided the all-too-common tendency to work with young people, who after conversion tend to get extracted from their people and leave the area for various reasons, including their inability to arrange a marriage. Parshall has emphasized that those professing the Lord were encouraged to wait on baptism until several could be baptized at the same time, thus establishing a comradery, a built-in support group to withstand the inevitable reaction.

Those most promising in "being able to teach others also" were invited to the missionaries' town nearby, after working in the fields, for an "overnight evening school," allowing them to get back to their crops the next morning. Instead of responding to the new believers' request for money, jobs, and other kinds of help, the missionaries turned the felt needs back to the believers, who were encouraged to ask God to provide, rather than the "wealthy westerners." The new believers could then experience a God who provides in their own milieu. This long-range approach served to build up the sincere and separate out the chaff.

West Java, Indonesia

According to Southern Baptist missionary Avery Willis, more than two million Javanese were baptized from 1965 to 1971. Willis's dissertation, published as *Indonesian Revival: Why Two Million Came to Christ* (1977), is an analytical account of an extraordinary instance of great church growth among Javanese Muslims. Willis's book is the only adequate report of the event that comprehensively deals with both the supernatural and human factors. Willis writes of "God's finger" engineering the events that led up to this multitude of Muslims becoming followers of Christ. But God often uses a "glove": the religious, political, cultural, and social milieu in which Javanese live.

> The more than two million baptisms in Indonesia's fantastic church growth among the Javanese, and the eleven reasons cited for that growth support our basic thesis that God prepares peoples and countries for response to the gospel through a confluence of anthropological, political, sociological, economic, cultural, and religious factors (p. 210).

An abortive Communist coup attempt on September 30, 1965 plunged Indonesia into a blood bath of recrimination, and brought death to approximately half a million people. These traumatic events sent a tremor through the country that left millions scrambling for an identity. For approximately two million, Christianity offered the best alternative.

After interviewing 500 firsthand witnesses, Willis concluded that both Muslims and Marxists were disillusioned by the power struggle between them, which is foreign to the native peace-honoring Javanese psyche. In analyzing eleven factors that influenced these conversions, the Javanese characterized their spiritual need as "emptiness of soul" or "not at peace." Apparently their former backgrounds of animism, mysticism, and Islam failed to meet the felt needs of the moment.

When asked, "What attracted you to Christianity that was not in your former religion?" the answers, in order of prominence, were: the promise of eternal life, peace, forgiveness, fellowship, power, love, and progress. Contrary to popular rumor, miracles were listed as the last factor on all lists as being an influencing reason for Muslims becoming Christians. When the government gave a blanket authorization for all Communists to be killed, many leftists who were still God-fearers and at least nominally Muslim were astonished at the rancor and recriminations of fellow Muslims, and thus fled for protection wherever they could get it. Hence, the actions of the government were the second biggest factor influencing conversion—protection was third.

Providentially, the churches in Java for the most part did not participate in the battle between the Muslims and the Communists, but commonly took in those fleeing who, while looking for protection, claimed they wanted to become "Christians." The Christians gave the protection and the Word of God by insisting that "the inquirers" go through the traditional bottleneck of individual decision, catechism, and attendance in the established churches.

Willis grieves, however, that only a fraction of the opportunity was grasped because the westernized Indonesian churches, for the most part, failed to cooperate with the cultural and political events by receiving people into the church as whole villages. In fact, the greatest part of the church growth came when villages converted *themselves*, as untrained laymen started Bible studies and house churches in their villages without waiting for church officials to approve. Thus, the greatest church growth among the Javanese lay more in multiplying new congregations than in adding members to existing ones. The denominations that started more new house churches in more new places were the ones who had the greater church growth. Most of the house churches came into being by one person asking for religious instruction and then opening his home to friends and neighbors when a lay teacher would come.

Willis further points out that, unlike other areas in the Muslim world, by the 1960s many Javanese churches had become rooted in Javanese culture. Therefore, Javanese Muslims could become Christians without being separated from their own people. Not only had these churches already conformed culturally to external practices and methods of communication, such as dance and drama, but they also "Javanesed" the gospel according to three of their religious traditions: *Kejawen*, the animistic indigenous religion, *Kebatinan*, Javanese mysticism, and Islam. In other words, the churches that made the Javanese feel most at home and least foreign had the most church growth (p. 125).

Some other interesting variables brought out by Willis's study are:

- 84 percent said that their family was influential in their decision to become a Christian. Only 15.3 percent said that their families opposed their decisions.
- 86 percent of the post-1965 converts had Christian friends prior to their conversion, so perhaps 80 percent of the two million new converts were influenced to some degree by significant others—friends or family who were already Christians or at least sympathizers.
- Two-thirds of the 500 interviewees who became Christians between 1960 and 1971 did so in whole village people movements, led by their village leaders. This follows the traditional pattern of decision-making based on *Mufakat* (consensus).

This explains why the vast majority of the new converts came from villages with coherent face to face leadership, as opposed to cities. The churches that were working primarily in cities saw relatively little church growth in comparison. What growth they did see was incorporating village people who moved to the city for economic reasons after becoming Christians (pp. 125–28).

Mombasa, Kenya

Another instance of church growth among Muslims has occurred in the last four years in Mombasa, Kenya. The World Home Bible League teamed up with Southern Baptist missionary Ralph Bethea who had been quite fruitful with church growth in Tulsa, Oklahoma. According to a letter from John DeVries of the World Home Bible League to Livingstone, Bethea took responsibility for five Baptist churches in the Mombasa area with 357 believers and the work grew to 22,000 baptized believers and over a hundred house churches in three years. DeVries has twice documented that 25 percent, or 6,500, of the new believers are former Muslims! A true advocate of "the priesthood of the believer," Bethea motivates the laity to plant new house churches wherever they live, teaching that the church is a community, not a building.

Although these five Baptist churches were thirty years old and not oriented to growth in this largely Muslim city of over a million people, Bethea's vision to see 100,000 people saved was contagious. He pushed the existing believers to start a house meeting where they would read the book of Acts once a week for five weeks. Through an emphasis on prayer, revival, and cleansing, the gentle work of the Holy Spirit was apparently experienced by the 300 original believers, who then began to share answered prayer with Muslim neighbors. "We started letting people know that if you've got a problem, Jesus has the answer. We started visiting Muslims in Mombasa, asking them if we could bring them a blessing (*baraka*) in the Name of Jesus," explained Bethea. Strangers welcomed these Christians and often fed them during these visits. Muslims expressed a high regard for prayer in the name of Jesus and generally expected powerful results.

Christians praying for Muslims established a new bond between them. The house churches among Muslims were formed after a Muslim experienced an answer to prayer. He would call the Christian back and relate the answer in the presence of his relatives and friends who would then celebrate together. The Christian would offer prayer for the whole group, as well as an invitation to study the Bible.

Previously, most of the Christians in the original core of the five churches had lost ties with the Muslim community. But as the Muslims requested them to come and pray for them, Christians were drawn into their homes.

Istanbul, Izmir, and Ankara, Turkey

In the illustrations from Bangladesh, Java, and Kenya, it should be noted that in those places missionaries are still allowed to function as missionaries, and that there is an existing church that, though reluctantly, did accept the new Muslim believers. In those countries it is not illegal for Muslims to be followers of Christ. Turkey, however, is a political environment where neither missionary visas are granted, nor is it considered acceptable for a Muslim to become a Christian. Thus church growth has not been nearly so great. Even though the congregations are tiny, it is a great encouragement that churches of Muslim converts are emerging in several cities of Turkey.

This fruit can be traced back to two American young men with Operation Mobilization, and a Swiss with WEC International who went to Turkey as tourists in 1961. Keeping a very low profile, these men encouraged O.M. to send teams of young people on tourist visas throughout the country, distributing Bible portions, Christian books, and correspondence course invitations in Turkish. The tracts appealed to perceived felt needs of the Turks, and hundreds, particularly of the more educated, wrote to a Swiss address to receive a Bible correspondence course.

Over the years many have requested a visit by a Christian and thus the course was useful in identifying seekers. In recent years it has become possible to advertise a modern translation of the New Testament in popular magazines, with the responses coming to an Istanbul address. This has ferreted out even more seekers. Church growth accelerated when Turks, converted while guest workers in Germany, came back to Turkey to be witnesses for Christ. Campus Crusade addressed the quantitative problem of few witnesses by sending in more than 100 summer workers to share the "Four spiritual laws" with anyone who could speak English. Amazingly, a church of over 30 mostly single men (unfortunately, mostly without jobs) remains the strongest gathering of Muslim Turks in Christ's Name in Istanbul. Fortified by a significantly growing force of missionaries holding secular jobs, these congregations have persevered with 6 to 30 believers meeting weekly for worship. Some of the believers were converted in isolation in rural areas, then afterward came to the cities for jobs and fellowship. In several other cities, 3 to 8 converts also meet. Everyone church planting among Muslims will want to continually monitor what is happening in Turkey.

Later, we will analyze how Muslim convert churches in Algeria and among the Sundanese of Bandung, Java came into being.

What do these "samples" of church growth among Muslims tell us, if anything? What do they have in common?

1. In each case there were appropriately gifted change agents who were focused on the task of church growth among Muslims.
2. In each case there was a reasonably wide sowing of the "good news," with change agents available to discuss and interpret in the target people's language.
3. Except in Turkey, the expatriates involved were able to take a secondary role, so in fact, nationals were doing the church planting while being "coached" and encouraged by expatriates.
4. In the case of Bangladesh and Indonesia, significant church growth came through groups of inquirers being baptized at the same time. They were already related to one another and followed already established natural leaders. In Turkey that was not true, and the churches are tiny in comparison. In Mombasa, the house churches had a core of relatives and friends who were at least Kenyans, if not Muslims. That the Muslims seemingly had few "intellectual barriers" and were responsive through felt needs being met would indicate that they were probably mostly rural, less educated people who most likely had moved to the city in recent years. Like those in Bangladesh, the Muslims in Mombasa are more animistic than orthodox in their Islam, hence the response to the "empowerment" aspect of the Good News.

Part 2

The Prerequisites
for Planting Churches
in Muslim Cities

The Change Agent's Role

The Quantitative Issue

In 1978, there existed only five or six male missionaries in Morocco who spoke Arabic sufficiently to teach the Bible. Between them they averaged three hours a week sharing the gospel with unconverted Muslims. Five men for three hours a week is hardly sufficient for the three million people in Rabat and Casablanca, not to mention the other cities of Morocco. Wherever the church of Jesus Christ exists today we normally find a history of a sustained well-manned effort over years. Thus, a major missiological problem related to church planting in Muslim cities is quantitative. Cairo is a city of 13 million Muslims, and as late as 1983 it did not have a church planting team from any agency or denomination. There still cannot be identified one person in Baghdad, Iraq, there for the express purpose of starting a church among the 92 percent Muslim majority. At this writing, only one part-time bivocational missionary to Muslims has been identified in Damascus, Syria. The six million Aceh of Northern Sumatra saw their first church planting couple in 1991. India—with its 100 million Muslims—has the second or third largest Muslim population anywhere, and yet less than two dozen Indians, and very few expatriates, are giving themselves full-time to church planting in the over thirty cities with a huge Muslim population.

Only three men who knew Pushtu could be identified ministering among the six million Pathans of Pakistan in 1989. Until recently, only three men had been making disciples among the six million Baluch there. Extremely few labor among the 15 million Malays of Malaysia and Indonesia. Thus it is not realistic to envision church growth in Muslim cities until there are many more change agents available.

Nationals

What about the churches in Egypt, Jordan, Syria, Iraq, Pakistan, India, Bangladesh, Indonesia, and Malaysia? Is it not common knowledge that two-thirds world mission agencies are multiplying and growing? The chairman of COMIBAM, a Latin American organization to encourage worldwide mission involvement, Edison Quieroz of Brazil, says:

> It renews my excitement to see that God is using the church of the two-thirds world to reach the unreached in this generation. God in his sovereignty, grace, and power is moving the Church to accomplish the task to preach the gospel to every nation. We know that many doors are closed for missionaries from the West, but those same doors are open to missionaries from other parts of the world (Pate 1989:vi).

To what degree are such statements aspirations, versus actually placing change-agents in residence in Muslim cities? *From Every People* (Pate 1989) is the most recent, carefully documented handbook of two-thirds world mission agencies. Pate has determined that there are approximately 36,000 two-thirds world missionaries with 1100 nonwestern agencies. But a close count reveals that less than a hundred two-thirds world missionaries are seeking to plant churches in Muslim cities outside of sub-Sahara Africa. For example, the indigenous Indian agency, Evangelize Every Muslim in India, based in Vellore, Tamil Nadu, has three missionaries. Other agencies such as the Ishmaelite Salvation Association of Bangalore, India—which claims 70 workers, mostly among Muslims—work only part-time among Muslims, mostly witnessing in the streets with little clear intention of church planting.

It is obviously encouraging when Christians come to understand and practice biblical truth. But to assume that even revitalized Christians will then automatically sense direction from God to open their hearts, homes, and churches to their Muslim neighbors, is to be naively ignorant of history, culture, and human nature. Don Brown, of the Africa Inland Mission, claims that some tribes in sub-Sahara Africa became Muslim because of their historic enmity with a neighboring tribe that became Christian. Yugoslavia and the peoples of the ex-Soviet Union also demonstrate the power of ancient hatred between people groups. Christiansen says emphatically: "Surely no one is blind to the fact that at a generous estimate not one in ten missionaries in Pakistan is really doing anything to propagate knowledge of Christianity among the Muslim masses. And among national Christians in Pakistan the figure would probably be not one in a hundred. The question then arises, 'From whence do the Muslim people have any knowledge of the Good News which would make them want to accept it?'" (1977:128).

In a serious discussion, a leading elder of a Presbyterian Church in Cairo, who was very evangelistic among Coptic Christians, was asked about what was being done by the Egyptian Christians on behalf of the 90 percent of Cairo that is Muslim. "After all, Ramses, don't we believe that the Muslims are going to Hell?" Looking to his left and right, he whispered, "Best place for them!"

An interview with a Christian leader who represents the Protestant Church to the Egyptian government revealed a similar antipathy toward the idea of church planting among Muslims. "Don't try to bring Muslims into our churches, our people are not ready for them." Then, revealing the dominance of his cultural grid over his theology, he appealed, "And why break their (Muslim) father's heart?" A great confirmation of McGavran's homogeneous unit principle.

One more illustration should suffice. A Muslim female Egyptian university graduate was converted in the United States. After returning to Cairo she sought to participate in the singles group at the leading downtown Protestant church. After a while, a young Christian woman whom the Muslim convert considered her friend blurted out, "Why do you keep coming here? Don't you realize you just make it difficult for us?"

The point is that we cannot assume that the existing national Christians will take up the task to establish congregations among the Muslims in their city. Cultural blindness, historical enmity, and fear of government oppression are among the reasons why many otherwise vital churches do not own the goal of ministry among Muslims. It is not the task of the expatriate to scold them, but to demonstrate that it is possible for Muslims to be genuinely converted and become fully productive members of the church. As in Bangladesh, it will most likely take efforts beyond the activity of the existing churches, after which existing denominations will hopefully receive their new brothers and sisters in Christ who have "proven themselves." All this says is that a lot more expatriate missionaries are vital to the cause of seeing the Muslim world evangelized for Christ.

North American Church Involvement

To "go and make disciples of all nations" and related commands of the Lord Jesus Christ were not given to individuals, but to the *ekklē-sias*—the local communities of believers. Recognizing this truth, there is a new movement of scattered North American and British churches that are deciding to adopt an unreached people group somewhere else in the world. Apostolic mission is being redefined as churches that send teams to establish new churches in neglected cities among unreached peoples.

Mission-minded churches are realizing that to fulfill their apostolic mission responsibility they need to think in terms of starting a sister church, not merely 15 miles down the road, but perhaps 13,000 miles down the road, in Kuwait or Kuala Lumpur. Michael Griffiths (1972) has proposed that the most biblical pattern of sending missionaries is for church leadership to "draft" its best people to start a sister church (Acts 13:1–3). Thus it should be the local church or fellowship of churches (denomination if you like) that sends the missionary, not a mission agency.

A sending church may well choose to delegate its authority for supervising its missionary to a mission agency if it decides it is not equipped to give the on-site management that a church planting effort requires, but the sending church must realize that the missionary is their responsibility, both while home and while overseas, even when they are in partnership with an agency.

Such a stance reflects a new era in sending church/mission agency relationships. When a mission agency receives an inquiry about ministry in a Muslim city, they should immediately be in touch with the leadership of that person's church to begin the process of decision-making together. And not only in sending, but in equipping and supervising that missionary until the work has been accomplished. For example, Frontiers will not service a missionary candidate until they have a written request from that person's sending church to do so. They also will not move that missionary to a different city or team without involving the home church's leadership in the decision.

Underwriting the missionary's finances is also the sending church's problem—not primarily the task of the mission agency or the individual missionary. If the sending church is too small to totally finance a person's service on a church planting team, it is their responsibility to network with likeminded churches, utilizing church members' abilities to ensure that their missionaries' needs are fully met.

There are at least ten steps toward involving a local church in establishing a sister church in a Muslim city.

1. The leaders can follow the example of the Antioch elders and ask God what he would have them trust God for. This might start with a small group of two or three asking God to move the church leadership with compassion for the Muslim world. As George Mueller of Bristol, England, allegedly exhorted: "If one desires anything for God's glory, keep asking, keep knocking, persevere until prayers are answered to fulfill the burden that God has given." God wants to give many congregations in North and Latin America, Africa, and Asia a vision—determination to make a significant contribution toward fulfilling the Great Commission among the world's one billion Muslims.

2. Design a mission weekend conference around the theme of church planting among Muslims. Bring in speakers who could help impart the vision not only from the pulpit, but in Sunday school classes, with the missions committee, and at lunch with the elders.

3. Hold a day-long Muslim awareness seminar for those who want to envision the steps involved in meeting, evangelizing, and church planting among Muslims.

4. Infuse prayer meetings with requests in obedience to Matthew 9:38, continually asking God to raise up laborers from your church for specific Muslim cities and people groups. Give out a sheet listing Muslim cities that are still waiting for their first church.

5. Organize some people to get involved with a local international student/immigrant outreach to Muslims. If an ongoing program cannot be found, someone in another city who is doing it can come to the church to train people in a host family program that does hospitality evangelism for Muslims. International Students, Inc. is one effective group that helps churches in such a program. Or an outreach leader from a like-minded church in another city could teach how their church got involved with international students or immigrant Muslims in their city.

6. Distribute pamphlets and bulletin inserts on the needs of the Muslim world. Make books and tapes readily available to interested parties who want a deeper understanding of the challenge of the Muslim world.

7. Sow seeds to keep the dream of starting a sister church in a Muslim city alive. People who feel they do not want to support another missionary who is merely passing through can get a renewed excitement about missions when they understand it is their own church starting a sister church among an unreached Muslim group in Karachi, Kuala Lumpur, Cairo, or Khartoum.

8. Begin to lay plans for sending a church planting team (perhaps as a joint venture with two or three sister churches) into a Muslim city. Make contact with a mission agency that is willing to facilitate and coach the process step by step.

9. Identify a team leader (or potential leader) who has a track record. Underwrite any needs of going full time at the Zwemer Institute for Muslim Studies (or an equivalent course) and then assign the leader to an existing church planting team in the Muslim world as an apprentice for two years. During that time the church would be holding a candidate school of their own, preparing others to

join this leader on the team to start a sister church in a Muslim city.

10. Continually involve the church leadership in praying and planning about which Muslim city to adopt. Part of that planning will be setting aside an increasingly larger portion of the missions budget to underwrite the project. Contacting mission agencies or the "Adopt-A-People" Clearing House at the United States Center for World Mission (USCWM), in Pasadena, California, will help determine which Muslim people groups still need a church to adopt them.

The USCWM provides an "Adopt-A-People" kit that can be distributed at an elders retreat. For example, Emmanuel Faith Community Church in Escondido, California, has adopted the Kurds in Iraq. The Grace Brethren Church in Long Beach, California, has adopted the Soninke in Keyes, Mali. Christ Community Church in Monrovia, California, has adopted the Albanian Muslims in Tirane, Albania. First United Methodist Church in Williamstown, New Jersey, has adopted the Hui Muslims of Northcentral China. Grace Church of Richfield, Minnesota, and Hope Church of Austin, Texas, are determined to start a sister church among the Turks in Istanbul. Moody Church in Chicago has adopted the Sousi Berbers of Morocco. Open Door Fellowship, Phoenix, Arizona, has sent a church planting team to Manama, Bahrain, including their most experienced elder.

The church in Antioch chose the two most qualified leaders of their congregation, Paul and Barnabas, to start new churches. Obviously, those "selected" by the church must have confirmed their own deep sense of being sent by God. The most solid formula for being "called" to the mission field is a combination of the individual (or family's) sense of direction by God, combined with a decision by the church leaders to send them—after a careful evaluation and the recommendation of an experienced mission agency. This kind of "three-fold cord will not be easily broken" (Eccles. 4:12) when the powers of darkness intimidate new missionaries with negative thoughts that they are not qualified and should not have come to that Muslim city.

For a church to recommend a candidate to a church planting effort requires that person to get prefield training and experience in the context of the sending church. Has that church seen the person do what he or she will be called on to do overseas? If it is evangelism and discipling, what indications have been shown in Tunbridge Wells to convince the elders that the same could be done in Tripoli, Libya?

Has this person ministered in close cooperation with other believers? Is it evident that people enjoy working with this person, or are there personality traits that tend to short circuit ministry efforts or relationships with other believers?

To minimize culture shock in the Muslim city, it is important that missionary candidates log at least a hundred hours with Muslims in their home country with accountability to a person in the sending church. What has gone well? What "holes" in the individual's preparation have been revealed by involvement with Muslims?

It is important that change agents become proficient in the language of their target people. Language acquisition techniques must be learned. Then the language can be acquired step by step, when face to face with Muslims. How well a person did in high school Spanish or French, however, is seldom an indication of future success in Baluch or Malay. There is a considerable difference in motivation between an adolescent and a committed adult missionary, not to mention the advantage of concentrated immersion 30 hours a week.

The Church Planter Defined

How do people know if they are supposed to be part of a church planting operation in a Muslim city? How does God indicate to individuals that they are to do this? What do church planters actually do? If different people on a team play different roles, how do we address the question of qualifications?

Church planter Wendell Evans of Arab World Ministries traces the term "church planter" to 1 Corinthians 3:6, where Paul writes, "I planted . . . Apollos watered . . . God made it grow." However, "church planter" is not a term used in Scripture as such. Today we use it in a much broader sense than the scriptural connotation of initial sowing of the seed through the preaching of the gospel.

The term "church planting" refers to the whole process of evangelizing, discipling, training, and organizing a group of believers to a level of development permitting it to function as a viable church independent of the agent(s) who brought it into being.

Church planters, then, are the catalytic, human agents of the divine process of church development, from the point of planting the seed through that of seeing believers gathered in Jesus' Name, and finally to that of seeing the viable entity function apart from the catalyst (Evans 1982:4).

From this definition we can conclude the following:

- The church planter's role in a given city is temporary, but the church is to be permanent.
- The culmination of the church planter's task is the transfer of authority and responsibility from the local church to men qualified to lead (2 Tim. 2:2).
- The church planter's priority should be finding and preparing the individuals whom God has chosen to lead that particular church (Acts 20:17–35).

Church planting, then, focuses on three main activities: proclaiming the gospel to those who are unsaved; discipling those who accept the gospel; and mentoring qualified men to serve as elders. The Word of God must be *proclaimed*. Preaching, speaking, reasoning, persuading, explaining, proving, testifying, and arguing persuasively are activities recorded in the book of Acts. "They spoke so effectively that a great number of Jews and Gentiles believed" (Acts 14:1). "Speaking boldly for the Lord, who confirmed the message of his grace by enabling them to do miraculous signs and wonders" (Acts 14:3). "They continued to preach the good news" (Acts 14:7). "They preached the good news . . . and won a large number of disciples" (Acts 14:21). It is virtually impossible to overemphasize the key role God intends the local church to take in the process of training and confirming church planters to the Muslim world.

Does this mean that a person is not called to be a church planter if he has not had experiences similar to these obviously successful endeavors recorded in the book of Acts? Christianity is an integration of idealism and realism. We are a people who are committed to continual growth, "pressing on towards the goal" (Phil. 3:14), committed to upgrading. Therefore, when a mission agency is looking for colleagues, in fact, it is looking for attitudes and aptitudes that would indicate potential, not necessarily provenness. Part of maturity is awareness that one must be an apprentice, eager for God's life-long training program. People who develop fastest are those who are in touch with their deficiencies and who are determined to become effective whatever it takes.

In his manuscript, "Pioneer Church Planting," Magnuson (1987) maintains that in discerning a calling to be a missionary to Muslims we must avoid two extremes. One is insisting on a special supernatural appearance or revelation as God met Saul on the Damascus Road, and the other is swinging the pendulum, as did Keith Green, by asserting that because we've all been given our marching orders in the Great Commission, everyone should be a cross-cultural worker with an unreached people unless God specifically shuts the door!

Magnuson points out that the two most prominent factors in people being set aside for missionary work in the New Testament are (1) the commendation of a local church, and (2) an invitation from existing church planters. Perhaps the sending church first senses a "call" to do something about an unchurched area, and then looks for people who have the willingness and ability to do that kind of work (Magnuson 1987:7–8).

For individuals serious about discerning their appointment from God to establish churches among Muslims, the single most important factor is previous active participation in the life of a church; to understand what a church is and how it functions, and to have practical experience in laboring to build up a church body. The church should be looking for those who have shown both a sense of burden, and evidence of being equipped (or gifted) to do some of the work of church planting as evidenced by their ministry in that church.

Church leaders should be aware that God may call out the leaders of that church, but missionaries will certainly come from among those who are effectively ministering with their church. Thus, rather than "calling," a better concept for the individual and sending churches to consider might be stewardship. "How can this person be best used to accomplish God's purposes for our church?"

Individuals being set apart for church planting among Muslims need not be perfected in the ministry skills necessary. Most of the missionaries in the New Testament received on the job training. Timothy was very young when he first accompanied Paul. Apollos, though very gifted, still needed to be upgraded by Priscilla and Aquilla. In any case, no one individual has all the gifts needed to do the work. The commandments are given plurally to the church as a team, and church planters in New Testament times worked in teams. Rather than looking for "super apostles" who can do all the work by themselves, the churches and agencies should be looking for those who can make a significant contribution to a team church planting effort. Their strengths should balance the weaknesses of others on the team.

It is time to demythologize Christian ministry. Too many still imagine that in the Lord's service all you need to do is make yourself available; then God in some magical way will make you effective. Too many perceive Bible school or seminary as a "car wash": Apply to a theological institution, go passively through it like a car through the car wash, and come out the other end three years later ready to make and teach disciples. Unfortunately, there may be few mentors in any particular theological institution who have the time and structure conducive to disciple a would-be missionary into an effective disciple-maker among Muslims. Most seminaries were established to prepare pastors for the middle class pastorate, not to prepare people for cross-cultural church planting overseas. Therefore, would-be pioneer missionaries need to ask themselves not which college is best for them, but under which persons can they apprentice who are proven in the knowledge and skills desired?

Characteristics Sought by Agencies

A "Go for It Spirit"

Church planters need a deep sense of being apprehended by God to accomplish his purposes where there is no church, or where a fledgling church still needs co-workers from the outside.

A Realist

A church planter is a person with a soldier's mentality who understands New Testament Christianity with its emphasis on suffering, who realizes that jeopardizing the physical and emotional health of self and family is normative, who is able to trust God for family needs.

A Learner

A church planter asks, "How can I do this better?" Although needing a basic introduction to a number of subjects before leaving for the field, even more important is a commitment to learning after arrival from colleagues, from the nationals, and from participant observation.

A Team Player

Candidates need not ask, "Am I the missionary type?" but rather, "What contribution can I make to a team effort to establish churches in a Muslim city?" Hopefully their agency will want to utilize them in the area of their strengths, but unless they have a team mentality, experience shows that missionaries easily drift into designing their own behavioral patterns and "territory," which often make little contribution toward the church planting goals.

Marketable

Most Muslim countries understandably do not offer missionary visas. It has been wrongly assumed in the past that this means a country is "closed to the gospel." These countries do not offer missionary visas for several reasons:

- Muslim leaders teach that Islam abrogates Christianity and therefore their people should not be confused by being taught it.
- The missionary enterprise is not understood by Muslims since they do not have the equivalent. Despite rumors to the contrary, Islamic theological institutions train religious teachers to disciple their own adherents. Muslim mission agencies aimed at converting people from other religions are few and small. The propagation of Islam to the non-Muslim world is often more an apologetical effort to make Islam respectable to westerners than it is a serious attempt to convert them.

■ Most governments have a policy of replacing foreigners as quickly as possible with nationals. Even if the society is tolerant about the teaching of other religions, as in India, nationalism would dictate that an Indian, Indonesian, or Pakistani hold the job of teaching Christianity in their country, not a foreigner. Thus the denying of a missionary visa may not necessarily mean an opposition to the teaching of Christianity as much as trying to preserve jobs for their own citizens.

■ Missionary visas were invented by colonial governments who forced Muslim peoples to accept the presence of missionaries. The presence of professional religious teachers from other countries perpetuates a perception of paternalism among Muslim peoples.

■ There is a negative emotive connotation to the word "missionary." One museum in China has displays describing the Christian missionary doctors not as benevolent, dedicated people who sacrificed to serve the Chinese, but as agents of their own governments who came to China to do medical experiments on the Chinese people that were banned in the West! Missionaries are commonly portrayed in Muslim cultures as C.I.A. agents, or at best well-paid agents of large Christian organizations who bribe sick or weak minded poor people to change their religion. Missionaries are also criticized for their "unmanliness" in proselytizing children who do not know Islam well enough to defend themselves.

■ Nevertheless, obedient Christians realize that Christ Jesus did not say go and make disciples of all peoples if you can get a missionary visa. The missionary visa has been available only for about 100 years. Christians today find themselves in the same position as Christians did for 1800 years before missionary visas were invented. To not be granted a special visa to proselytize is normative. Thus everyone on a church planting team in a Muslim city needs to be marketable to the host government. There are at least six legitimate ways a bivocational missionary can obtain a residence visa in a Muslim city:

• by holding a full-time job in a project or business because of a skill or experience not common among nationals

- by holding a part-time job teaching or providing a desired service
- by obtaining a student visa
- by obtaining a visa to retire there (if over 55 years old)
- by befriending an influential Muslim who can obtain a resident visa
- by being part of a team that is starting a business or project
- by being a spouse of one of the above

The adage, "It's not what you know but who you know" is even more of a reality in the East.

Critical Faculties

Tragically, a large percentage of the missionaries across the world are neither gifted to self-analyze or evaluate their ministry, nor do they have access to "middle management" supervisors who can do evaluations for them. Therefore, much mission work has tended to be the perpetuation of the ineffective in the name of faithfulness. The youth director of a large suburban church has much more input, supervision, evaluation, and helpful team synergy in one year than the vast majority of missionaries receive in a decade. Missionaries are neither lazy nor lacking in dedication, but dedication without goal setting and problem-solving skills can lead to poor stewardship of personnel and finances. Many serving overseas find themselves in an impasse because they are not trained to find a third, fourth, or fifth option.

For example, Chinese Christian leaders in Malaysia have come to erroneous conclusions about ministry among Malay Muslims there. Their position is based on their awareness that in the past some have been imprisoned or expelled for evangelism. It is commonly concluded that because of persecution, not biblical injunction, it is not God's will to attempt evangelism among the Malays. In any case, true to the homogeneous unit principle, Chinese pastors in Kuala Lumpur are especially burdened with the many Chinese there who do not have a saving knowledge of Christ.

Assuming it is the will of God that Malays have the same reasonable opportunity to consider the claims of Christ on their life as the Chinese or Tamils, it behooves the churches outside Malaysia to send some men and women gifted in analysis and problem-solving. They will find a way to make disciples among the Malays even though it has not yet been accomplished successfully.

Experience bears out McGavran's contention that Muslims who would be intolerant of a witness from their near neighbors, with whom they have a historical enmity, may be quite open to hearing the same message from another nationality, particularly if that person's social ranking is adequate. This is even more true if the one sharing the gospel is doing it in a culturally appropriate way, avoiding putting the Muslim on the defensive. This is assuming the prior question of trust. Warm, respectful, human relationships—once established—remove the likelihood of a Muslim friend reporting the conversation to the police. Often it is not the "offense of the cross" that closes Muslims to a reflectful consideration of Christ, but the offensiveness of the messenger. That kind of problem can be solved.

Foundational Knowledge

Later, the need to be acquainted with one's adopted country's culture, religion, language, value system, and so forth will be addressed. But what about theological training? Each member of a church planting team must know the Scriptures well enough to understand and teach basic Christian doctrine. Before going into the field, they should know how to respond to typical Muslim misunderstandings of Christianity. Muslims expect the Christian to be able to show what the Bible teaches and how it addresses the issues that are relevant to them.

How well one needs to know the Bible and systematic theology would depend on that individual's role in the church planting effort. Team members responsible for a well digging project will not be required to either argue against a deuteral-Isaiah hypothesis, or necessarily be able to invalidate "The Gospel of Barnabas." However, each should be able to introduce a sincere seeker with any sincere question to a co-worker who can address it.

Thus we reiterate that, of the various persons involved in the church planting ministry, since not everyone has the same role to play in the corporate ministry of proclaiming the gospel, not everyone needs the same knowledge. In some cases in Acts the proclamation is in the plural, "we" or "they" proclaimed the Word, but in other cases the focus is on

Paul or some other individual speaker. Thus we would conclude that proclaiming the Word to unbelievers is not the major ministry of every individual on the church planting team. There are different roles for individuals in regards to proclamation; some who are not able to minister to groups might be quite effective on a one to one basis or in a living room to one family.

Some persons hesitate to join a missionary team because they cannot relate to the book of Acts. Doug Magnuson in North Africa feels that Paul and his companions did not have a gift for evangelism far beyond that of Christian workers today. The essential qualification for what was done in the book of Acts was a thorough understanding of the gospel, especially in terms of God working throughout history, and an ability to communicate it effectively to others. Paul more than once indicated that his preaching was not with "eloquence or superior wisdom," but was done "in weakness and fear, and with much trembling" (1 Cor. 2:1, 3). Paul claimed, therefore, that any response was not due to something special in himself, but to a working of the Spirit of God (1 Cor. 2:4). "I may not be a trained speaker, but I do have knowledge" (2 Cor. 11:6).

Paul asks for prayer, for opportunities to proclaim with clarity (Col. 4:3–4), for the right words to speak, and for fearlessness (Eph. 6:19–20). Paul was "receptor-oriented" and God-oriented simultaneously. Others were similarly gifted in teaching the Word of God and were exhorted to do such a ministry for the upbuilding of the church. Silas, recruited by Paul, had a prophetic gift he used to "encourage and strengthen the brothers" (Acts 15:32). Titus was instructed by Paul to teach, rebuke, encourage and warn with "all authority" (Titus 2:15).

Timothy, another of Paul's co-workers, was exhorted to devote himself to preaching and teaching (1 Tim. 4:13), and to correctly handle the word of truth (2 Tim. 2:15), using it for teaching, rebuking, correcting, training, and encouraging through "careful instruction" (2 Tim. 3:16–4:2). These skills, still basic for ministry today, demand a commitment to keep growing in an understanding of the Word of God, and an ability to "teach others also" (2 Tim. 2:2). Such knowledge can be better learned in the midst of the ministry than at seminary.

A Work Ethic

In too many cases there have been missionaries who have worked far fewer hours at their ministry each week than their supporters in the sending churches. Because many missionaries are unsupervised, they can too easily allow the week to be dominated by domestic duties, writing to supporters, or preparing a Bible study or two. It seems rather superfluous looking for a "redemptive analogy" to bring a breakthrough in a ministry if preoccupation with existence allows only 3 to 6 hours a week for bringing people to Christ. One gifted missionary, fluent in the language, was spending up to twenty hours a week doing banking for the other missionaries! The banking could have been done by a retired self-supporting team member or volunteer who spoke a little French, thereby freeing this excellent missionary for direct ministry with Muslims.

The Apostle Paul writes of the schemes of the wicked one (2 Cor. 2:11). These schemes are not limited to getting one to quit or fall into immorality. Some of the schemes are simply to distract from concentrating on the task one was sent overseas to do. Sadly, mission agencies get too many applications from young people who have been in school their entire lives. They have not been patterned to a 40 hour a week job for more than a few weeks.

Therefore, would-be missionaries often come with an unrealistic idea of what a normal work week entails. The donor to missionaries who works for IBM, Woolworths, or sells houses has a boss to please, quotas to make, and hours to keep whether or not his wife is depressed or kids are sick. The farmer does not have the luxury of taking off a week for prayer during harvest season. The mission agency needs to justify to the sending church that the contribution of their missionary warrants the cost. One missionary with five children went to France to serve as the maintenance man in a Bible correspondence school. As his family continued to increase it became evident that it cost far more to support them than they could justify. In contrast, if a church can send facilitator-types with families who can start a business and thereby provide residence for three more couples who can make disciples, then the investment is justified.

Emotional Stability

There are two kinds of Christians: those mostly focused on themselves, and those mostly focused on the needs of others. Sending churches and mission agencies are looking for people who have both the will and the capacity to be "givers." This assumes a substantial level of emotional health. Well meaning and dedicated people thinking of the mission field, who because of their difficult backgrounds have an emotional vacuum, may need such a high degree of maintenance that there is little point in sending them overseas as missionaries. A growing, secure person is eager for psychological assessment—eager in fact to obtain all the pastoral care available toward becoming a person who can maintain joy and a capacity to serve others in the midst of difficult circumstances.

It is common knowledge that some missionaries supplement and encourage their colleagues, and others drain and distract their co-workers to the detriment of the work. A basic element of emotional and spiritual growth is an attitude that sees vulnerability as a strength. Mature individuals are not threatened when people want to correct their deficiencies. A missionary must model to the converted Muslim that a disciple is one who welcomes assistance from every side toward becoming a person of God and an increasingly effective servant.

Adequate in Communication Skills

Missionary life is no occupation for the recluse. Introverts especially need to realize that nearly all on a church planting team have high expectations laid on them to communicate—to their prayer partners, to their sending churches, to their mission agency, to their colleagues, and most important of all, to the people they have come to minister. It is vital that all members of a church planting team among Muslims know the areas in which they are expected to communicate well. The need to communicate effectively will vary according to one's role, but there seems little place on a church planting team for people who are so private that almost no one knows what they are doing or thinking.

Grateful Servants of God (1 Thess. 1:7–10)

Whatever one's function might be, God, sending churches, and mission agencies are looking for grateful people who deeply understand what a privilege it is to be set apart by a church, to be a co-worker with

God and one's colleagues in accomplishing God's purposes. It may be possible to be an indifferent "professional" when employed in an ecclesiastical position in the West, but Muslims will soon discern whether you are a person with a deep sense of calling, gratefully teamed up with the living God, or merely a paid propagandist of religion.

Marital Status

As the sending church decides whom to send—who could make the most effective contribution to a church planting effort—the discussion inevitably comes to the advantages and disadvantages of singles versus families. The Roman Catholic and Mormon churches have abundantly demonstrated that single workers can spend much more time among the target peoples, free from the cares of family life. On the other hand, since marriages are arranged and the single life is seldom an option to Muslims, a single man or woman over thirty is continually suspect. Single men are not always welcome in the homes of more conservative Muslims.

Sometimes single missionaries find themselves limited to ministering to other singles, usually students. Far from home in a strange city a single man also faces greater temptation to fall into sexual immorality.

Is there a place for singles in the family-oriented Muslim world? In North Africa, several of the most effective missionaries in the last twenty-five years have been single women. However, an overall evaluation would probably reveal that only one of every five or six single women has the emotional capacity to live more than two to four years as an unmarried Christian worker in a Muslim city.

Increasingly progressive mission agencies are encouraging single women whose churches want to send them to the Muslim world to focus on goals appropriate for a two-year term. Then they, the church, and their agencies can discern whether God has given them the capacity to minister singly over a long term in that culture. If not, they are encouraged to return home without a sense of failure, knowing that they have made a significant contribution to the on-going team effort. Interestingly, the single women who historically have been effective usually found that most of their fruit in disciple-making came when they were beyond 35 years of age and had enjoyed long-term relationships with

Muslim families. Their singleness had become accepted. They became a significant trusted person to the extended families to whom they ministered. In some cases it was important that they be "sponsored" by a respected Muslim family who would continually uphold their reputation as a "good woman."

Ironically, in many Muslim cultures it is more acceptable to be a divorced person than to never have been married. "At least her father was able to get some family to accept her once" runs the gossip.

Those who are ministering effectively as single people have in common that they are pleasant individuals who can fit in with either an expatriate or a Muslim family. The single person who is preoccupied with a desire to get married is probably not called to be single, and may be too inward-looking to effectively minister beyond a short term overseas. Such people need to be given an assignment at home while they are single, or until it is no longer an issue for them.

It is likely that the most effective change agents among Muslims will be families in which a man's love for his wife and children is evident to the on-looker. A household that is not well managed, or where fear, frustration, or anger prevails, is not likely to be very productive in ministry. The familial qualifications for an elder would be basic to the change agent on a church planting team.

Studies of the IFMA (Interdenominational Foreign Mission Association) have shown the most frequent reason that missionaries returned to their home country prematurely was because of their inability to work and live with co-workers. Present trends, however, indicate that the most prominent reason is that they could not adjust to rearing a family in a Muslim country as a bivocational missionary. This may be because of the inordinate expectations of western evangelical culture on parents today. In the past, missionaries had a reputation for neglecting their children (whether it was true or not). Today's missionary candidates are highly conscious of psychological issues that often result in a paralyzing fear of not being adequate parents. This concern may be exacerbated by an increasingly large number of candidates whose parents are divorced and who themselves suffered some kind of deprivation.

Whatever the reasons, young missionary parents seem to be disproportionately anxious about protecting their children, and doubt it is possible in a Muslim area. These overriding concerns have dramatically increased the number of missionaries returning home when their children are between 8 to 14 years of age. It also has greatly increased the percentage of parents who insist on home schooling. Facing up to this reality, Marguerite Kraft suggests that team and ministry continuity could be designed so that a family could return home for 4 to 5 years if the children need to.

If possible, pioneer church planting teams that face educational challenges for their children should recruit single teachers for two years at a time to set up their own "one room" M.K. school, utilizing materials approved by the parents.

These important issues, however, are beyond the scope of this book. It is feared that if missionaries leave their adopted Muslim people group soon after they have become fluent in the language, have their mistakes behind them, and have become a trusted person and effective communicator—as well as having reached an age when they are more likely to be listened to—this generation is not going to be any more effective in church planting among Muslims than those of the past. Furthermore, there is a consensus among mission executives that a very small percentage of families who leave the field for more than two years ever return.

If the vast majority of mission effort among Muslims continues to be done by people in their twenties and early thirties who are still in the apprentice stage, then we are working in opposition to cultures who normally take truth from their "elders"—those over 50 years old. Recent experiments with early retirees supplementing teams in Turkey, Morocco, and Egypt look like a partial answer to this problem. They also provide much welcomed "grandparents" for the children.

Home schooling is back in vogue, and it does enable families to go where there are no affordable English medium schools. However, most mothers home-schooling their children are going to have difficulty learning the Muslims' language, and will not be spending sufficient time with Muslim mothers. The expatriate mother, then, is in danger of not becoming "at home" in the culture, which will make it even more difficult for her to persevere there.

It is important that sending churches and agencies help aspiring missionaries to understand which expectations on parents are biblical absolutes, and which may simply be trendy, cultural, or a question of personal preference (possibly motivated by fear). These issues are so paramount that Parshall (1977) expressed his conviction that those sensing an assignment from God to do pioneer church planting should seriously consider whether he is not also leading them to have zero to two children. Though it can be argued that most segments of Muslim cultures would not comprehend limiting a family by birth control, it is not necessary to inform them "why God has not given more children."

In summary, those seeking to do church planting among Muslims must give problem-solving attention to these issues, believing that the God who sends has the answers to the problems of rearing a family or being single in a Muslim city. Surely it is basic to fully trust that the God who wants to use his servants to rescue the Muslims will be faithful in meeting the needs of his faithful servants and those of their children. If they are not sufficiently "at home" when their children reach teenage years, there may be some serious flaw in the enculturation process. Until strong national leadership can take the work forward, it must be determined what it takes to stay in a Muslim city, lest the missionaries find themselves on a merry-go-round that yields no more fruit than efforts of the past.

5

Making Critical Choices

Which people should be targeted? With whom should the change agent team up? What should the change agent's identity be? Augustine reportedly taught, "Love the Lord your God with all your heart, soul, strength, and mind, and do what you want." There is a sense in which God does not mind which Muslim city or which segment of that population is targeted, since almost any society of Muslims would qualify as "laying down one's life for the brethren" (1 John 3:16), or "preaching the gospel where Christ was not known" (Rom. 15:20). Therefore, it may be more directive to begin where a bridge or an open door is evident.

To Whom

One missionary is going to a city in Saudi Arabia where he spent several years as a child, because his father worked there. He has friends who are welcoming him and is thus fulfilling the principle of Matthew 10:11–14: "Whatever town or village you enter, search for some worthy person there and stay at his house until you leave." Commonly in Muslim contexts it is important to have a sponsor, a leading citizen who is respected by your target community. Being the friend of Abu Daud automatically gives you legitimacy in the neighborhood. In many parts of the Muslim world it is similar to biblical times, where receptivity is related to who you know will receive you.

Bivocational missionaries are strongly encouraged to make friends in high places. Friends can be called upon to rescue them when under the threat of expulsion or prison. A large percentage of missionaries to Muslim countries who have been asked to leave would not have been required to do so (at least not as soon) had they adequately enmeshed themselves in the society. A local sheriff in Algiers apologized profusely, while serving coffee to a missionary colleague, because he was not able to renew the English teacher's missionary visa. This government official had been friendly toward the missionary for years, but pleaded he was too low in the pecking order to reverse the handed down decision. One wonders whether it would have been different if the missionary had joined the local Rotary Club. What if his wife had taught English to the children of one of the prestigious families? By contrast, one woman's family has become friends with the ruler of an Arab country. She teaches ice skating to children of the ruling family and serves on the ruler's committee for the special Olympics. Another worker has befriended the chief of police in an Arab capital. The chief has put his reputation in jeopardy by telling this missionary, "If any of the religious mullahs give you any trouble, let me know and we'll put them back in their place."

To overcome the opposition of the Muslim fundamentalists, we can utilize the ideology of the liberal or noble minded in high places. They may defend Christian activity under the principle of freedom, and their desire to see Islam perceived as tolerant. A bivocational missionary in the Arab Gulf made friends with such a man who was the editor of two newspapers and eleven magazines. This highly educated Oxford graduate was aware of the missionary's purposes, yet he was willing to sponsor missionaries as businessmen because of his conviction that deeply spiritual and sacrificial Christians in business are a needed example for his country.

Parshall recommends that missionaries live as close to their target culture as they can, without endangering the mental or physical health of their family. This injunction recognizes that missionaries have differing capacities to adapt. Some are gifted to live among the abject poor, others with the lower middle classes, and others still should seek to make their influence felt among the upper middle class.

One idealistic couple from an elitist Atlantic seaboard college moved into the slums of Tunis, Tunisia, intending (in their minds) to follow the example of the Lord Jesus. It is doubtful whether this particular couple could have adapted to the slums of Philadelphia, much less Tunis. The Tunisian slumdwellers, unable to comprehend the Americans' motives, and being totally unaccustomed to Europeans living in their quarter, threw stones at the children and the windows, and left human excrement on their doorstep. Such reactions by the Muslims left these missionaries devastated both emotionally and physically. They left the Muslim world permanently.

This same couple might have been effective among Tunisians who administer or teach at the University of Tunis. Change agents should normally begin with those closest to them culturally, where the communication gap is most narrow. After some time, some will be able to live and work in the slums, among the garbage collectors and rickshaw drivers. Viv Grigg (1984) and others have demonstrated that those truly assigned by God to live in the slums are enabled to do so as they learn to adapt and know their limits.

New Muslim converts will be most likely to witness to someone at, or slightly below, their own social status. Once there is a well-established group of Tunisian or Aceh believers, for example, who are confident in their walk with the Lord and their place in society, as they mature in Christ they will be able to "go into the streets and gather in the poor, crippled, and blind" (Luke 14:13). However, as McGavran (1980) points out, to prematurely attempt to link a rural farmer, a middle class merchant, and a member of the royal family into a church body is unrealistic in any culture.

For western Christians to piously insist that new Muslim believers from every strata of society move in and out of one another's homes as supportive friends (because they are equals in Christ) is missing the fact that few western evangelicals have close friends in several social stratas. In most Muslim cultures, close social interchange is often limited to other long-known families. Therefore, this work advocates that expatriates focus on heads of families among a particular social segment of the city.

In any case, change agents must begin with a certain social economic segment of society with which they can gain substantial depth of affinity and communication. If they are constantly looked at as the rich English curiously visiting the slums, it may be a long time before serious negotiations over the claims of Christ are possible, due to the lack of sufficient trust and rapport.

It is one thing to know which strata of society to begin with, but what about the more basic question of which people? How would you know if you were to go to Iranians, Nigerians, or the Hui in China? It is a biblical given that God prepares his servants comprehensively. Therefore, change agents reflect on whomever God has caused to cross their paths to that point. Have they met a number of Iranians and enjoyed their food and various aspects of their values and worldview? This may be some indication that they would function substantially well in the Middle East. Perhaps they realize an affinity to sub-Saharan Africans or Muslims of the Indian subcontinent, or perhaps the Chinese or Southeast Asians. A Germanic personality might do much better among the Hui in China than among the Arabs in Dubai. Another might prefer to minister to Mediterranean people. He would need to enjoy the Arab who slaps him on the back after knowing him five minutes saying "You are my best friend. I like you too (sic) much." It is difficult to make disciples if one cannot make friends. To make friends, it is vital to be able to enjoy people and the basic ethos of their culture.

Paul the apostle had sufficient affinity with his target people. He could speak of sacrificing his life, even being poured out like a drink offering, in the same breath with: "I am glad and rejoice with all of you. So you too should be glad and rejoice with me" (Phil. 2:17–18).

Different Kinds of Callings

Over the last century, God has enabled pioneer church planters to determine their place of ministry in a number of different ways. Here is a partial list:

- Going out to the people one met at home or on travels.
- Feeling a call to a particular social segment, for example, students, businessmen, medical professionals, street people, prisoners, or the abject poor.

- Having the imagination caught by a particular country or continent. (Before 1970 it was not uncommon to meet missionaries who professed they "knew" from childhood they were supposed to go to Africa.) Some intuitively sense that God wants them to work among Muslims, Buddhists, or Bibleless tribes.
- Sensing direction to a particular organization or agency, for example, Campus Crusade, Arab World Ministries, Frontiers, Operation Mobilization, or the mission agency of one's denomination.
- Going through the local church. The church leaders may appeal to members to go to a certain unreached people. If the church is feeling led to adopt the Kurds, some from that church should first consider this possibility. It is also quite acceptable for would-be missionaries to offer themselves to their church's or denomination's mission agency, with the conviction that the leaders can decide best where they are most needed and where their gifts best fit.
- Being led by God to a co-worker. Timothy was recruited by Paul and his home church confirmed that he should go out to be Paul's apprentice. Timothy apparently did not know where he was going, or to which people, except that some would be Jews and some Gentiles. Some hear of a particular work (for example, Viggo Olson in Bangladesh or Chris Marintika in Java) and sense God leading them to work with it. Others may be recruited by a team leader of a new church planting effort with whom they feel a rapport and likemindedness—even though they may feel no particular compassion for the Uzbeks of Afghanistan.
- Feeling drawn to a particular kind of ministry or profession. Some have gone with World Vision to feed impoverished Muslims in The Sahel, North Africa, or to be doctor in TEAM's hospital in Pakistan; or have acquired a degree in teaching English or chemistry, and afterward looked for an opportunity to teach as part of a church planting team in a Muslim city.
- Going where there is a response. Some are encouraged by church growth thinking, or by their church leaders. Would-be missionaries to the Muslim world have often been discouraged by the elders in their church, who have considered Muslim work an

exercise in futility. "Why don't you go where the Lord's work-ing?" Some church mission committees, programmed by the American business ethos, advocate the would-be church planter go where the donors get "the most results for their financial investment."

For whatever motive, it is not necessarily unbiblical to place the reapers where the harvest seems most ripe. Agencies can help deter-mine where a people movement may be starting. In 1992, such a con-viction to give priority to the presently responsive might lead one to work with Iranians, in Bangladesh, or with the Sundanese of West Java. However, it is inappropriate to register a particular Muslim people as unresponsive where the number of actual presentations of the claims of Christ under appropriate circumstances in the Muslims' language have been more or less negligible—or at least far too few to label the people unresponsive. It would be more accurate to label such societies as yet untested.

McGavran taught that in any given city, the change agents must con-tinually filter through the various segments of society to identify those who manifest the greatest felt needs for what the gospel offers. For exam-ple, a church planting team has been working in an affluent suburb of Istanbul for years, finding very few Turks who are concerned about pleas-ing even Allah (never mind Christ). Not many reveal concern for the final judgment of which both the Koran and Bible speak.

The team decided to divide up, in order to test the response in two other cities, as well as to upgrade their skills for detecting spiritual hunger within their chosen subset of Istanbul. In Kingston, Ontario, if Chris-tians want to identify neighbors who are "seeking the Lord" or being "drawn by the Father" (depending on one's theology) they might start a neighborhood Bible study and invite their neighbors face to face. If neighbors show up professing that they "always wanted to get into the Bible," it is reasonable to conclude that this person is moving toward Christ.

How would a church planting team in Istanbul discern who was inter-ested or seeking the Lord? In each city, the church planting team will need to establish and continually refine a system of counsel with the first converts, one that will alert them to the signs of responsiveness, so they will spend their limited time with the people most likely to become followers of Christ.

As Whom

How should change agents identify themselves and their associates? Historically, mission agencies have been the assumed vehicle for a church planting team. It is possible, of course, to go to a Muslim city as an ambassador for Christ without being related to an established mission agency. In fact, Ralph Winter estimates that roughly 100,000 western evangelical Christians hold jobs overseas—perhaps several thousand in Muslim countries.

Therefore, it is argued, a good strategy is to go overseas at a government's expense, on a very adequate salary from a multi-national corporation, or to get hired by a Muslim company or institution. To do so avoids the unenviable task of raising one's own salary from donors. Often overseas positions include benefit packages, including school expenses for children, medical insurance, and even air fare back home annually. Theoretically, the "tent-maker" could stay close to his local church, still have a commissioning service, be continually prayed for, and could avoid the possibly distasteful or confining subculture of a fundamentalistic mission agency.

Is this not the era of the tent-makers? Some pastors even prefer this model because their church gets credit for having a missionary out there in the Arab Gulf without needing to pay any of the expenses!

A seminary graduate has the option to pastor an international church for westerners in a Muslim city. Although his first responsibility is to the western Christians needing a shepherd, there are opportunities to also minister to the needs of the missionaries, and possibly he could occasionally minister to Muslims himself if the church board does not forbid it out of concern for legalities. Indeed, it would be helpful if the international churches in Muslim cities were pastored by men with a heart for the Muslims, who in turn would encourage others seeking to plant churches, or at least witness to Muslims. Christy Wilson of Afghanistan, Dudley Woodbury of Saudi Arabia, and Paul Smith in Fez, Morocco (before he took a team to the Kurds in Iraq) are excellent examples of pastors to the missionaries who also served as coaches for church planting efforts.

Unfortunately, as Michael Griffiths points out in *Give Up Your Small Ambitions* (1970), very few people are effective at two major tasks. The examples of individual tent-makers with full-time jobs who have made a measurable contribution to planting a church among Muslims are rare. There have been some outstanding characters who worked a full-time job, learned the language well, and made disciples, but the vast majority of ordinary people accomplish very little among Muslims without a team of like-minded people combining their skills, time, and contacts.

Without a coordinating mission agency, it is difficult to establish and maintain a team. Of course, many larger churches can send out a whole team and by-pass the existing mission agencies, but by doing so they themselves become a tiny mission agency that most likely is unable to give adequate services and supervision to the church planting team.

Normally, churches are not planted among Muslims unless several people in a given city see establishing a church as their primary task. These workers are held responsible for staying focused on the task. The workers must learn the language and culture well, with adequate supervision and coaching. There must be sufficient freedom and time for majoring in making disciples, as well as a back-up agency committed to continuity of the church planting effort—even if there is a complete turnover of personnel.

Of course, people on a church planting team in a restricted access country may need to take a job in the city to establish their residence. It is strongly advised, however, that a church planting team either start their own business, which gives them ultimate freedom to minister in association and in their own chosen time frame, or that they at least get hired by Muslims and work for Muslims, staying in the Muslim milieu. Those who work for western companies may get much higher salaries, but they will usually find, to their great disappointment, that it is the western companies more than the Muslims who forbid the propagation of Christianity. The company that has a multi-million dollar contract does not want to lose it because one of its employees was "messing with the native's religion."

Historically, a case could be made that the British and French governments have been a greater hindrance to the propagation of the gospel than any of the Muslim governments. For example, William Carey, when he launched out to India, had to take up residence in a Danish colony there because he was barred from preaching the gospel to Indians by his own British government.

Another advantage in working for Muslims is that most Muslim cultures are not workaholic, management by objective oriented, like large western firms. There is ample time to share one's values and worldview on the job when working with Muslims. In western culture, witnessing on "company time" is considered unethical. Such a notion is unfathomable in a people before profits culture.

Finally, those who work for western companies tend to find themselves living in a nice, but isolated, foreigners' ghetto, segregated from the people to whom they came to minister. Therefore, it is a premise of this text that being in connection with, and responsible to, a ministry team accountable to a missions agency is most conducive to effective church planting.

Ethics

Increasing numbers of committed world Christians, both connected to and unattached from mission agencies, are taking up posts among Muslims where no missionary visas are offered. Are they ethically required to identify themselves as missionaries or not? Do people who are clearly sent out by a church to make disciples, and who are understood at home to have missionary intentions (secular job or not), need to declare themselves "missionaries" to the host government? If they do not, are they agents of deceit, living a lie before their adopted people by portraying themselves as English teachers, artists, businesspeople, students, and so on? Does it make a difference ethically if they report only to their church and are not supervised by a mission agency?

I know several former missionaries who have renounced their membership or attachment to a mission agency, hoping to alleviate the agony of getting discovered, or their guilt for being "deceitful," fearing they will eventually be confronted with the question, "Are you a missionary?" or "Have you been sent by a missionary organization?" By resigning from their agency (or never joining one) they hope to be seen as having greater integrity, being less of a deceiver, one who pretends to be one thing, but who is actually there for a much different reason.

However, the uneasiness is not usually resolved by resigning from an agency. The independents still know that they are there to see Muslims become Christians, but they did not tell their employer that on their application.

No one debates that a Christian must be an honest person, and also be perceived as such. Who is going to receive the gospel from a person who is not perceived as good? Is it possible to be missionaries, yet not be *officially* missionaries? How shall we deal with this question?

A Muslim may not understand the change agent's deepest motivations since the Muslim has not yet entered the Kingdom of Christ. Easterners normally do not think of religion as evangelical westerners do: as a personal response, a decision to give themselves to God, to enter into God's family or remain apart from it. To Muslims, religion is the house in which they have been born. Hence, in the Muslim's view, any effort to convert a Muslim to Christianity is essentially robbery committed against the established Islamic community. Becoming a Christian is an act of betrayal on the part of the Muslim, running counter to the laws of family, and perhaps even nature. Most Muslims are unable, or unwilling, to see conversion as a choice or contract that a person can make solely based on a desire to please or obey God. It will be extremely rare for any Muslim to consider someone involved in disciple-making as noble, or even reasonable, even though Christians see it as a consistent application of the Christian faith. To most Muslims, only an insensitive, arrogantly superior, colonialistic-minded, brain-washed fanatic would ever make it the point of his life to see Muslims "change their religion." Reproach or accusations of dishonesty and trickery, therefore, though essentially unjustified, are unavoidable (2 Cor. 6:8). Disciple-makers must be deeply rooted in the conviction that it is their obligation to help bring about a reconciliation between the Savior and their Muslim friends.

Change agents must live in the awareness that they are simply trying to be obedient to the Lord, not arrogantly trying to make a conquest, but merely carrying out Christ's orders. The so-called ethical doubts may arise from North-Atlantic cultural conditioning, manipulated by a people incapable of seeing the missionary's true motives. Obviously, missionaries would be perceived as good if Muslims could understand their true purpose: to show the way to forgiveness and power over sin.

Furthermore, it seems impossible to function as an ambassador for Christ, breathing the urgency of a rescue operation, without it becoming quite evident to those around you! Sooner or later a witnessing Christian will be confronted with the indicting questions: "Are you a missionary?" "Are you trying to change the religion of the people here?" "Do you believe Muslims need to be followers of Christ?"

More often, Muslims don't bother with questions, but dogmatically inform you of what they are sure of: "We know you have been sent by your government to convert our people!" No matter what you answer to any of the above you are as guilty as the Muslims choose to make you. There is no evidence that any Christian worker has ever met a Muslim who, when aware of the "tent-makers" true purpose, saw his agenda become more acceptable simply because the worker was not officially attached to a missions agency.

It is difficult for a Muslim to even conceive of an independent agent. Suppose they are told that friends and family (or church) are the ones praying and paying for one's endeavor to convert Muslims? Tent-makers are not considered more noble, or seen as having more integrity because they do not belong to a mission society. There is no evidence that being independent of an agency makes a disciple-making Christian among Muslims more acceptable, or in any less danger of expulsion.

Perhaps it will be helpful if we discern between two different issues.

1. What is the basis on which one is applying for a residence visa?
2. How does one's worldview affect civil disobedience?

In biblical times, it is doubtful that the people of the Roman empire thought of Paul and his New Testament church planting team as "missionaries" by profession, since the category or vocation was not common. Most likely, they were seen, as Jesus himself, as a person with a profession who had also become a religious teacher with disciples. It is unlikely that Paul introduced himself as an "apostle" (Latin for missionary) to non-Christians.

Thus, when you apply for a visa, you simply consider what options exist or are offered to a foreigner in that particular country and choose the one most appropriate. If it is possible to get a job as an English teacher, you are saying that you want to be in their country and, in order to do so, you are willing to take the option they are offering you to be an English teacher. If it would be helpful to your sense of integrity, you might consider asking the consul if they offer a visa to be a religious teacher of Christianity. If they say no, you could then ask if they object to foreign teachers or businessmen being Christians and practicing their religion. Muslims generally pride themselves in saying that Christians are free to practice their religion, including discussing it with Muslim friends.

Do any Muslims apply to the United States Embassy for a missionary visa to be a missionary to the Americans? Some possibly apply to be chaplains to Muslims studying in, or migrated to, the United States (the equivalent of applying to be a pastor to expatriate Christians in Morocco). But good Muslims, no matter what their profession, would be happy to spread their faith. So it is not difficult to explain to Muslims that no matter what job we might hold, spreading the "good news" and seeing people get right with God is much more important to us.

Would we be offended if we discovered that a Yemeni Muslim in Detroit supported himself by repairing shoes, but turned his shoe repair shop into a place to discuss the merits of Islam with Americans? If anything, we would admire him. Would this not be true in reverse in the Muslim world? If we discover, in questioning our shoe repairman, that in fact he is supported from Al Ahzar University as part of a Muslim missionary society, we might be surprised to know we are objects of Islamic missionary work, but we would not likely be offended or accuse him of having no integrity simply because he is fixing shoes. If he came to America under the only provision immigration gave him, as long as he was also doing what his visa stipulated, we would not think him unethical.

So to get a visa to Kuwait on the understanding that the member of a church planting team is going to teach English means that, among other things, he must be teaching English. If she has a visa on the basis of being an artist, she must paint, or if to export rugs, it should result in buying and exporting. But like good Muslims, biblical Christians are not materialists. Our purposes are much higher, as are the priorities of noble Muslims, Hindus, or Buddhists. When one has a significant trust relationship with Muslims, they will be eager to hear about our higher purpose and calling from God. Why are you really in Constantine? Because God sent you!

Andrew Van der Bijl (Brother Andrew) addresses the issue of the necessity of civil disobedience. He has publicly encouraged Christians to go where they are not invited. "There are no closed countries as long as you are willing to not come back out!" Muslims may not take Christians seriously until they are willing to fill up the jails of Muslim countries. If Mohandas Gandhi, for a cause that he felt was just, could introduce nonviolent civil disobedience, why would it be thought inappropriate for Christians to do the same? As when they are told that they may not take up residence in a Muslim city to make disciples, in obedience to the Lord Jesus Christ?

Andrew Van der Bijl (Brother Andrew) teaches that Christians can in all righteousness break certain laws. William Tyndale opposed King James to make the Bible available to England in English. Adoniram Judson, pioneer Baptist missionary to Burma, George Vins in the Soviet Union, and Watchman Nee in China were all imprisoned—condemned by the action of the constituted authorities because they broke the law. Why were there believers in prison at the time the New Testament was being written? Why have Christians been imprisoned throughout the history of the church until this very day? These believers, like the apostles Peter and John, decided to obey God rather than man. They decided they would not obey the civil laws when those laws transgressed the express will of God. In fact, we may have to break the law of man and of governments in order to keep the law of God (Bijl 1985).

If civil disobedience is right in relation to nuclear weapons, racism, or abortion, how much more in our obedience to the King of kings to go make disciples of all *ethnos*? Should we finish what the Lord Jesus Christ commanded us to do, or should we stop short because of the mistaken perspectives and directives of Muslim rulers?

With Whom

Aside from the futility of thinking that a witness will have more integrity by not working with missionary co-workers, it is crucial to face the implications of not being accountable to a missions agency. Nearly all workers with Muslims are working beyond their skills or experience. Few are Paul-type apostles. Most will continually have difficulties merely "becoming at home" in their adopted culture, not to mention becoming a change agent within it. Few are natural missionary types, heavily endowed with dramatic gifts to singlehandedly preach and teach and plant churches. Most, however, can make a significant contribution as part of a church planting team.

History shows that only a few "loner" types have been sufficiently gifted, independent, and strong in their relationship with God to recruit nationals alone, to work so quickly that they could overcome the disadvantages of being without an expatriate missionary team. Although going alone is an option, it is important to realize that a Muslim city without a church is territory under the wicked one's control (Matt. 12:29; 2 Cor. 10:4).

Why would anyone want to make themselves any more vulnerable to the schemes of Satan than necessary? Christians have more protection where they are subject to shepherds (Acts 20:28–29). The people who are so immature emotionally that they fear authority more than they covet the wisdom of the elders whom God has placed in their lives are not likely to persevere at the church planting task. Finally, an independent worker is a poor model to the Muslim convert. So whether a person seeking to plant churches in Muslim cities is attracted to a mission agency or not, it is a tenet of this work that the Lord's commands are in the plural "you." God normally intends for us to serve with a team of people whose gifts and pastoral care are complementary.

What Is a Church Planting Team, Then?

The paradigm in the book of Acts involves several people working together to enter into a given city, become significant trusted residents or sponsored guests, and proclaim the good news of Jesus Christ as change agents, then making disciples whose supreme loyalty is to Christ, and enabling these new believers to assemble together to represent Christ in that area as his ambassadors.

Although different church planting teams may have different entry strategies, as well as different ways to become identified with their adopted people, they have in common one overriding purpose: to plant churches with their own national leadership among the Muslim citizens of that city. We say "churches" because this work, as mentioned above, endorses the homogeneous unit principle, which understands that new believers will want fellowship and worship with their own kind of people. There may need to be different fellowships within a given city that would cater to the more urbane, westernized Muslim versus the more eastern rural Muslim, as well as house fellowships for the educated or semiliterate. Transportation problems may demand that there be several flocks around the city for accessibility, so each self-contained neighborhood might have their own congregation.

Church planting teams need members with a variety of gifts and experience in order to be fruitful. But the three most important components that every team must have before they can even begin are described below.

The Three Components of a New Testament Missionary Team

The Team Leader

This spearhead person is something of an entrepreneur (whether an extrovert or an introvert), gifted at getting the process started, and helping the rest of the team envision the steps necessary to leave the home country and take up residence in a Muslim city. This team leader must continue to motivate and problem solve as colleagues face a series of impasses and disappointments. This is the one who constantly breeds an attitude that the task is do-able.

However, Frontiers has ascertained in recent years that a pioneer church planting team in many cases needs a different kind of leader for the second stage of the effort than it did for the initial stage. The founder of a church planting effort, like a creative entrepreneur starting a church at home, is often a person with different skills and personality traits than the one who can take over an effort with effective personnel and resource management.

The first-stage team leader is often a "big picture" person with good motivational skills, minimal caution, and an optimism that is contagious—the kind of person who can help people envision the work before it is started and thus give team members the security to attempt something they would normally not. After approximately two years, however, team members getting settled into a culture often feel that they may have greater insights than the original team leader. Typically, they begin to vie for control of the team's policies and strategy. They also usually manifest a need for increased pastoral care, which the pioneer team leader may not be skilled to provide.

The first-stage team leader then begins to think of team members as too independent or rebellious. It may be time to move that team leader on, to start a new work that does not demand so much managing of people and follow-through on details. At this point, the team needs a second-stage team leader who is more skilled and experienced in pastoral care and administration. Such a team leader is more appropriately sensitive to the task of patiently discipling national elders into shepherds of the new flock.

Both these team leaders, however, must concentrate on the church planting process, leaving the church establishing business enterprise or relief project to other people who can give themselves to that task. If the project leader is also the team leader, the church planting process tends to suffer because of a preoccupation with establishing the business or project.

The "People" People

Whether they are called disciple-makers, ministers, or nurturers, it is clear that a number of people-oriented tasks must be accomplished in the church planting effort. But not all "disciple-makers" have the same skills. Ephesians 4:11 implies that even those who minister directly to people will have different gifts:

FRIEND MAKERS

Someone on the church planting team must be able to meet strangers in such a way that there is a desire to continue the relationship. This person is able to introduce a Muslim friend to others with different gifts or ministry skills.

HOSTS

If there is one common element among Muslims, from North Africa to the Philippines, it may be their hospitality. Therefore, the change agents must likewise be perceived as hospitable, generous persons. Some of the wives and mothers can major in hospitality since their home (as opposed to a church building) will be their major site of ministry. Asians from Istanbul to Jarkarta will quickly perceive how welcome they are in a home. In the Middle East, mores about visiting homes are quite different from those in the West.

In the West, one does not normally go to a friend's for dinner until invited at a specific time on a specific day. The westerner is honoring a friend with an invitation to dinner. In the Middle East it is the opposite. The Arab or Turk honors friends by showing up unexpectedly for dinner. Therefore, Muslims will often visit and expect to be enthusiastically forced to stay and eat. The missionary who does not become known as generous and hospitable will find that any proclamation of the goodness of God is heard as hollow and truncated. Muslims, even in the cities, tend to live in cultures not unlike Luke 11:5. The man in this passage had someone visit him extremely late at night. The host was obligated to lay out at least an elementary meal immediately. In fact, his reputation was so intricately involved that he left his home at midnight and pounded on the door of a local friend to borrow three loaves of bread. It is fascinating that the host is turned down at first, but refuses to leave his neighbor's door until the man gets up and gives him as much as he needs.

An even more astonishing story is found in Genesis 18:3–8, when the angels stop by to visit Abraham. Although Abraham calls it "a bit of bread," he insists on sacrificing a sheep for a meal that would take half a day to prepare before the angels are allowed to depart and accomplish their task. And the Muslims consider Abraham the first Muslim!

EVANGELISTS

This study defines an evangelist as one who has been gifted by God to effectively help people understand their sinful nature and their need for a Savior. Most, even when trained in evangelistic techniques, do not find those to whom they speak convicted and concerned about their sin and the judgment they face in the future. But people are motivated to reconcile with God when spoken to by a gifted evangelist. Therefore the church planting team cannot afford to leave home without them. The team must also be on the search for such gifted persons among the first Muslim converts. Without evangelists, the tendency is to allow friendship evangelism to be almost entirely friendship, with little persuasive evangelism. If the church planting team does not see people actually "turn to the Lord," and switch their allegiance to the Lord Jesus Christ, it may be because they have not sufficiently involved team members with a gifted evangelist. If a team does not have such a gifted evangelist, one answer is to have a traveling evangelist visit church planting teams, meet the team members' interested friends, and then lead them to Christ. Mazhar Mallouhi serves in such a capacity for Frontiers' teams in the Middle East.

PASTORS

Evangelists typically leave follow-up to others. Because of their unique instincts, evangelists want to find someone new to confront with the claims of Christ. In their minds, follow-up is somebody else's job, and indeed it is. When Scripture speaks of God giving pastors to the church, it is not referring to senior administrators of a local church, but to those who are gifted at building up new believers in the faith.

Pastors are marked by mercy, grace orientation, and patience so that they can persevere with new believers until they develop mature biblical life patterns. A discerning sending church may rightly send someone to a church planting team who has never led a soul to Christ. The strength of these people, however, may be in nurturing several new believers who can eventually teach others, or have some other effective ministry on their own. In a Muslim city, introducing Muslims to Christ is difficult, but it is the easier task. After a Muslim becomes a follower of Christ, hundreds of hours of loving nurture are usually needed. Only those with the pastoral gift have the patience to give the needed time and support. How else will new believers learn to pray, and feed themselves on the Scriptures, and stay loyal in a mutually encouraging fellowship?

PROPHETS

The prophetic mission and gift belong to those who have been anointed and called of God to emphasize purity in the church. These persons tend to come across as critical because they have a tendency to see what is wrong in the church and in society. Because prophets hold up God's highest standards, they tend not to go out as missionaries, nor do they encourage the sending church to send others out, convinced that "we're not mature enough as Christians to export any missionaries." However, merely sharing Christ in the Muslim world may not be adequate.

Perhaps we will not see a breakthrough in a Muslim city or neighborhood until we have tough, gifted spokespersons in the mold of the Old Testament prophets. Muslims everywhere (like Christendom) tend to be indifferent, complacent, self-seeking, and seldom place a high value on pleasing God or keeping his commandments. It may come as a shock to would-be missionaries to Muslims, but the most difficult thing in Muslim cities such as Istanbul or Jakarta is to find Muslims who feel a need to be closer to God, find forgiveness, or have assurance of salvation.

The Muslim editor of two newspapers in Bahrain told of how he was fed up with the hypocrisy of the religious Saudi Arabians. He proceeded to tell stories of how Saudis would come to Bahrain and hold wild parties—getting drunk and fighting over Iranian prostitutes—although they would stop without fail for ten minutes, five times a day, for ritual prayer. They then condemned him because he did not do the required prayers.

Who can call the "hypocrites" of the Muslim cities to repentance? Will it be necessary to recruit older, righteous men with prophetic gifts to join church planting efforts, even if for a few weeks at a time, utilizing gifted interpreters?

There has also been a recent call for prophets who receive information supernaturally from God: to expose sin, give direction to individuals and the church, and even to let God's servants know what God is doing in terms of engineering events to bring people to himself. It would be interesting to witness how such a gift would serve a pioneer church planting effort.

TEACHERS

Someone has to deal thoroughly with the hard questions Muslims ask. Although theological objections are not the foremost reasons why Muslims do not submit to Christ, they certainly are significant obstacles. A church planting team needs teachers who can patiently articulate the differences between the Muslim and the biblical concepts of God.

Apologetics may not win many Muslims to Christ, but it is often vital for clearing the way so Muslims can more openly consider the claims of Christ on their life. The new believers will also be bombarded by Islamic teachers, brought in by the converts' family to win them back. Unless converts know why they believe, as well as in whom they believe, they will often falter.

Missionaries gifted as teachers are often introverts, relatively shy, and find evangelism—which takes aggressive initiative—difficult. Therefore, the church planting team must find ways to utilize teachers, consistent with their nature and gifts. For example, one team in university evangelism in Basel, Switzerland, included Andrew, a brilliant student from Cambridge University. Andrew shyly asked to be relieved of the duty of "button-holing" students at the university with the intention of getting them into a conversation about Christ. "You just stay here in the church basement near the university, Andrew, make some coffee and wait." The rest of the team went out to the university where they engaged students in conversation. Those considered "divine appointments" were invited back to the church, to have coffee and talk to a friend who could answer any question they had! Andrew had absorbed volumes of apologetics. Once back to the church, someone would instigate a conversation by saying, "Andrew, this is Fritz. Fritz was asking me how the God of the Old Testament could command his followers to massacre women and children along with the enemy soldiers. How have you dealt with that problem, Andrew?"

Andrew would quietly pour a cup of coffee and deal with Fritz's obstacles to faith for the next two or three hours. One of the team, more gifted as an evangelist, would sit quietly until the appropriate moment and then confront Fritz with, "Is there any reason, Fritz, why you wouldn't want to turn your life over to Jesus Christ right now?"

The Facilitators

The third component of the New Testament missionary team is the facilitator. These are people who either have marketable skills or who can start a business or project that will enable the church planting team to gain residence in a city, and that will minister to the practical-logistical needs of the team so they can function well in that city for a number of years.

Dr. Robert Pickett is an example. He has taught appropriate technology and international development at Purdue University, Azusa Pacific University, and William Carey International University. Although he is not able to leave his home situation and take up residence in the Muslim world, he was willing to go with a church planting team to the capital of a Muslim country that had never been known to have missionaries. Because of Pickett's expertise and many degrees, he was accepted by that government as the chief advisor of a church planting team starting an agricultural project in this totally unreached area of South Asia. The project has enabled team members to make many friends among the leaders and elders of that community.

Pickett returned annually, to have tea with officials and make sure that they were satisfied with the project, as well as to advise the team on technological matters. Once the team ingratiated themselves to the Muslim leaders, they no longer had to depend on Pickett's status or presence, and gained a considerable amount of freedom for sharing their faith and teaching the tenets of Christianity, particularly on Christian holidays. From these more formal occasions, they were able to ferret out inquisitive individuals for investigative Bible studies.

The facilitator component would include those who teach at the schools for the missionaries' children or who start one in a Muslim city, accountants, Bible translators, and operators of the development project or business that keeps the disciple-makers in the country. The church planting team in Istanbul, Turkey, has recruited a teacher for their one room schoolhouse, to coordinate the correspondence courses for the children of their eight families. Without this missionary kid teacher, these bivocational missionaries would need to pay $3,000 to $5,000 annually per child for the international school. Home schooling, as was previously mentioned, would greatly limit the mother's ability to spend time with neighborhood women.

In Cairo, Egypt, a couple in their sixties run errands, do airport runs, and provide hospitality to enable the missionaries to concentrate on logging hours with Muslims. This warmhearted couple also serves as surrogate grandparents for the missionaries' kids, as well as "Mom and Pop" for some of the young missionaries who may be very gifted, but are still in their twenties and therefore have not experienced a great deal of life.

Team members in facilitator roles can view themselves as "witnesses" in the same way laity or salaried church staff (secretaries, sexton, administrator) might see themselves as a vital part of the witness at home. The facilitator's job on the team, however, is not evangelism/discipleship, but helping others who are more directly gifted in those aspects of ministry. Obviously, facilitators need to be just as convinced of God's call to their particular role as evangelists need to be of theirs. Kent Schriber writes of a unique facilitator role.

> In Turkish society we see friendship evangelism as one key to the establishment of congregations. However, it is extremely difficult for husbands and wives with young children to pursue deep relationships with Turkish families because visiting usually must be done in the evenings, after 8:30 p.m., and babysitters are not available in the way they might be in the west. Therefore, one is forced to bring children on such visits. It becomes very difficult to focus all of one's energies into "finding the opening for witness" in a new language, relate properly in a new culture, and still mind one's children so that they do not misbehave (according to Turkish standards) at someone's home, especially when they're probably overtired.
>
> Because of these complications, most missionaries with young children simply do not visit Turkish friends regularly in the evenings. This prevents deep levels of trust with Turks to be built up. (Turkish families usually have relatives to watch their children.) Turks may bring their children with them to visit you, but remember, they are not trying to be a "change agent" in a second culture and second language.
>
> It is conceivable, therefore, that it would be very strategic to have perhaps short termers on a church planting team who see as their primary role being a "nanny," to free up gifted evangelists and disciple-makers. Is this not parallel to the Philippian church's sending of Epaphroditus to help Paul with his practical needs so that Paul could effectively minister his gifts? (Phil. 2:25–30).

How a Team Functions

Most bivocational missionaries will need to take a 15 to 40 hour a week job or a university course that may or may not be conducive to direct ministry. Therefore, a team may need two or three people ministering to have the equivalent of one full-time missionary. Beyond the time involved in employment, rearing a family in a Muslim city can seldom be done efficiently. It tends to take more time than it would in the home country, thereby leaving even less time for direct ministry.

As noted, it is rare to deploy several in a Muslim city who are all gifted in evangelism and teaching. Therefore, a church planting team needs at least 6 to 12 adults who can share their complementary ministry strengths. Ten persons (as opposed to two or three) making friends and confronting Muslims, are obviously more likely to ferret out those who, in the language of Scripture, "were appointed for eternal life" (Acts 13:48). Assuming that in the city of Kabul, Afghanistan—like in the ancient city of Corinth—"the Lord has many people" (Acts 18:10), logistics dictate that there be a sufficient number of searchers to find them.

This team approach to church planting assures that the work will continue, even if one or two couples must return because of a child having a learning disability or a parent needing support in the home country. One person may not have the capacity to live in a Muslim culture, another may develop an illness that demands a return home for treatment. Unless at least six adults seek to plant a church together, normal attrition can reduce the effort to naught.

Human nature demands accountability. It is not what is expected, but what is inspected that gets done. Many workers overseas have a tendency to get distracted (if not derailed) and as alluded to above, often see their time used up without making progress toward the goal that brought them to a Muslim city.

North Americans in particular are accustomed to an educational system that tells them which pages to read for the next day and motivates with a pop quiz and grades every few weeks. When they go on to business they face performance reviews. Missionaries, on the other hand, have historically been turned loose to go do "whatever missionaries do" with far too little supervision, management, or performance review. Particularly in interdenominational missions, one has the distinct impression that there has been more accountability to keep the rules and regulations of the mission society than to accomplish anything in ministry. Some Christian leaders, particularly in Britain, have suggested that management by objectives is beneath the dignity of God. Some missionaries, therefore, who began with carefully monitored goals, have been led away from them by leaders who devalue such notions as "California businessmen's optimism."

Right or wrong, this is a generation that demands a sense of fulfillment. Most people with a great commitment to Christ and the willingness to die to self, still find themselves programmed to ask questions like "Is this me?" or "Does this fit my gifts and personality?" It is vital that missionary candidates adequately think through and discuss these issues with their team leaders prior to moving to a Muslim city.

For example, a seminary graduate who envisions himself teaching eager believers will be greatly frustrated when he realizes, upon arriving in Kuala Lumpur, that there are neither any Malay believers to teach, nor will he soon have the facility in Malay to teach even if there were! This is often a crushing blow to the ego and sense of self-worth. This partly explains why some with excellent references from First Church in Sydney, and voted most likely to succeed on the mission field, often return after two years. Unknown to any, including themselves, many cannot function without the congregational affirmation and recognition that a position in the home church provides.

Can we envision then that different people with different gifts are needed at different times during a ten-year church planting process? Some are more gifted to pioneer a work than to persevere with an embryo congregation that seems to disappear off the surface of the earth in alternate months. Indeed, teachers will be needed to build up the believers, but perhaps they should not come until there are ten or twenty believers taking a stand for Christ who are desirous of teaching.

One kind of gifted team leader is needed to get a team into Tashkent, Uzbekistan, to work among the Uzbeks. But once that work has a beachhead, he may need to turn that team over to another, more managerial team leader who has some pastoral gifts, and then move on to another city that has no pioneers at all. Hopefully there are a sufficient number of mission agencies that can work with this kind of diversity rather than condemn it.

Generally, mission societies have a screening process that works against the spontaneous entrepreneur. Older agencies tend to be biased toward the cooperative, soft-spoken worker who will take orders and not overly question established policies. Such an ethos does indeed enhance harmony, but when that same society sends such a compliant person into a pioneer situation in a Muslim city such as Pristina, Yugoslavia, to work with the Albanian Muslims, they may discover that he is paralyzed without a manager to guide him clearly through the church planting process.

Those who work best within highly structured situations are often unable to work in an open-ended, unstructured pioneer situation where there are no precedents, few guidelines, and no manual of step-by-step procedure. Such persons should not be sent out until there is a clearly defined ministry structure with an overseer prepared to supervise them.

There is another seldom addressed reason to have a team ministry. Some Muslim converts do not continue to follow Christ because they have known only one Christian: the missionary who brought them to Christ. This gives the Muslim no opportunity, as Magnuson sees it, to experience the fullness of Christ (Col. 1:19). If the church (Eph. 1:22–23) is the fullness of Christ, then a team will be more fully representative of the church than any one individual.

For example, I recruited three Indian brothers in Hyderabad, India, who after some time with me had an opportunity to go on an evangelistic trip with newly arrived (now Operation Mobilization leader) Ray Eicher. When they came back a month later, full of enthusiasm, they unguardedly blurted out, "Brother Greg, you taught us so much, but we've been so inspired by brother Ray's life!" They were more motivated to serve Christ after spending time with my colleague.

Particularly in the Muslim world, where distrust is both endemic and of epidemic proportions, it is vital for Muslim inquirers to see how believers should love one another. A team enables Christ's prayer, recorded in John 17:20–23, to be answered. Francis Schaeffer called this supernatural interrelating in mutual love "the final apologetic" (1970:2).

The team is a "proto-church" and not a church per se. The apostolic church planting team is a temporary structure whose function is to establish churches. Although it is an incomplete model of the various aspects of church life, it can stand in the gap until the planted church takes over the task of demonstrating the fullness of Christ to that Muslim city.

The church planting team must also be a model for interpersonal relationships, especially in conflict resolution. When the fruits of the Spirit are evident and lifestyles of servanthood are manifested, including the modeling of repentance, forgiveness, and reconciliation, Muslims are often deeply impressed. Assuming that human beings everywhere desire reconciliation and loving relationships, decision-making by a team through prayerful interaction, mutual submission, and shepherding—plus joyful worshipping together—may be the most powerful evangelism, and an essential model for church life.

A team provides pastoral care for itself so that each member will remain fit for serving God. Paul exhorts the elders to "keep watch over yourselves" (Acts 20:28), and "Teach and admonish one another with all wisdom" (Col. 3:16). A team needs to be more than a number of families related to the same mission agency that happen to be in the same city. They need to be a group of interdependent people committed to one another's welfare in the spirit of Philippians 2:3, "consider others better than yourselves."

The team that prays together is more likely to stay together. It is a strange phenomenon of evangelical subculture that we talk much about prayer but are extremely reluctant to initiate it. Perhaps even missionaries fear that someone will feel they are self-righteous if they initiate a time of prayer on the spot. Why is it not natural to stop several times a day and turn a fear or a frustration to God (Phil. 4:6)? "Devote yourselves to prayer, being watchful and thankful. And pray for us, too, that God may open a door for our message, so that we may proclaim the mystery of Christ . . . clearly. Be wise . . . make the most of every opportunity" (Col. 4:2–5).

Too often missionaries have rewritten Philippians 4:6 to say "Be anxious about everything, but don't take time for prayer and petition—presenting your requests to God—because you know in your heart that you are not thankful, even though your theology tells you to be so." There is little mystery as to why the peace of God does not transcend our understanding or guard our hearts and minds when individuals do not utilize their team for stress management. Twelve-step Alcoholics Anonymous groups seem to practice sharing of fears and struggles more often and with a greater level of trust than most missionaries.

Even those who have some ability to confront Muslims with the claims of Christ often find themselves at an impasse. They do not know how to go further with their Muslim friend. It is common to lack discernment on how responsive a Muslim friend actually is. Perhaps the missionary has decided to relax with his Muslim friend or family, but is no longer dealing with the issues of salvation. What is needed is an evangelism partner with whom periodic review of progress can be monitored. A teammate can be a sounding board. "What would you do in my situation? How would you respond to this? How would you get around this barrier?" Or again it may simply be that a teammate has more of the evangelistic gift. A Muslim might be prepared by one team member, but will respond to direct confrontation by a teammate who is a skilled evangelist. The Muslim will hopefully listen to another because he is a friend of his friend, and therefore has credibility. This is "tag-team" evangelism.

In Chapter 9—*The Proclamation*—a Syrian, middle-class, Muslim convert's methodology will be illustrated. He is a gifted evangelist on a one-to-one level. He has been effectively used by God to lead Arab Muslims to Christ, who were nurtured to the brink of decision for over two years or more by a western missionary. It may be that Muslims are more willing to submit to Christ in the presence of another from a Muslim background whom they respect, than to do so with a westerner, which may have overtones of losing face. (In some circumstances the opposite could be true.) National or expatriate, normally a Muslim is only open if the messenger is perceived as an equal or as someone higher in social status than the receptor.

The team is a training place. Paul was a follower on Barnabas's team, due to Barnabas's greater experience in the work, until Paul became a leader himself. Barnabas and Paul took John Mark with them as their "helper" (Acts 13:5), and Timothy and Erastus are later called "helpers" of Paul (Acts 19:22). In Acts 20:4, we see that Paul was continually picking up trainees from each place where a church was established, well aware that he had to reproduce himself if the new churches were going to get enough shepherding.

Thus this study recommends that a church planting effort have a team leader who is taking responsibility for the team and the team's final decisions. If a team is to model the plurality of elders for house churches, which can live in a hostile society, the team leader will want to demonstrate to the Muslim believers how the church planting team shares responsibility and authority. The men who are newer on the team, and especially to the task of church planting, will naturally tend to defer to those who are more experienced, but the team leader must be ready for more gifted people (or at least differently gifted) taking over some of the functions as soon as possible to multiply the ministry.

One church planting team in the Middle East had several families who were quite content to submit to the ideas and style of the strong team leader for the first two years. But after they began to feel at home in the country, and did their own analysis of the culture, they began to propose what they thought were better ideas. The team leader, not prepared for a transition time, saw them as rebellious, disloyal, and immature. His reaction was to withdraw from them, which resulted in a schism with the team finally rejecting him as their leader.

A more mature team leader, like Barnabas, will be ready when team members want to "try it their way," and will give them the freedom to experiment without paternalism. If team leaders do not know how to nurture new team members into taking greater responsibility, they are likely to know little about discipling converted Muslims into taking leadership responsibility in the fledgling church.

Finally, a successful church planting team is a group that is composed of people who are confident of their convictions to the point that they do not need to have others conform to them in order to feel secure. Thus, although it is important that they have substantial agreement in their theological stances, the team members need to be able to easily discuss everything from formulas of sanctification to ecclesiology and contextualization in a non-censorious environment. George Verwer demonstrated this kind of leadership by saying that he would be equally happy to have either George Whitefield—a Calvinist—or John Wesley—an Armenian—on his team. Verwer built up an appreciation for diversity in God's church. Team life means being able to share fears and to question anything without impugning motives or demanding uniformity.

The team leader must have an understanding of the big picture and be prepared to tolerate ambiguity and inconsistency, even steps backward, in order to assist the team to persevere without schism, in keeping with the goal of producing a congregation that will have the same kind of resiliency. The goal is to have a nonjudgmental grace orientation to co-workers.

The primary reason why missionaries do not always function in the kinds of teams described above is because many do not know how to practice basic biblical principles of interpersonal relationships. It is important that through team fellowship the problem of members' sinful nature be continually addressed. It should not be a shock, but it should be considered normal that there are times when various team members are ugly, unreasonable, and judgmental.

It is important as well for all to be aware that, due to our being reared by sinners in a fallen world, none of us have escaped emotional damage. All missionaries, like all other Christians everywhere, have blind spots, that is, areas where we do not recognize sin, selfishness, self-centeredness, or neurotic addictive behavior and how it affects our colleagues.

Thus it is vital that a team know how to practice reconciliation according to Matthew 5:23–24 and 18:15–17. The Bible is very practical in its instructions on how to maintain biblical, supportive relationships that lead to a much higher standard than just mutual tolerance. Experience shows that missionaries do not often follow these instructions seriously. And when they do not, they allow a wedge to develop between them, until a multitude of sins cover love.

6

Establishing Significant Relationships

Whether it is called bonding, enculturation, becoming at home with the people, "becoming a Muslim to the Muslims," or incarnational evangelism, the change agent must identify what is involved in becoming a significant trusted friend from whom the Muslims can take truth. What can one do to become at home among an adopted people in an adopted city?

Leaving your culture for another culture within another country that is intrinsically hostile to your purposes is not normal. It is important to reinforce yourself with the consciousness that God is sending you, and your church and mission agency are in partnership with you, lest you conclude it was your own irrational idea. Hopefully you will be aware of every other person in that city who is there for the same purposes. All evangelicals who sense direction by God to start his church in that city, regardless of mission or church affiliation, are part of "God's team" there. It is important to work as closely as possible with as many other church planting aspirants as seems appropriate. The Muslim cities are different from other mission fields because no person or organization has been singularly fruitful. Workers among Muslims have a certain comradery that change agents in Latin America or animist Africa may have lost, because of competition for the loyalty of converts. Those working in

Muslim cities need to pool their experience and skills, and counsel each other over obstacles.

Enculturation

Although the concepts were not new, Thomas and Elizabeth Brewster (1984) repackaged, in step-by-step detail, how to make new friends in an unreached city. They teach both how to learn the language and how to become a respected guest in the chosen subculture. It is important to realize, however, that the Brewsters' bonding techniques come more naturally to some temperaments than others.

For example, two equally dedicated couples with similar training take up residence in Constantine, Algeria, for the purpose of church planting. The Carsons, without hardly thinking about it, find themselves meeting someone on the street who takes them to his family for lunch. An uncle in that Muslim family has a friend who is a house agent who that very day promises to take them out house hunting. It actually does not happen for three more days because of holidays, but the Carsons meanwhile find themselves invited to various Algerian homes, and even out to a village for a feast, having been taken under the care of their new friends. In due time—even though they are hardly able to communicate, except in a few sentences of French—the Carsons are shown an apartment that can be rented from a distant cousin of the first family who took them in.

The Algerians, sensing that the Carsons want to be among Algerians, enjoy these Canadians and find it a break from daily monotony to have foreigners in their midst. This Muslim extended family completely takes possession of them. This seems so wonderful to the Carsons that they are eager to communicate these obviously divinely arranged events in their next prayer letter.

Suppose, however, that the Smiths come to Algeria on the same airplane, but do not have the same extroversion or happenstance to link up with a Muslim family. They might be sitting in their hotel room, stunned and disappointed that the Carsons have disappeared for several days. What happened to their agreed concept of a team? When they finally get an opportunity to complain to the Carsons, the Carsons may react defensively with lectures about their purpose being to spend time with Muslims, not westerners.

Hence, the close team concept examined earlier of expatriates, working together and encouraging one another, may militate against an equally important concept of making close friends among the Muslims, living in a Muslim milieu, and avoiding the tendency to set up a little America in one's apartment or between four apartments (a modern version of the earlier missionary compound). The expatriate team members need to help one another to fully enculturate.

Some western co-workers will have their needs met through Muslim friends easier than others. Some will have more need to spend time in a weekly game of bridge with another missionary couple, a behavior that may appear quite absurd to a third team family that never plays cards for relaxation. It has been noted that some people will be on the team primarily to keep the other expatriates functioning. These "facilitator" team members will understandably be spending more time with expatriates than those who are majoring in evangelism and disciple-making.

Accepting the change agent is the beginning point in a Muslim conversion. For trust to become a reality, expatriates must accept themselves as often being inconsistent and irrational, thereby developing an accepting attitude toward both the Muslims and their co-workers, which in turn can lead to a reciprocal respect in interpersonal relationships. It is essential that they learn to laugh the "laugh of faith," which begins by seeing one's own behavior as a product of individual culture, temperament, and parental script, not necessarily the way things are universally supposed to be.

Westerners find it difficult to deal with Muslims making what they perceive as empty promises, until they enculturate. For example, a request in a given shop is often met with, "Of course!" After a promise that a car will be fixed by tomorrow, the tent-maker, ten days later, is furious when he discovers that work has not even begun on his car, much less been finished. This is an opportunity to learn how things happen there. In this context, it is not profitable to become "a prophet cursing doom on these ungodly liars." He needs to conclude that he has not been among these people long enough to pick up their actual messages. Courtesy demands that the shop owner not embarrass the foreigner by saying no, so he promises to do it even though he knows he cannot keep the promise. Another difficult part of the bonding process involves learning how to recognize sincerity among Muslim friends. One first-term couple wrote a letter asking for advice.

> I had heard it said and even said myself that Jesus does not want us to be doormats for the world. But what did he mean when he said, "But I tell you, Do not resist an evil person. If someone strikes you on the right cheek, turn to him the other also. And if someone wants to sue you and take your tunic, let him have your cloak as well. If someone forces you to go one mile, go with him two miles. Give to the one who asks you, and do not turn away from the one who wants to borrow from you" (Matthew 5:39–42).
>
> Morocco has forced me to come to terms with this passage as never before.
>
> Hakim, my Moroccan friend, and I have spent many hours together running errands and talking. Several difficult misunderstandings have caused me to distrust his motives. Hakim was kicked out of his home by his step-father, has no job, and very little hope of finding one soon since unemployment is estimated at 40 percent here in Casablanca.
>
> Hakim refuses to go back to his home (where he admits good Moroccans his age should be and where he would have all his needs met) because he would lose face. So, he relies on his friends (including me) to meet his needs and does little to repay us.
>
> I suspect Hakim finds that soft-hearted foreigners feel guilty about their abundant possessions in contrast to most Moroccans' meager possessions. Foreigners, therefore, tend to readily part with some of their wealth. Stories abound that Moroccans make friends with foreigners for what can be gained materially. For a while, it seemed that Hakim and I had a genuine friendship, but after a while his visits were long enough to be polite, but ended with a request for a small loan (for which he has no means to repay) or to borrow my overcoat on a rainy day ("The man with two tunics should share with him who has none" Luke 3:11).
>
> Of course, friendships in the West also involve mixed motives.
>
> We accept some and others offend us. The trick here in Morocco is to get our acceptance/offense expectations lined up with theirs. My problem is that the Scripture passage mentioned above does not give me the choice of deciding the motive so I can eliminate who I can help and not help thereby.

Obviously I don't like being exploited, but was not the Lord exploited? Did he not heal and feed some who were only looking after themselves? "You are looking for me, not because you saw miraculous signs, but because you ate the loaves and had your fill" (John 6:26).

What this American bivocational missionary in Morocco seems to be missing is input from a Moroccan mentor, someone who is recognized as a noble person and whose behavior should be emulated. He also needs to consider the value of spending time with what Christiansen referred to as a "marginal misfit" who is not an employed family head.

Understanding the rules of reciprocity and the issue of face-saving is not easy for a westerner in an eastern context. An incident from Lebanon in 1968 may illustrate. Mazhar became an author and distributor for a western mission agency that published Christian books in Arabic. Mazhar was able to get a Muslim publisher to buy 2,000 copies of his novel written for Muslims that emotionally presents the beauty and claims of Christ.

As a necessary cultural courtesy, Mazhar bought 20 copies of *The Life of Muhammad* from the Muslim publisher, thereby enabling the Muslim to save face with other Muslims, explaining that they traded Muslim books for Christian books. The western missionary in charge of the literature mission, however, insisted that Mazhar return the Muslim books to the Muslim publisher, lest the Muslims think that the Christians were acknowledging Muhammad to be on the same level as Christ. Mazhar protested that the 20 books could be thrown away; anything but returned. He knew that as soon as he returned the Islamic books, the Muslim company would return the 2,000 Christian books. The missionary forced Mazhar to return the 20 books on Muhammad, which did indeed result in the 2,000 Christian books being given back.

What the missionary understood as integrity was a lack of understanding of reciprocal obligations and courtesy within Arab culture. The Muslim publisher could not accept the 2,000 Christian books (even though he planned to sell them for profit) without getting the Christians to take at least a few Muslim books. Here it seems that the missionary's conscience was more locked into his own culture than into a biblical definition of integrity.

Fortunately, the less provincial in a chosen neighborhood of a Muslim city will realize that foreigners do not know how to act properly in their midst. There is a grace period, but care must be taken to quickly learn what is regarded as good manners, courtesy, generosity, and nobleness in that particular culture or subculture. Wendell Evans told of a conference in Casablanca, where some Moroccan believers complained that some missionaries still did not practice local courtesies after ten years. Marvin Mayers says it is imperative to become consciously aware of the stratification system operating in the society and to know where one fits in it. Missionaries may at times feel constrained to spend time with people either below or above their assigned rank in the society, but they should be aware when they are breaking the rules. They should be ready to give a reason for their behavior that can be appreciated by the host people.

In the Arab Gulf a bivocational missionary/civil engineer working as a consultant on a business project was asked by a 20-year-old Bahraini for a New Testament. As delighted as this engineer was by the prospect of putting the Word of God in his hands, Jack was sufficiently aware of the principle of trust to realize that he should not give the young man a Bible without first requiring him to obtain permission from his father. The father initially was negative, but after realizing that the foreigner was honoring him as the head of the family and was not going to undermine his authority, the father invited Jack to his home for dinner. In a propitious moment, when the Arab father would not lose face, he asked Jack for two copies of the New Testament—one for himself, and one which he as the head of the family could present to his son.

Doing things their way, working toward becoming an insider in the culture, is what Sherwood Lingenfelter, Marvin Mayers, and Phil Parshall sometimes label "incarnational evangelism," because the Lord Jesus is our supreme example of a foreign change agent. Jesus became so at home in Palestinian society, it was difficult for most to believe that he was anything other than Joseph the carpenter's son, a self-taught Rabbi totally able to communicate in the forms and nuances of his adopted society.

Muslims need this kind of missionary because when they meet westerners they generally hold the stance that becoming a Christian is not only apostasy and betrayal to God and family, but it is also unnatural. For most Muslims, to consider becoming Christians is as unthinkable as a western Christian contemplating a sex change! The disciple-makers must realize that they do not begin at zero with a Muslim, but at minus ten. Christians are westerners, and westerners are commonly thought to be irreligious.

One missionary was startled when, after twenty years of service in North Africa, her Muslim friends showed amazement when they discovered that she prayed. Because she didn't pray openly and ritually (Matt. 6:6) as they did, the Muslim ladies assumed that she had no prayer life at all. They were delighted to discover that she reads a Holy Book, prays, and wants to keep God's commandments. "We never met a Christian who believed in God," she was told.

Lingenfelter contends that the challenge is to become a 150 percent person. An Iranian living in Los Angeles understands this intuitively. He has taken on many American ways and even the local jargon. He has become 75 percent Iranian and 75 percent southern Californian. He has become bicultural for the most part, at home in both Iran and California.

To become 150 percent persons is more than an ordinary challenge. Discarding or setting aside something of one's America-ness or one's social or church identity is almost sacrilege to many people. Our way of life is often equated with godliness and we defend vigorously its apparent rightness.

We forget the example set by Christ who "being in very nature God" did not cling to that identity but instead became not only a Jew, but a servant among Jews (Phil. 2:6–7). We must love the people to whom we minister so much that we are willing to enter their culture as children, to learn how to speak as they speak, play as they play, eat what they eat, sleep where they sleep, study what they study, and thus earn their respect and admiration (Lingenfelter 1986:25).

Lingenfelter admits that such effort creates anxiety, especially when guests feel unwanted or burdensome to their hosts because language is so limited. They feel that they must be boring to their Muslim friends after the first few visits. Still, "the individual who is not ready to give up being an American for a time and to begin learning as a child is not ready for the challenge of cross cultural ministry" (1986:25).

Language and Value Learning

Learning the language(s) fluently and intimately is, more often than not, an extremely wearisome and tedious adventure. One missionary to the Arab World (who requested anonymity) wrote,

> As a conversational instrument, my Arabic is useless. I am limited to greetings, street directions, words for food and thank-yous. To live in Arabic is to live in a labyrinth of false turns and double meanings. No sentence means quite what it says. Every word is potentially a talisman conjuring the ghosts of the entire family of words from which it comes.
>
> The devious complexity of Arabic grammar is legendary. It is a language which is perfectly constructed for saying nothing with enormous eloquence; a language of pure manners in which there are hardly any literal meanings at all, and in which symbolic gesture is everything. Arabic makes English look simple-minded, and French a mere jargon of cost accountants. Even to peer through a chink in the wall of the language is enough to glimpse the depth and darkness of that forest of ambiguity.

Lingenfelter asserts that many people mistakenly believe that mastering a language means automatically imbibing the culture. Those who operate under this misconception may not learn what Edward Hall calls the "silent language of culture" (Hall 1959:3). Language is but one of ten primary message systems found in every culture. The other nine message systems are also crucial for becoming at home in the adopted culture:

1. Temporality (the attitude toward time, routine, and schedule)
2. Territoriality (space, property)
3. Exploitation (the methods of control, the use and sharing of resources)
4. Association (family, kin, community)
5. Subsistence (work, division of labor)
6. Bisexuality (differing modes of speech, dress, and conduct between men and women)

7. Learning (observation, modeling, instruction)
8. Play (humor, games, jokes)
9. Defense (health procedures, special conflicts, warding off evil spirits).

Since each message system has its own rules on how it affects communications, each one must be understood and integrated into new patterns of lifestyle (pp. 38–59). Because there is such a wide spectrum of different Muslim cultures—from North Africa to Northwest China to Southeast Asia—each missionary must determine to learn their adopted culture's "message system."

Don Larson in his essay, "The Viable Missionary: Learner-Trader-Storyteller," reiterates that "there is often a wide gap in the missionary's conception of his role and how it is viewed by the non-Christians of his adopted community. He may see himself as a servant of the Lord, but they may see him as a servant of the CIA. It is extremely difficult for an outsider to teach, or sell, or accuse an insider" (Larson 1981:443). Larson warns that you do not want to parade yourself around in your adopted community as some kind of a freak, misfit, spy, or someone who is useless.

> This matter of community viability is often overlooked. It should not be. The local residents must feel good about my presence in their community. The Muslim may expect the outsider to learn his viewpoint before the outsider can teach effectively about a new gospel. The Muslims will tend to measure Christ's ambassador by their own ethical standards before they will tolerate being perceived as sinners by the Bible's standards (1981:444).

Larson's principle of order is important: learner before teacher, buyer before seller, accused before accuser. For the first three months we are merely learners. We are learning the language in such a way that the Muslims know we are serious because they see us learning more each day. Below is a summary of Larson's own classic instruction:

> I spend my mornings with a language helper (in a structured program or one that I design on my own) from which I elicit the kinds of materials

that I need to talk to people in the afternoons. I show him how to drill me on these materials and then spend a good portion of the morning in practice. Then in the afternoon I go into public places and make whatever contacts are natural with local residents, talking to them as best I can with my limited proficiency—starting the very first day. With each conversation partner I get a little more practice and a little more proficiency from the first day on. At the end of my first three months I've established identity with dozens of people and reached the point where I can make simple statements, ask and answer simple questions, find my way around, learning the meaning of new words on the spot and most importantly, experience some measure of "at-homeness" in my adopted community. I cannot learn the "whole language" in three months, but I can learn to initiate conversations, control them in a limited way and learn a little more about the language from everyone I meet.

For the next three months, I would add the role of the trader, trading experience and insight with people of my adopted community, sharing as fellow human beings. Equipped with a set of 8 x 10 photographs of life in my home country, I can use the afternoons using the photos as part of my show and tell demonstration, talking about the way others live, make their livings, what they do for enjoyment, how they hurt, etc. establishing with my new friends that I'm one who is serious about the ultimates of life and death and our purpose on earth and God. I also become a bridge between the people of this (Muslim city) and the larger world.

Story-teller. When I begin my seventh month I shift emphasis again to the role of story-teller. I learn to tell a very simple story to the people I meet and respond to their inquiries as best I can. The stories that I tell are based on the wanderings of the people of Israel, the coming of Christ, the formation of God's new people, the movement of the church into all the world and how it is coming to this particular (Muslim) city. And finally I tell my own story of my encounter with Christ and my walk as a Christian. During the mornings I develop these stories and practice them intensively, then in the afternoon I go into the community as I've been doing for six months, but now to encounter people as a story teller. Hopefully by the end of the third three months, I'm beginning to discover those whom God has prepared to know more and eventually know the Lord Jesus Christ as Savior" (1981:447, 449).

Structure is necessary for many team members. Many task-oriented missionaries can only be effective if they have structure. They need to be able to schedule their own activities and work independent of others while staying integrated with other team members and their ministries. Some co-workers experience great aggravation when they are interrupted by Muslims who stay around for two hours without revealing the point of their visit.

The Arab method of accomplishing goals is often unfathomable to the uninitiated. Missionaries in a person-oriented culture often fail to grasp the importance of interaction without defined agenda. Person-oriented westerners function better in most Muslim societies where the individual in one's presence takes priority over a name in a schedule book. Much can be learned from the Arabs who will not answer the phone while they are having a cup of coffee with a guest. They are honoring their guest by not allowing a person using an impersonal electronic device to interrupt their face to face conversation. If that other person wants to see the host badly enough, he will show up on his doorstep.

The majority of the church planting team will need to be "people" people, willing to spend hundreds of hours with Muslim friends, often unrewarded by decisions or declarations of faith. Leaders of a church in South Carolina were once asked to send a certain young man to Tunisia. They pointed out that he had not been exactly brilliant in his theological studies, and that his preaching and teaching were neither inspiring nor well organized. They were judging his potential as a missionary by the standards of ministry for a middle-class American church. Had they noticed that he had spent three years with two young men who had gone from spiritual babes to strong, reproducing Christians? Galen had the gift and temperament to spend hundreds of hours "pastoring" new Muslim believers, a gift many "preachers" lack.

Five Muslim men were converted at the American University of Beirut in 1971. To the missionary's surprise, they showed up on his doorstep for supper almost every night following. Being responsible for twenty-five missionaries locally and another 75 in surrounding countries, he did not have the time to disciple them. He needed team members like Galen with the time and gifts to nurture them.

For goal-oriented workaholics, casual conversation can be more of a burden than a hundred tasks. Outwardly they appear to be listening, but inwardly they are thinking of all the things that they could be doing instead. This kind of temperament finds it difficult to concentrate on individuals when there is so much to be done for mankind! The body is present, but the mind is somewhere else working on some other task. What a contrast to the apostle Paul who could say, "We were gentle among you, like a mother caring for her little children. We loved you so much that we were delighted to share with you not only the gospel of God, but our lives as well, because you had become so dear to us" (1 Thess. 2:7–8).

Making Friends and Mentors

How are friends made in a Muslim city? One colleague in Cairo confessed that he found it very difficult to make friends among the Muslims there. Could it be because he is gifted more as a teacher/scholar than a pastor, so when he is with Egyptians he feels a need to lecture to them?

My wife Sally and I found it is easier to make friends with Muslims if we were dependent on them. When moving into an apartment building, we would quickly knock on the opposite door and always get invited in. In the Middle East it is quite impolite to ask anyone their business before sitting them down and giving them tea. If a man was not home, I would turn back and the Muslim woman would invite Sally (Sarah there) in.

After 15 minutes of light talk we might reveal to these Muslim neighbors that we were lonely foreigners and we did not know how to make friends in this new neighborhood. Was there any way they could help us? We appealed to their innate sense of hospitality. If they were not the ones who were willing or able to spend time with us, usually they would at least get us connected with someone who was. It can be frustrating in a city context, where the men work long hours and perhaps have a long commute. Urban pressures give them less time for visiting than in the rural-oriented past. In some cities, or at some socio-economic levels, men may find that they can have more relaxing relationships in their workplace, the shops, coffee houses, or recreation places, than by visiting in one another's homes.

Missionary wives, however, can knock on the doors of the apartments in their building for a cup of sugar, instructions for buying or preparing food, or help on how to light the hot water heater. Mothers easily meet in the playground as their children naturally migrate toward one another. An expatriate's offer to watch a Muslim's children or to entrust hers with them is an effective way of bonding with another family (it also enhances the Turkish, Arabic, Baluch, or Sundanese of the children).

Once they communicate their needs and desires, and show themselves to be mutually helpful, it is gratifying to see how even urban Muslims are willing to get involved in the lives of expatriates. In Beirut my landlord once called me up to his apartment for a serious father/son discussion (he was 50 and I was 30, but he realized that my father was dead and felt that someone had to fill in). In total seriousness, he advised me "not to divorce my wife and marry my mistress." I was a little bit taken back that he assumed I had a mistress, but because of his obvious caring fatherly spirit, I found myself thanking him for his wise advice and assured him that I would take it! The bonding process had begun.

Whether on family issues or other areas of acculturation, it is vital that would-be change agents secure both a language helper and respected mentor for the length of their stay in an adopted culture. It may take two or three efforts to find someone who will be honest about how you are coming across to Muslims in the neighborhood.

For example, Arabs tend to depend upon outsiders to intervene in disputes. If a relationship is drifting or you sense that you may have offended a friend but can get nowhere in restoring the relationship, you need to find out how Arabs approach this problem. Does an intermediary or mediator need to be brought in? Missionaries must insist they are a foolish Singaporean, Scot, or Swiss and that they are eager to avoid mistakes or offenses. If they keep asking questions, Muslims will eventually believe that they actually want correction. You will likely get more advice than you want!

Muslim women tend to be more free in giving advice to western mothers since they are generally more provincial and therefore know "the only proper way" of doing things. Even urban Muslim women will take the kitchen utensils out of a western woman's hands to show her how to cook rice properly. They may be quite judgmental with regard to how the western woman clothes or feeds her children. The missionary does well to at least act like she is going to do it their way, even though it may mean unwrapping three layers off her baby as soon as the Muslim woman is out of sight.

Once a relationship of trust with a less provincial Muslim mentor is established, it becomes naturally reciprocal for church planters to share their values through their life story. This can be done in a culturally sensitive way so that it not only makes sense to the befriended Muslim family, but also creates admiration for church planters, who are doing what they believe God and Jesus want them to do.

It is important that Muslim friends perceive missionaries as being consistent with their understanding of God's commandments. Some have been surprised when Muslims give them advice on how to more effectively communicate the gospel to their fellow Muslims! A colleague in Tunisia who was seeking to understand his Muslim neighbors' actual value system (as opposed to what orthodox Islam teaches) asked around until he found some "Muslim evangelists." These young Muslim men wanted to help nominal Muslims become active (not dissimilar to pastors in America seeking to assist nominal Christians in becoming active churchgoers).

The expatriate learned from the Muslim evangelists five different Arabic words for "sin" with various levels of severity. They appreciated his zeal for God more than most Tunisians did, and even tried on one occasion to get him to do the Muslim prayers in the mosque and say the creed, "There is no God but Allah and Muhammad is his prophet." When my colleague, with a smile, communicated that he could not in good conscience do that, they were not alienated but laughed with him, saying, "You can't blame us for trying."

Cam Townsend, the founder of the Wycliffe Bible Translators, was a model for making friends in his adopted culture. Townsend was one of the first to articulate the homogeneous unit principle, that each tribal people group needs to have the Scriptures in their own language, translated with an appropriate ethno-historic, contextualized hermeneutic. He also understood how to get things done in the culture of his host country. He would treat suspicious Catholics and Marxists warmly. He deeply understood the need to have "sponsors" consistent with our Lord's instructions in Matthew 10. Townsend knew how to become an ally of a Mexican government official. He understood that influence comes through relationships. Unlike many before and after him, he showed appreciation to the host government and counted it a privilege to live within their boundaries.

Townsend made it a point to remember the important milestones in the lives of many Latin American friends, such as a wedding, a funeral, or someone gravely ill, in which case he hurried to their bedside. He did everything he could to be of service to President Cardenas of Mexico, although it took away from precious mission time. It bothered him that in Guatemala and Mexico even his own missionaries often identified too closely with the American community and its political views. Townsend spent so much of his time cultivating Mexican friends that he was often charged with having "secular," instead of Christian, involvements.

You need to find a mentor like Townsend in your adopted country, who can teach you how friendships can be established that are not easily broken by jealousy or a cultural faux pas. How can one be perceived as hospitable and generous, or in the words of Scripture, be full of "goodness, kindness, patience, and longsuffering" (Gal. 5:22 KJV) in the Muslim's eyes, as opposed to being exploited (as the missionary in Casablanca experienced) or as merely being an object of amusement or suspicion?

Without relationships, communication is minimal. It was assumed for many years that if a person could either hear or read the Gospel words describing the incarnation, atonement, and needed response, that the messengers had fulfilled their obligation, both to God and to that particular segment of lost humanity. Missionaries rarely entered the receptor's space, and very seldom with the preparation that would cause a Muslim to make a positive inquiry toward the message being communicated.

In other words, particularly in Muslim societies, preaching the Good News was actually giving out bad news. Because of the failure to monitor what receptors were hearing, it was assumed that they were terribly ungrateful people, turning their backs on the self-sacrifice of the incarnate God. Arabs were simply perceived as being stubborn in their sin. But most only take truth from "our kind of people"—those who are "us," not "them." The Lord Jesus, in the incarnation, clearly demonstrated the need to become an insider in order to impart eternal truth, to sit where they sit, to weep with those who weep, to rejoice with those who rejoice, and to be a friend of sinners.

For many years I was perceived not as a friend of sinners, but as an enemy of sinners, a condemner of those who were different. I was understood to be one who believed in three gods; who held a doctrine that God had sex with a human being, Mary (the mother of God); and was myself a blasphemer, elevating one of the prophets, Jesus, to the level of Almighty God. Is it any wonder that the Arab Muslim was as minimally receptive as I am when a Jehovah's Witness or humanist devalues the Lord Jesus Christ?

The Apostle Paul speaks about becoming a Jew to the Jews and a lawless one to those that were not reared within the Jewish law, becoming "all things to all men so that by all possible means I might save some" (1 Cor. 9:22). Although this text is often quoted, there do not seem to be many westerners who have discovered how to apply it among Muslims.

Trust

Most western Christians are so intimidated by accounts of resistance that they would not seriously consider moving to a Muslim city. Those who do go, unwittingly confirm the seeming impossibility of seeing Muslims transfer their loyalty to the lordship of Christ and openly standing for him in their own society. Normally one cannot make disciples until friends are made. People do not voluntarily follow someone they do not like (except when they have ulterior motives), particularly in a society where conformity to tradition, the family's values (and therefore religion), and group decision-making present formidable obstacles for the change agent. Therefore progress demands a knowledge of what Muslim acquaintances or friends actually think. Where are they coming from? With what are they struggling? What various feelings are they experiencing when invited to bow their will to the living, resurrected Christ?

Mazhar in North Africa is now one of my closest friends. What makes us friends is that we have gone through both hard and joyful experiences together over the past 19 years. We feel loyalty toward one another, and the desire to be mutual enablers for the rest of our lives.

Yet upon reflection, I realize that Mazhar is the only Middle Easterner who has ever fully opened his heart to me. And even he does it with ambivalence. When he complains about circumstances and other people's failure (what this one and that one should do), it is not easy to discern when he is hurt, why he is angry, how a matter affects him, or what he really wants.

What does it take, then, or under what conditions can a middle-class Anglo-American and a nonwesternized, middle-class, Arab Muslim (still in a Muslim culture) communicate with integrity? Can we talk to each other in such a way that neither one is suspiciously searching for the other's hidden agenda? Is it possible to achieve a relationship of openness and vulnerability? Can we share doubts, fears, struggles, and a sense of personal failure?

Before these issues can be addressed, some preliminary questions need to be asked. Does the goal of communication with integrity—or bonding, as described earlier—have a cultural bias itself? Is this a western definition of friendship, of effective communication, and therefore limited in its usefulness? To what degree does the question itself reflect a twentieth-century, American, middle-class culture as opposed to universal human needs?

The ambassadors for Christ must first define what constitutes friendship, "being straight," or integrity in relationships within their own middle-class, twentieth-century, Christian culture. Then they can ask the same questions of their adopted people. They should be able to clearly distinguish between their own value system or personal preferences and that of the targeted people. How does either contrast with their understanding of biblical values and lifestyle?

David Lyth, an English physician in the Arab Gulf, feels that Arab men do not have the deep, trusting, sharing type relationships with others that many westerners desire. He sees Arabs as turbulent people whose relationships are always in tension. Their concern is to maintain their reputation at all costs, often by devaluing the reputation of others. This reflects a deep insecurity, which Lyth believes originates in Islam. Islam has bred a concern for external purity and conformity, but fails to acknowledge that a man is truly depraved or that pure motives are important.

Lyth, sharing his personal experience with the author, related this story.

> I drew very close to a Muslim who is a fisherman, and in the past we have wept together and even prayed together. My wife and I were even commissioned by his family to find him a wife, and the story takes many twists. Finally he found a bride, is now engaged, but has declared that he will not be seeing much of us in the future on a regular basis. When we meet, he is still the warm, charming friend that he was before, but that deep commitment is gone. Also, at the hospital where I work, a Muslim doctor who had professed to be a close friend went to other Muslims and relayed things that I had told him in utmost confidence, fully aware that this would hurt our relationship and my standing here.
>
> I conclude, then, that we must not be idealistic in the quest for deep relationships, but we must accept these people as they are, ride the waves, rejoice when there are good relationships, and don't weep too much when relationships fall apart. We must have goals that are appropriate to the particular people that God has put us amongst (1986).

Doug Magnuson wrote the author in 1987.

> Even in our own culture, we have deep relationships with only a very few people. Furthermore, the deepest, most ideal relationship is not necessary for having a significant impact on people. A more important goal would be to have people's respect as a person of integrity, a person of my word, someone who is consistent (rather than vacillating in my character). In other words, we can't control the other person. It takes two people to have a relationship of trust, integrity, and affection. We will meet some Muslims who will enter with us into a deep and honest relationship. But I believe that this will be the exception.

To become socialized, one needs to stay with a Muslim family and pay close attention to what each family member is feeling when things are happening. Keep a diary of what it is about different situations that makes people feel happy, sad, hostile, or anxious. Magnuson continues:

> I would have to say honestly that, although I have many good relationships with men here, I don't have one that could be called fully open, vulnerable, or without guile. In every good relationship I have, there are lim-

its. My friend M, for example, is probably my best friend. We share many interests (like basketball), often have what seems to me to be a sort of "fellowship" due to our shared belief in God. And because of his carefully practiced Islamic faith, he is very consistent in relating to me. I know I can count on him if I am in need. But his (or I should say, our) faith is also the biggest barrier in our relationship, because I know that his first allegiance is to God and to Islam, not to me. If there is a conflict, he will follow what he knows from Islam.

There are others with whom I have a good relationship (enough to be a "change agent" in their lives) but I always feel that there are many unseen things (motives, views, etc.) under the surface, which I can't take into account in relating to the person.

The North American director of Middle East Media, who lived in Cairo for several years, writes:

We Westerners simply define friendship differently. We Americans give less hours to friendship, i.e., our house is not always open even to our friends. In our culture, an appointment is usually agreed on to see your buddies. I always found it rather uncomfortable to be around Egyptian friends because their demands were so intense (by my Western norms), and I felt hemmed in.

Even though I was aware of what was happening and had developed some helpful coping strategies, gleaned from my missiological studies, I still did not overcome, at my emotional level, my negative feelings about those demands. I wanted friendship on my terms, although, of course, I knew I had gone to Egypt to "lay down my life" etc. It's one thing to lay down one's life in intent, but it's much harder to surrender your space, freedom, time, and emotional need for quiet once you're there (1987).

Another missionary, with over twenty years of experience, confesses: "Communication with integrity with Muslim males? I never got near that point, or only rarely. But then, I think most missionaries to Muslims have the same problem." And another: "There's nothing like a good fight from time to time. It doesn't prove there's communication. It may destroy it, but then again, some things may come out that might not get said otherwise. Manipulation is a way of life both for we Westerners and also for Muslims. Do we really expect to get beyond that with a lot of people?"

"We Westerners just move too fast," another missionary observed. "It takes six months for someone to figure out and believe that you're not a complete, obvious, paid fake or CIA agent."

Turning from the missionaries in the field to the anthropologists, Edward T. Hall wrote about the same issues. How are Arabs different from North Americans? The basic difference is that Arabs are highly "contexted." They examine the entire circumstance in which events are happening in order to understand them. Their words are only a small part of their communication. In a low context culture, which depends on the verbal message and less on the context, you get down to business very quickly. The high context culture takes considerably longer because the people have developed a need to know about you before a relationship can develop.

In the Middle East, if you aren't willing to take the time to sit down and have coffee with people, and talk about family matters, you are perceived to be rude and have a problem. You must learn to wait and not be too eager to talk business. Learn to make what we call chit-chat. If you don't, you can't go to the next step. It's a little bit like a courtship, and without all the preliminaries, sex becomes just like rape.

Hall has incredible insight:

> People will be watching you and getting to know you, developing feelings about you. They're probably even watching the pupils of your eyes to judge your responses to different topics. . . . That's one of the reasons why they use a closer conversational distance than we do. . . . By watching the pupils they can respond rapidly to mood changes. We're taught in the U.S. not to stare . . . If you stare at someone, it is too intense, too sexy, or too hostile. . . . They're . . . coding, sort of synthesizing their reactions. They say to themselves, 'How do I feel about this person?' In contemporary American terms: 'What kind of vibes am I getting from him?' . . . They're picking up thermal, olfactory, and kinesthetic cues also.
>
> A lot of touching goes on during conversations in the Middle East. . . . In general, Arabs know more about each other than we do. The group is smaller and more intimate, and there are differences in what people take for granted in negotiating. . . . This is because people need to

discover what kind of cards the other fellow is holding. We think that price is everything. In this sense, we're kind of naive. Profit isn't as important to these people as a human relationship.

. . . We had learned that Americans were getting down to business much too fast in the Middle East. They were skipping important steps in the action chain. . . . An action chain is a behavioral sequence with two or more participating organisms, in which there are standard steps for reaching a goal. If you leave out one of those steps, . . . people are confused and have trouble completing the chain.

. . . The trouble is it's hard to get an American to take each step seriously and to be coached. Most Americans are too eager to buy and reluctant to take coaching. Only actors and athletes are accustomed to being coached. Doctors and industrialists and lawyers [and can we add missionaries?] don't take directions very well (1979:47–53).

7

Proclaiming the Message

George Jennings (1977), professor of anthropology and U.S. Director of MECO-Middle East Christian Outreach, believes that effective communication with Muslims depends in large measure upon considerable appreciation of contrasting ideologies and psychological sets represented in the cross-cultural encounter. It is vital to understand the ethos of your own culture and subculture (the ideals and values that dominate and tend to control the behavior patterns within a society), and then look for those same nuances in the Muslim subculture within which you are seeking to communicate.

What is in your Muslim friend's worldview that needs to be appreciated with empathy, in order to build the needed rapport that will facilitate him in taking your worldview seriously? All too often, well-intentioned missionaries to Muslims find themselves seeking to defeat the Muslim with western logic, unaware that their memorized arguments from formal education may be addressing questions that few Muslims are asking.

To decry Mohammad for his failings is to forget his heroism, and the merit of his efforts in calling Arabs to seriously obey the one true God. To focus on Koranic contradictions and errors is to miss its teaching about God's activity in nature, or the ethical duties of mankind. To attack Islam because of what it has failed to do, is to forget both its contributions to European culture and Christianity's failure to change its own societies.

Thus, to first desire to refute and destroy Islam is an unproductive method. It causes the Muslim to become defensive, thereby hardened and prejudiced against Christ and the cross. The natural reaction of anyone whose beliefs are being attacked is to maintain them even more resolutely, and to discover better reasons for holding them.

The result of missionary preaching during the past century and a half demonstrates with tragic clarity how unproductive a frontal attack launched on the intellectual level has been. An insightful Pakistani colleague feels that the best of modern missionaries to Islam pursue a mode of approach that (while not totally neglected by their predecessors) was seldom quite trusted to bear full fruit: the method of intimate and personal loving service, of sympathetic testimony, and relentless, united prayer for Muslims befriended.

Conversations with former Muslims reveals that the essence of conversion is a direct experience of encountering Christ as a living, heavenly personage who forgives sins. Muslims are led to that experience by being helped to envision how their deepest needs can be satisfied by a living, caring, powerful Messiah who, if called upon, is personally available as the mediator between God and people (1 Tim. 2:5).

In Karachi, another Pakistani colleague, Jonah, reports that former Muslims were attracted to Christ through ever-deepening friendships with disciple-makers; through a gentle guided study of the New Testament; through leisurely conversations; and through praying directly with them to a God who is near and can bring peace to their troubled mind. Christian messengers need to remind themselves that the prime purpose of conversation or communication in the West is often the impartation of information or knowledge. The prime purpose of communication in the East, however, is to establish or enhance relationships. To the westerner, the most important thing is what is communicated; to the easterner, the "how" of communication is more important than the "what." For you it is probably important that the communication be clear; to the Middle Eastern person it is important that the communication leave a favorable impression, that is, it makes the other person feel good. We westerners are oriented toward facts; most Muslims belong to cultures oriented toward people.

Thus, the natural eastern tendency is to say what will please the listener rather than what the speaker really thinks. To the Muslim, this is social politeness. To a westerner it is deception. But our straightforwardness is often experienced as discourtesy to a Middle Easterner. Often, proclamation between the westerner and Middle Easterner is unfruitful because the Middle Easterner is not so interested in what you are saying, but is trying to figure out why you are saying it.

Muslims are constantly looking for an ulterior motive. They may be so busy determining motives that they miss the point of the message. If this is true, we can understand the necessity for long contact with Muslim friends until they can eventually internalize the missionary's motives. Now you can understand why relationships with many Muslim people at first seem warm and hospitable but later turn cold. If we as westerners focus on what Muslims are saying on the cognitive level alone, we may be quite perplexed when their subsequent behavior is inconsistent with what they have told us. If it is observed that a Muslim friend acts one way around the westerner and another way around other Muslims, it is likely that his concerns are in a different place than his cognitive positions. He will attempt to function with a westerner to meet the expectations of the westerner. However, the Muslim value system includes a deep emotional commitment to Muslim traditions, allegiance to family, national honor, and so forth; so their deeper loyalties will often prevent them from taking the Christian message seriously.

Identifying Seekers

When the Apostle Paul was ministering in Corinth, he apparently suffered doubts concerning the viability of his ministry, to the extent that God deemed it necessary to give him a vision. In it he was told, "Do not be afraid. Keep on speaking. Do not be silent. For I am with you and no one is going to attack and harm you because I have many people in this city" (Acts 18:9–10).

So, in "apostolic succession," the modern day apostle to an unreached Muslim city must assume that God is in the process of opening the eyes of Muslims, whom he has chosen to live eternally in his Kingdom. With this understanding, church planters can move about in their adopted Muslim city assured that they are going to be given divine appointments with Muslims who are going to follow Christ. Still, there are human factors to overcome that need to be addressed. To do so, let us assume the following:

- The change agents have established a residence, and a reputation as good people.
- They have learned the language well enough to enter fully into the lives of their target people and teach the Scriptures.
- In the process of acquiring the language; getting a place in society; and learning the values, interests, and worldview of their adopted people, they have met two or three hundred Muslims; they have established friendly relationships with dozens, and are praying daily for God to lead them to divine appointments with those that he has been preparing to gather into his assembly in that city.

Now, what would a model Christian worker do then? A couple of years ago, for two consecutive evenings, I accompanied Mazhar, my Arab friend, to the coffee shop next to Hussein's mosque in the Poet's Quarter of Cairo, Egypt. Men sit in groups of two to six around tiny, wobbly tables to drink mint tea or Arabic coffee, smoke cigarettes or bubble pipes, and discuss politics, religion, philosophy, or often, women and survival.

Mazhar had met Anis in the post office. Anis invited us to meet him at 10 p.m. at the coffee house. A lower, middle-class postal clerk in the daytime, Anis comes alive as a self-professed poet and proponent of the Wafd opposition party in the evenings. There were no places to sit in the coffee house, so after checking two other nearby coffee houses, we took our coffee to the street and sat on the sidewalk below the mosque.

A sheik (religious leader) from Sudan had staked out a 12 by 6 foot piece of sidewalk, covered by cardboard, to articulate the ideas of his Sufi sect. Anis knew one of the men in the circle, and after profuse greetings were exchanged, we were welcomed to join in the Thursday evening (before Friday, the holy day) discussions.

Mazhar was our spokesman, so he sat cross-legged directly opposite the sheik. The forum began with Mazhar, the Frontiers team leader in Cairo, and myself sitting across from the sheik and five of his adherents. After a flurry of profuse greetings and introductions, the oldest man in the group, an Egyptian in a wool galabiya, refused to sit until we complied with his demand to order something to drink. We gave in and requested tea, which was ordered by the old man simply by shouting across the street in the direction of a coffee house. With the tea, which was loaded with at least four teaspoons of sugar, came a large crepe with white powdered sugar on a newspaper. It was placed in the center of the circle for us to eat communally.

The repartee began with exchanges of best wishes for health. Then Mazhar took a book out of the sheik's hand, which was the writing of a twelfth-century Sufi philosopher. Professing exuberant enthusiasm for the philosopher, Mazhar gained instant rapport, and went on to inform the sheik that the philosopher had found hidden meanings in the Koran that spoke of Christ!

Since Sufis are much less rigid than Sunis, the sheik seemed able to receive that idea, particularly since it was peppered with effusive statements by Mazhar about how he could see God in the eyes of the sheik, how "the sheik's presence brings light to a dark part of the city," and other similar affirmations.

To build rapport with the other Muslims, who were Egyptians, Mazhar told a story of an Egyptian who was living in Morocco. He had asked Mazhar to bring back a handful of dirt just so he could "smell the beauty of the Egyptian soil." Actually, I would not have wanted to put my nose in the dirt of that area of Cairo, but the poets won out over the pragmatists.

Mazhar then went on to quote David's psalm of repentance to the group (in Arabic), and the sheik returned the favor by quoting a portion from the Koran. At this point no one knew where to take the conversation, so it lightened into the topic of the different dialects spoken across the Muslim world, everyone choosing a dialect to belittle that was not represented by the present company. The sheik then spoke about the civil war in his own country, Sudan, which could be perceived as being between Christians and Muslims. Mazhar refused to let sides be taken up and dismissed the whole thing as politics, nothing to do with the will of the common people. Aware of their helplessness in the political realm, assent was quickly achieved.

Mazhar went on about the universality of God's love, and the need to focus on him and his ways—a proposition on which it was also easy to gain assent. Going as far as he could go with such an audience, Mazhar made an appointment to see the sheik the next day. We broke into blessings, handshakes, and salutations, put on our shoes, and departed.

The next afternoon the sheik from Sudan, a handsome man of about 35 years, dressed in what seemed to be his only robe and turban, met us enthusiastically at the prearranged point in front of Al Azhar Mosque, Islam's symbol of strength and education. I guessed wrongly that he would want to meet with us away from the prying eyes of the Sufi brothers. To my surprise, he walked us right back to the coffee shop which had served us the night before.

He apparently was honored there and is probably granted credit. His simple, village garb was deceiving. I came to realize that he was from an educated, middle-class family in Sudan. His brothers both held fairly high, white collar jobs: one in the Arab Gulf and one in Europe. Ahmed had obviously turned his back on middle-class values and was looking for a better country, "a heavenly one" (Heb. 11:14–16).

Over three glasses of super-sweet tea, face to face, Mazhar emanated the love of the Lord Jesus for this man, brought his New Testament out of his shirt pocket, and after kissing it, read 1 Corinthians 15. I watched the face of the sheik closely, to see if he would revolt at the obviously anti-Islamic proposition that the Lord Jesus indeed died on the cross as an atonement for our sins, and rose again, breaking the power of death. Mazhar completed the reading, kissed the New Testament, and held it to his forehead before returning it to his shirt pocket.

All the sheik could manage to say was, "I've never talked to a Christian who could explain these things to me." He asked if he could have Mazhar's copy of the Injil (New Testament). Mazhar told him that this copy was very precious, because a very special friend's name was in the front cover (Ahmad's—from the night before), but of course the sheik could have a New Testament if he would come to Paul's home to get it (thus insuring a follow-through visit). Leaving that seed to germinate, with the sheik open for more, following the pattern of the Lord Jesus himself, Mazhar moved us on to yet a third mosque to visit an old religious leader.

This old sheik warmly greeted Mazhar (and politely, me) with bright eyes and a burst of "Praise the Lord. Praise the Lord." (Muslims say that commonly—Al hamdallah.) The sheik, who was not yet able to reveal to other Muslims his attachment to Jesus, led us to a quiet corner of the mosque where Mazhar, in Muslim chanting style, read the Scriptures and had the sheik repeat each verse after him.

Sensing the sheik's discomfort with the presence of a westerner, Mazhar sent me off to the center of the mosque to pray, with my face on the mat, while he continued exhorting, studying, and praying with the sheik who had opened his heart to the Lord through Mazhar five years earlier. In January 1990, while visiting Mazhar, I had the joy of meeting Anis again, the post office clerk, now a faithful follower of Christ who attends a house meeting of Christians.

The next step in proclamation is bringing the Muslim to decision. Fraser (1979) applies an "Engel" scale to Muslims' spiritual decision process. Major decisions in most societies, particularly those involving lifestyle changes such as marriage, vocation, or religious allegiance, are made only by the family clan or community after a relatively significant period of deliberation. The decision for Muslims to switch their allegiance—from their family and Islam, as they understand it—to the personage of Jesus Christ as a contemporary living leader with whom they can communicate, is a gigantic one.

Such a decision to swim upstream, against the strong tide of feelings and opinions of significant others, cannot be made quickly by intelligent, sensitive people. Assuming that science is the investigation of reality, including how God works in human beings, it is useful to pose questions about the process by which either a group or individual among a target people would make a radical new commitment.

Fraser, therefore, suggests constructing a model of stages, or steps that known Muslim converts have gone through as they awakened to the power of God and responded to Christ. Commonly in missions, examinations of the decision-making processes involved in conversion have been avoided, because of an uneasy feeling that such research invades a sacred area belonging to God alone. To some, being concerned with human motivations, and factors that increase the likelihood of favorable response, implies the reduction of the gospel of Christ to the same level as Madison Avenue sales techniques. But here we would invoke the maxim, "All truth is God's truth," regardless of who might bring it to our attention.

John Stott, a British theologian and evangelist, would hardly be prone to "California or Madison Avenue techniques." He writes:

> Some say rather piously that the Holy Spirit is Himself the complete and satisfactory solution to the problem of communication and indeed when He is present and active, then communication ceases to be a problem. What on earth does such a statement mean? Do we now have liberty to be as obscure, confused and irrelevant as we like, and the Holy Spirit will make all things plain? To use the Holy Spirit to rationalize our laziness is nearer to blasphemy than piety (1975:127).

Predisposing Factors

Most people are reluctant to make new consequential commitments. Under most conditions they prefer to keep what they already believe intact, even if it means ignoring massive evidence to the contrary. This is even more true with taking a new religious position, except by certain marginal or risk-taking persons.

Therefore, for conversion to take place, there must be certain tensions, problems, or predisposing factors that push people out of their normal stance. Such factors might include a combination of physical conditions, political situations, or initiatives by the leadership of those with whom they most identify. Without such predisposing conditions, large movements to Christ do not take place. This is illustrated by the Javanese example of church growth in Chapter 10.

To what extent are there opportunities for Muslim friends to alter their religious commitment? Often there is more anonymity in the urban context and therefore more freedom than in a face to face rural society. On the other hand, Muslims in the city may be so economically dependent on relatives, friends, or their boss that anti-social activity would carry an even greater penalty than it might for an independent farmer in Bangladesh who has his own ox, plow, and water supply.

However, most Muslim cities will tolerate a great variety of belief within the spectrum of Islam. Could a group of people find freedom to fully follow Christ if they were still perceived as Muslims? The Amadiya (a sect in Pakistan acknowledging a prophet after Mohammed) have been officially censored as non-Muslims, but their critical mass is large enough for them to continue. What has enabled tens of thousands of Iranian Muslims to become Bahai, despite persecution and imprisonment? Missionaries in Turkey reported in 1984 that over 20,000 Muslim Turks had become Jehovah Witnesses in Istanbul. What can be learned from this people movement out of Islam? An important study could be made of Muslims switching to other non-Christian religions.

How are those whom God is drawing to himself, or who are seeking God on his terms, discovered or identified? There are people groups and individuals (cf. Cornelius, Acts 10) who are already embarked on a search for which faith in Christ is the answer. When they encounter the evangelistic appeal, with insight into who God in Christ Jesus is, they are ready to believe.

It is common sense that unless people are dissatisfied with their present integration of social, emotional, and religious factors, they generally would be quite unmotivated to give consideration to another religion. It is no accident that large movements into the Christian church have occurred under situations of significant social and cultural change, and largely from among parts of the population who felt themselves peculiarly disadvantaged, so it was in their best interests to follow respected leaders who were adopting those changes.

The maxim, "the sheep go where the grass is good," not only applies to American church growth, but to Muslim peoples as well. If Christians look within themselves, they will realize that a good percentage of the motivation that brought them to Christ was because turning from their past ways and moving into obedience to Christ seemed to be well within their own self-interests. It is unrealistic to hold a loftier ideal up to our Muslim friends.

However, an individual or group may be unaware of their needs or feelings of discontentment until they encounter an appeal that brings those needs to the surface, and offers an alternative that is seen as a realistic solution. Instead of thinking that the proclamation of the gospel will create a need, the Good News must be sown as widely and intensely as possible depending upon the Holy Spirit of God to cause paths to cross with those with whom he is dealing—drawing to himself—preparing the way through social, economic, and historical circumstances.

Must the right to be heard be earned? What does this truism mean? The vast majority of persons who submit to the reign of Christ in their lives do so on the basis of a recommendation from a significant other in their lives. It might be a parent, relative, best friend, respected teacher, or one considered an authority who communicated through the media.

In the early church it appears that a man, as head of a family in a paternalistic society, could carry his whole family into the faith, whereas an isolated decision of a wife might remain solitary. All people have prejudices as to whom they respect and to whom they will give a hearing. The agent of evangelism must adopt a role in a Muslim city that provides the appropriate balance of human compassion and confrontation, which is conducive to being taken seriously in the matters of redemption.

There is a tension between the role of a prophet ("thus saith the Lord"), which points out sin and failure, and that of being a nurturing friend. At times one must sacrifice empathy and risk rejection in order to motivate Muslim friends to consider their ways. Among simpler, rural-oriented people (even if they are in a primary city due to migration) evangelists who are perceived as healers or exorcists tend to be besieged by Muslims with a felt need for protection from the *Jinn* (evil spirits). One Egyptian Pentecostal pastor in Alexandria, Egypt, for example, finds that he has more Muslims seeking his help than he can service. His methods of exorcism, both directly, and by providing holy water (which Muslims are instructed in Jesus' Name to throw on the walls of their home) raise eyebrows among westerners and westernized nationals. Hiebert (1982) would remind us, however, that this pastor is gaining a hearing for the gospel because he is dealing with the "excluded middle"—the spirit world—unfruitfully ignored by western educated ministers of the gospel.

It is noteworthy that nonwesternized, rural-type, poor Muslims in Cairo seem to feel more at home in the incense-filled, highly liturgized, chanting, orthodox Coptic churches with Christians who share much of their same folk beliefs, than they do in the Bible-teaching, Presbyterian churches that cater to the upper middle-class, westernized Egyptians. What does this say about what less educated, rural-oriented Muslims in Cairo would need for a Christian worship service?

This is not saying that Muslims will not come to Christ in Cairo until they experience signs and wonders, but that ministry to Muslims must begin with felt needs. Where protection from evil spirits is a primary concern, Jesus must be demonstrated as the primary answer to that need—since he is. Parshall, reporting on fruitful church planting in rural Bangladesh, says: "There has been an appreciation of the supernatural on a practical level. Visions and dreams of spiritual significance have been fairly frequent. There is a simple faith that prayer is an instrument of change. Crying out to God and fasting are utilized to effect release from difficulty as well as to bring healing to the afflicted" (1980:24).

Though a noncharismatic himself, Parshall gently pleads that Christian ministry must involve itself where the Muslim has felt needs. Parshall quotes Bill Musk (an Anglican minister formerly among Muslims in Cairo); Charles Kraft, of Fuller Theological Seminary; William Miller, a Presbyterian (40 years in Iran); and Max Kershaw of International Students, to persuade workers among Muslims to accustom themselves to living daily in a world in touch with the supernatural.

A large percentage of Muslims giving testimony of their conversion include reference to a vision or dream of Jesus. The Muslim Imam—model, pattern-maker, leader (Surah 25:74, 36:11)—as an authoritative religious leader, is constantly visited with the expectation that he will disperse amulets and charms as aids to cure sickness, sexual impotence, ward off evil spirits, ensure the birth of sons, and bring good luck in business. Although these practices are more prevalent among village types, today's population of a major city like Cairo in the Muslim world may be 70 percent villagers.

The change agents then need to be totally familiar with how decisions are made among their target people. Who is involved? Is it all the family? The clan elders? If the male head of a family makes a commitment, is that likely to be a decision that the rest of the family will follow, or is the woman still holding her father and brothers as her ultimate authority? In a particular Muslim culture, are children most influenced by mother or father? How much power does a mother have over her adult sons and their families? Whose decision for Christ will best leave a door open to the other relatives? Protestant Christianity was established in North America through immigrants from Europe. Christianity was established in Europe through people movements, not one by one extraction from the pre-Christian tribes. What are the implications of our christianizing history for a Muslim city?

What about the method for registering the commitment? The issue of secret believers and baptism is highly debated. The missionaries who have an intimate relationship with Muslim inquirers, with whom they are discussing the implications of following Christ (and reading Scripture), can ask the Muslims how they feel followers of Isa should identify themselves. They can then ask Isa as their Lord to give them wisdom and direction.

The Decision Bolstering Process

Every Muslim falls somewhere along a continuum in terms of a saving relationship with Christ. At one extreme are those who have no direct knowledge of the gospel, but who know only what they have discovered through nature, their conscience, and whatever truth is found in their understanding of Islam and their culture. Others under orthodox Islamic teaching may be monotheists, aware that the disobedient will come under the judgment of the one true God. He is a God who has communicated through the prophets in history and through the holy books given to the prophets.

Some of these Muslims will have been instructed that there was a prophet named Isa who was given the Injil (New Testament). He was virgin born and is referred to in the Koran as the Word of God and the Spirit of God. Some of these have sat under a religious teacher who taught that Jesus Christ will be present at the judgment, and in fact may be personally involved with Mohammad in implementing God's will concerning who should go to Paradise and who should go to hell. A smaller group still will be aware that there are still people on the earth who are serious followers of Jesus Christ (not merely westerners who are called Christians) and who think that Muslims need to believe in Christ as they do. Most likely, these Muslims will have a negative attitude toward those who are propagandizers of the Christian religion for imputing less than godly motives to them.

Finally, an extremely small number of Muslims will have met an evangelical Christian who has helped them overcome their misconceptions about Christianity, and who may have even made the gospel message understandable to them. This small group will divide up into two still smaller groups: (1) those who understand the facts of the gospel, but not its implications, and (2) those who understand that Christians are on a life and death rescue mission; their Christian friends are fully convinced that they, as Muslims, are in trouble if they do not relinquish their dependence upon Islam and put it fully on what Christ did on that cross in history as a necessary ransom for their lives.

These in the second category are the few who recognize that they have a serious problem to resolve. Usually, a person with some gift in evangelism is involved in helping Muslims realize that they have a sin problem that Islam cannot cure. If Muslims move the next step on the responsive scale, they are deciding to act, making a contract with God and Christ Jesus (probably unable to internalize the concept that they themselves are one). This involves a turning to Christ, as their mediator/sin-bearer and, hopefully, their highest authority.

At this point conversion becomes a reality, and with the Holy Spirit's work of regeneration, our Muslim friend becomes a new creature in Christ Jesus (2 Cor. 5:17). It is helpful to approach a Muslim friend as one needing help. The conversation might go something like this:

Mohammad, I have really enjoyed our discussions about God over the last couple of years, but I really need your help these days on knowing what I should do.

You'll remember, Mohammad, my story on how I changed some years ago, from basically orienting my life around becoming wealthy and comfortable, to a person who had an experience with God that completely changed my goals in life. The more I came to understand God's will and commandments through the holy books and prayer, I realized that the Lord Jesus Messiah broke the power of death and is alive today, still telling us to go to all peoples of the world and tell them how they can be rescued from Shatam and eternal banishment from God.

My problem, Mohammad, is that I want you to be my friend, and I don't want to offend you, but as I understand God's commandments, I'm supposed to help as many people as I can to understand how prophet Isa came to earth to seek and save people from the terrible judgment that the Koran also talks about.

I would like to talk to you more about these things because I'm worried about you as one of my best friends, but I don't want to offend you, so I need your advice. What would you do if you were me?

Mohammad needs to feel that, from the perspective of the Injil, he is in trouble without a connection with the personage of Isa, the mediator (1 Tim. 2:5). He also needs to feel an appreciation for my concern for him. If he sees me merely pressuring him to switch camps, from Islam to Christianity, then I have become an agent of the opposition. If he sees and feels that I am going out of my way to help him find something extremely important, he is much more likely to take a serious look at the claims of Christ. My goal, then, is to have my Muslim friend feel that if the Christian's gospel is true, and he takes advantage of it, that would be good news indeed. And conversely, if it is true and he turns his back on it, there could be terrible consequences for him.

Assuming that a valid, life-regenerating commitment is made at some point, the Christian growth process begins. The first stage of post-decision evaluation is often accompanied by doubts and anxiety about the decision's validity, and the repercussions from the significant others in the Muslim's life. At this point it is common for Muslims to repudiate the experience as they count the cost afresh and conclude that they have nothing more than their western friend's ideas and approval versus those of their entire extended family and countrymen.

The new convert, therefore, is going to need group support within a context that will solidify belief. Finding other like-minded former Muslim believers, with whom they can bond as a new family member, is intensely important. A post-conversion period of evaluation, reassessment, instruction, and preparation is critical. It gives converts the internal and external strength to face typically encountered resistance and discouragement growing out of that commitment.

This is why the church planting team needs pastors to connect the new believer with others, until they become mutually supportive to the point that their boldness, not their fear, increases. Psychologically, for Muslims to assume that every person they have ever known is wrong, and that this (often young) foreigner is right about the most basic ultimates of life, is to be adopting a rather improbable position. That is why conversion to a group of already converted Muslims holds much more promise.

The human psyche feels extremely arrogant being one alone against a million. Of course, Muslims who want to defect from their Muslim country and family, and to identify with the West, may see becoming a Christian as part of that process—a decision that enhances their direction. Such people could make a genuine decision for Christ, but they are not ones on whom you could hope to build an indigenous church in a Muslim city. They, in their own mind, have already left the Muslim world.

Thus, it cannot be emphasized enough, how vital it is to steer and pray the Muslim inquirer both into a radical existential experience of meeting the Lord, and into assimilation within a local community of former Muslim believers. The converts are often reluctantly accepted into a fearful group of believers only after someone respected in the group will champion their cause.

A premier example of this is Barnabas, in Jerusalem, who "took him [Paul] and brought him to the apostles" (Acts 9:27). Barnabas was Saul's mediator, staking his own reputation on the genuineness of Paul's conversion. By "sponsoring" him, Barnabas enabled Paul to actually move in with some of the believers, internalizing his decision to switch communities and to be identified with the Christians, whom earlier he had persecuted. The family model was assumed and the other disciples were referred to as "the brothers" (Acts 9:30).

Normally, however, brothers do not function without parents. This means that someone must serve as the father and mother, transferring this role from the change agent to national shepherds as soon as possible (1 Thess. 2:7). The church in Algiers got established because one unintimidated older woman (who, amazingly, was married to an unconverted Muslim hajji) took in the new converts from Algiers University, encouraged them, and nurtured them in the Lord. She served as liaison between them and the missionaries until they could mature enough to become elders in the newly formed Muslim-convert church, there in the capital of Algeria.

Very little adequate research has been done, isolating the variables of how or why Muslims have been making commitments to Christ. If, for example, most of the converts in an area report that a vision of Jesus was an integral part of their decision for Christ, then it would be important to ascertain what was involved in the preconversion experience of those who had visions of Jesus.

Why would some have a vision of Jesus and others not? Becoming an effective disciple-maker among Muslims in a resistant culture may require as much study and problem-solving as becoming a doctor who must diagnose and treat accurately, or a civil engineer who must build a bridge over a swamp.

A superficial analysis might indicate that there is no typical pattern to Muslims switching their allegiance to Christ Jesus, but there may be common factors. For example, a review of the Muslim converts in Morocco, Algeria, and Tunisia indicated that most went through a period of getting acquainted with New Testament truth, through a combination of radio and correspondence courses from Spain or France.

Most were then followed up with one on one evangelistic Bible studies with an expatriate missionary. Several mentioned their participant observation of a missionary's family as the final apologetic that convinced them that the Christian message was indeed of God.

Some Christians make a dichotomy of science and God's work. Who would not scorn the Christian farmer who refuses to learn principles of farming, dismissing them as worldly, and professing that simply trusting in God will bring blessing on the harvest? Are Bible translators to be despised for utilizing the science of linguistics and computers? It is not a matter of "manipulating" people into the kingdom, but rather, of cooperating with the nature of things, people, and culture, as we attempt to be good stewards of the gospel we sow.

Missiologists commonly argue that many peoples who are considered "resistant," may not actually be rejecting the Christian faith. Their refusal to respond to the gospel may be because they perceive that they will be swallowed up by another distasteful people or culture. Suppose for a moment if the only followers of Christ in North America were Hispanic? No Afro-Americans or people of northern European stock. If Anglo-Americans had to go into a Spanish-speaking service, or even one in English that was dominated by Latin culture, how easily would they become followers of Christ? Thus, church growth theory argues that people become followers of Christ when they see that doing so is appropriate for their kind of people, and normally not until then. Pioneer workers have this same challenge before them in their given Muslim city.

I was walking through the streets of Karachi with a well-educated Bahai Muslim, who as a friend of colleagues, had a good understanding of the gospel and its implications. As a group of street sweepers (who were Christians of Hindu background) passed us, he wrinkled his nose and demanded of me how I could ask him to join those people! He could relate better to us, as westerners, than he could to poor Punjabi Christians in his own city who were citizens of his country.

While in Peshawar, Pakistan, I was told a joke by an Uzbek from Afghanistan that revealed how Uzbeks totally despise and devalue Pathan Afghans. He concluded that the Pathans were animals, not even at the level of a human being! And we are talking about a fellow citizen of Afghanistan. Where this kind of prejudice exists, it argues well why one church planting effort must exist in the city among the Pathans, and a separate effort among the Uzbeks. After both Uzbeks and Pathans have come to Christ, and have matured, they would be expected to recognize each other as brothers and sisters in the body of Christ—even as Americans expect it between Black, Hispanic, and Anglo churches in the United States. Yet, outside of an occasional special event, even different ethnic groups in the democratic, egalitarian United States of America seldom attend the same services.

When I visited Bangladesh, my untrained eyes and lack of experience caused me to perceive the Bengalis as a more or less homogeneous people. Then I read in *Crucial Issues in Bangladesh* how Peter McNee feels strongly that by "not realizing the importance of class distinctions, evangelistic work among Muslims is ineffective" (1976:2). If this is true in

Bangladesh, where most of the people speak Bengali, how much more true in India, Pakistan, Afghanistan, Indonesia, and Morocco?

In Alexandria, Egypt, a university graduate typically holds a government clerk's job for 60 dollars a month, despite the government's encouragement to be a "free market" entrepreneur, like the low class Coca-Cola® vendor, who makes 300 dollars a month. However, because of that graduate's family background, it is unthinkable to become a street merchant. How open would these same young people be to regularly attending an evangelistic Bible study dominated by those who sell cokes, vegetables, and used clothing in the street markets?

In the Indonesian church growth example in Chapter 4, it is important to note that the breakthrough of baptizing over a million Muslims in Java between 1965 and 1975 was almost entirely among the Javanese Muslims, not the Sundanese who also live in Java. Dixon (1984) reports that during those years the West Java Christian Church in the Sundanese areas did not grow significantly. He believes this to be because the church leaders were basically relativistic, and therefore did not cooperate with either Indonesian or foreign evangelical mission efforts involved in evangelism during those years. More important to the point here, is that the Javanese Muslims coming to Christ did not share their discovery with the Sundanese communities nearby, although they share a very crowded island.

Avery Willis gave the clue as to why there was a response among the Javanese Muslims and almost none among the Sundanese. By the 1960s, the Javanese churches had become rooted in Javanese culture, and therefore, Javanese Muslims perceived that they could become Christians without being separated from their own people. This has not been the perception of the Sundanese. But lest we think that contextualized communication was the primary factor in Javanese Muslims coming to Christ, note that Willis's study indicates that "84.7 percent of the Muslim converts said their family was influential in their decision to become a Christian; 86 percent of the post-1965 converts had Christian friends prior to their conversion; 67 percent of the 500 converts interviewed who became Christians between 1960 and 1971 did so within people movements usually led by their village leaders" (1977:125).

In contrast, Dixon (1984) reports that, since 1968, several parachurch organizations including Indonesians have foraged into West Java in an effort to win Sundanese Muslims. Dixon believes that they failed because of their traditional approaches. The witnesses were non-Sundanese using Indonesian language; their evangelism was aimed at individuals; they held western-style meetings; they tended to extract Muslims from Sundanese life; and they had no plan to develop local leadership.

The success of Chris Marintika and his Bible School, which reportedly demands that all students start a church before they are given their graduation certificate, is greatly admired in the West. Marintika has perhaps given Indonesian Christians more vision and hope for Muslim work than any Indonesian alive today. Marintika told the author, "Church planting is the best method of evangelism in Indonesia. We can do it relatively quietly while the giant sleeps." Marintika's vision is to see a church established in every one of the 50,000 villages of Indonesia that are still without one.

His method seems simple: A student spends four days in the classroom, and three days in the villages, trying to establish a congregation of at least 30 baptized believers. The newly formed church then becomes part of that particular student's denomination, and therefore legal in Indonesia. In the past six years, Marintika's students have planted over 300 churches.

However, it should be noted that these church planting efforts are among basically illiterate village people, not in an urban context. The church planting students may get a hearing because they are at least one social niche above the villagers. Also, all of the effort is being done among people groups who already have Muslim convert churches in the area, if not in that particular village. This is significant because the people being approached realize that some of their own are already Christians.

Sadly, very few of these graduates stay in Muslim church planting after they graduate because Marintika has promised to send them back to their sponsoring denominations. Thus, the existing Bible schools and seminaries are producing Christian workers for the people groups who already have churches. This is quite a different thing from establishing the very first churches among an unpenetrated people group, or in a particular section of a Muslim city where no Muslim convert churches exist.

Another reality interfering with communication of the gospel is the hangover of the Muslim perception that Europeans have always come to conquer them! Ali, a mature Muslim convert in Istanbul, told me about the head of the Turkish Communist party, who returned from exile in Paris to Istanbul only to be immediately arrested. It seems even the normally liberal newspaper editors applauded the arrest because he came to Turkey surrounded by European Communist leaders. The issue switched from communism to domination by imperialistic Europeans. As soon as the Turks felt that the Turkish leader of the Communist party was using Europeans to force himself back on the Turkish population, they reacted negatively to him, regardless of their stance on communism. Americans and Europeans working with Muslims must understand that, normally, Muslims do not separate religion and politics. Many conservative Muslims hold a reconstructionist worldview. God's will is to bring the kingdom of God to earth by putting all peoples under Sharia law—government as dictated by the Koran and the Islamic traditions. Therefore, anything associated with the West cannot be of God.

Western change agents must find a way to get disassociated from the image of Europeans forcing their culture on the Muslims. They must prepackage the Christian faith as "made in Palestine," and "assembled in Turkey by Turks."

Don McCurry quotes from Muhammad Husayn Haykal, a well-known Muslim writer in Egypt:

> Europe, however, does not conquer in order to spread a faith nor in order to spread a civilization. What it wants is to colonize; to this end it has made the Christian faith a tool and instrument. This is why the European missions never succeeded, for they were never sincere and their propaganda had ulterior motives (1979:185).

Missionaries quickly take offense and are hurt by this common imputation of less than godly motives. Perhaps no other tactic can more effectively demoralize and demotivate a missionary to Muslims. I remember as a college student giving up my summer to be a missionary in Mexico. While going door to door with Christian books and Bibles, a man angrily devalued my effort, summing it up as an effort to get rich by taking money from poor people. I was so unprepared for such a response that I literally sat down on the curb and wept.

Some do not have the strength of ego (or maturity in Christ) to minister to ungrateful people. Yet even if we can take abuse, and our motives are substantially good, if they are perceived as evil, our Christian witness will obviously be hindered. Thus it is vital that the disciple-makers among Muslims learn how to portray themselves in such a way, as Parshall emphasizes, that they are understood to be people of God, dedicated to helping others; sacrificially giving themselves to the cause of God.

The Arabs call it *Jihad* (striving for God) or *Dawa* (involved in a movement to spread the knowledge of God). Magnuson identified the most respected religious movement in his adopted subculture. He made an effort to get to know people in it, until its respected features could be readily understood, and its best aspects emulated.

Every Christian worker among Muslims needs to be familiar with the Koran (and if possible the Hadith). The Koran's assertions about Hell outnumber the New Testament's. Yet it is quite rare to meet a Muslim, like the great eleventh-century Sufi, al Ghazzali, who will reveal any fear of actually being destined to Hell.

Universalism is as common in Islamic cities as it is in Christendom. To an alarming degree, educated people across the world have elevated relativism and tolerance to the top of their worldview. Doing so almost automatically relegates Christianity and Islam to the smorgasbord of ethical teachings from which people are encouraged to pick and choose as they are comfortable.

Anthropologists will point out how urbanization, new industry, relocation, westernization, political changes, and so forth, can weaken the ties of traditional values held by the Muslim; but few point out that this same process usually weakens ties to religion in general. The urbanized Muslims who no longer practice Islam are generally even less interested in becoming religious Christians. Religion is not high on their value scale.

In Istanbul, until recently, frustration had been high because few had found Turks who were interested in serving and pleasing Allah, much less in becoming Christians. (They have had something of a break-through, however, since they developed a better system for finding the few who are seekers.) The secularization process is no friend of the gospel. Dissatisfaction with Islam may lead to change, but that person may need to go through an extended nonreligious period, or a personal crisis, before feeling a need to be connected to God at all.

Given the general state of mind of the vast majority of Muslims, particularly in the urban context, who believe that the universe is superintended by a friendly, undemanding creator, why would any rational Muslims want to alienate themselves from their own people? Why call attention to their low commitment to Islam and designate themselves Europeans by becoming Christian? The vast majority of Muslims in the cities want to be friendly, tolerant, and sustain a relationship with others that will cause no one to lose face.

In an increasingly competitive world, where one does not have much time for religious practice in any case, why waste time or endanger relationships by suggesting that anyone should change their religion? In an interview with a Sundanese religious teacher in Bandung, West Java, Indonesia, I was told that the ideal Sundanese is one who loves the language, loves the culture, and is given to hospitality. There was no mention of faithfulness to Islam!

Because of this overall relativistic, spiritual atmosphere, the position of missiologists who imply that harvest is only a few sociological adjustments away, is deceiving and naive. To the contrary, Islamic fundamentalism in revival may indicate which Muslims desire to please God, and who may best be discovered by a prophetic approach. Why do so few Christian workers today seriously consider warning Muslims of the Judgment to come, in the mode of Jonah, Haggai, John the Baptist (Luke 3:3–8), or even as Paul to the Athenians (Acts 17:30–31)?

People Movements

Thus far this study has focused on the necessity of establishing viable communities of former Muslims as opposed to individualistic conversions. There is a tendency for marginal people or social deviants who have a relatively low social status in the Muslim community to be more responsive. At this point, then, it is important to interpolate the guideline of 2 Timothy 2:2: "And the things you have heard me say in the presence of many witnesses entrust to reliable men who will also be qualified to teach others."

Here, understand "reliable men" to be a synonym for noble, high-minded persons who draw respect because they are perceived as the best of their particular subculture. The change agents are being told by the Apostle Paul to invest themselves first in people with integrity and character whose commitment to Christ, when made, will be most sincere and lasting.

Second, the injunction would narrow one's focus further to identify faithful people "who are able to teach others also." The concentration of the disciple-maker then, is not on communication, but on *communicators*, people who can motivate fellow Muslims to consider Christ, and who can lead them to a new understanding and redemptive decision. If the focus of evangelism is on faithful people who are able to teach others, then the evangelist can count on God's encompassing mercy to eventually welcome in everyone else regardless of social status.

However, that is not where missionaries must begin. The "weaker" people (Rom. 14:1–15:1; Acts 20:35) will need leadership, or "umbrella" people to protect them from the counterattacks—the human ones led by fanatical Muslims, and the supernatural attacks by principalities and powers from the kingdom of darkness. There will be no churches until there are leaders who command a following.

Begin then with those who come from a position of strength, who have respected families and can support themselves financially. Otherwise, not only will elders not be established, but the missionaries will also fall prey to Muslim accusations that they are subversively exploiting the weak. Thus, while effective communication is basic, we must go beyond communication if we are serious about establishing congregations with their own national leadership.

Steve Hawthorne (1987) differentiates between missiology and "communicology." Hawthorne sees it as progress that in recent years "communicate" has become an important term, as opposed to "preach," which has implied religious monologue with little thought to the receptor. We are learning to become "receptor oriented" instead of assuming that others can make sense out of what we are saying just because it is perfectly clear to us. In recent years, Don Richardson has provoked missionaries to search for "redemptive analogies," advocating a careful study of cultures for ways to use local proverbs and poetry to better communicate. There is also an emphasis on Scripture translation, to find "dynamic equivalency," which means trying to find the words that will make the same impact as was experienced by the original hearers.

But communication is not enough. If the pioneer church planting team persists in focusing on a communicology framework, it will be better equipped to talk sensitively to the people, but that is not sufficient. Hawthorne fears that if we are satisfied with only good communication, we stand in danger of only winning a few more converts, instead of being a catalyst to an entire people group coming to Christ. With Hawthorne, McGavran, and the church growth movement, there is concern about the prospect of a new generation of missionaries who communicate the gospel with utmost cultural sensitivity, yet fail to plant churches. This because they are not prepared to cooperate with the dynamics of society in triggering a people movement. Perhaps a shift in mentality, beyond cross-cultural communication, to a focus on people movements to Christ must be a priority for research. Is it possible to foment and feed movements of obedience to Christ that produce long-term reproducing congregations? It seems that the Apostle Paul counted on large segments of people believing and obeying, and saw it as normative: "so that all nations might believe and obey Him" (Rom. 16:26).

If the church planting team expects to witness to a few people, that is what will happen. If they expect to see a few being faithful to the Lord, that is likely what they will realize. If, from the beginning, the team and the sponsoring churches envision a congregation with its own elders living openly in faith and obedience to the living Lord Jesus Christ, they are much more likely to see such a congregation become a reality.

In many cases, missionaries communicate much more effectively than they give themselves credit for. What about the Muslims who have well understood the claims of Christ and yet refused to be baptized? For them the problem is not poor communication of the message, but their fixation on the obstacles or social consequences of conversion. Hawthorne asks then, "How will they see the gospel enfleshed in their own culture, by their own people so that it's a psychological possibility to consider living under Christ's lordship with minimal social dislocation? So the issue becomes not so much the contextualization of the truth in the thought forms of the culture, but rather, the creation of a way for people to follow Christ in keeping with the most godly ideals of their society."

In Algeria, a young man heard the radio broadcasts of the North Africa Mission from Marseilles and wrote in for a correspondence course. After completing one or two courses, he wrote again, asking if they could tell him where he could meet someone who could explain Christianity personally to him. He was advised to go into the capital and meet an American English teacher. He did so, and they began evangelistic Bible studies. After a number of weeks of Bible study without much happening, this Algerian Muslim came to the missionary's house while an Algerian Muslim convert was visiting.

The Christian Algerian invited his new acquaintance to accompany him to a prayer meeting. Joining four young Algerian Muslim converts, the newcomer was deeply moved as he listened to his fellow Algerians lift up their hearts to the Lord Jesus Christ with practical prayer requests. They seemed to be talking to God like they knew him personally! What was happening was the same experience alluded to in 1 Corinthians 14:24–25: "If an unbeliever comes in while everybody is prophesying, he will be convinced by all that he is a sinner and will be judged by all and the secrets of his heart will be laid bare. So he will fall down and worship God, exclaiming 'God is really among you.'"

This Algerian was immediately converted. He hurried back to his American missionary friend blurting out, "Why didn't you tell me there were other Algerians like me who believed in Christ? I would have become a Christian a long time ago." No Muslim wants to be the first to identify with Christianity. It is almost impossible for Muslims to envision themselves following Christ as the living Savior unless they know someone who is respected and has also taken this path with whom they can identify. Thus the key to evangelism among Muslims is for them to experience a vital congregation of joyful redeemed Muslims taking care of one another, and giving Christ the credit.

In researching a city with a people movement mentality, it is vital to delineate the various sets of people who have a common identity and ask the following questions:

- What sociological walls divide this people from other people?
- Where are the gateways of a particular people that allow influence from the outside?
- Who holds dual citizenship with this people and another segment of people at the same time?
- What are the channels of communication within this people set?
- Who has been a change agent among them in recent times?
- How are decisions made?
- How are leaders recognized?
- How are organizations formed? (1987:7)

Obviously, any given Muslim city is a network of intersecting sets. Some of these would be merely vocations or other kinds of commonality, but not a distinction relevant to their highest values or goals. For example, taxi drivers in Istanbul may or may not have intimacy and loyalty to one another. Distrust and competition may be so great that they avoid intimacy. On the other hand, Richard Slimbach in 1985 found the Muslim rickshaw drivers of Hyderabad, India, very responsive to being helped to form a union so that they could demand better working conditions from those who leased the bicycle rickshaws to them. Slimbach, and his wife Leslie, discovered their friendship toward one rickshaw family was soon known among dozens of others, so Leslie would often get picked up by a rickshaw driver she had never met who would refuse to take a fare from her. They saw a great potential for this cohesive group to respond to the gospel, but sadly, their own residency visa was not stable enough to keep them in India the required time necessary to be effective change agents.

The team must consciously integrate its efforts with the flow of the history of evangelization in a city. God is neither going to begin his work in that city when you arrive, nor stop it if or when you leave. A team is soon going to Damascus, for example, as the only known workers among Muslims there. They must take courage in remembering that God's church once thrived in that great city. History will remind both them and the Muslims of Damascus that an emerging congregation of Muslim people who worship the Lord Jesus Christ there is not unthinkable.

In recent years, ambassadors for Christ have taken up residence once again in the classic Muslim city of Kashgar, China, as students and teachers. Elderly Muslims there remember a congregation of Uygur (Turkic) Christians who existed there in the 1930s, the result of a Swedish mission. By blaming the godless Marxists for its extermination, Uygur nationalism might be inflamed with the idea of establishing their church once again. Two known Uygur believers already own the dream of their church becoming a reality in Kashgar once again.

In most cases the Muslim converts themselves will establish a church, not the expatriates. The cross-cultural disciple-maker has the job of finding the hungry, introducing them to Christ, and being a spiritual midwife until they are able to reproduce themselves. Perhaps not much will happen until the bivocational missionaries find an "Andrew," who will find his brother "Peter," who may find "Barnabas," who will challenge "Saul," and then the people movement will begin!

Finally, the team can look for parallel situations in other Muslim cities that might provide clues for the target city. Change agents must be available to coach one another. The first principle of church growth is to ask which Muslim cities have new churches becoming a reality? Why? What is there to learn? What might apply to Ujung Padang, a city in Indonesia with over a million Buganese Muslims? A breakthrough in one city may have elements that would help bring a breakthrough in another city. Thus the case study method becomes crucial in helping workers see patterns and avoid pitfalls. In Chapter 11, two very different situations are reviewed. Each illustrates different aspects of team church planting in specific cultural contexts.

Part **3**

The Task
of Planting Churches
in Muslim Cities

8

Characteristics of a Church Planted

Wendell Evans, a veteran of 25 years of church planting effort among Arabs in Morocco, Algeria, and Tunisia, admits that compiling guidelines on how to form Muslim convert churches in the Muslim world seems a presumptuous undertaking. "No one on the basis of visible results can yet claim to be an expert in the field. No definable method has so brilliantly succeeded as to become a model of procedure" (1982:1).

Nevertheless, as my mentor, Ralph Winter, teaches: progress comes from one person taking a risk by proposing "answers," and then with first-hand experience come forth furnishing more data. The process brings us closer to the truth. Evans is one of those brave pioneers who was willing to make an attempt to lay out guidelines that may help the process. Evans represents the conclusions of the leadership of Arab World Ministries, which as North Africa Mission, has labored in Muslim North Africa for over a century.

We must begin with a definition of the church to be established.

A Working Definition

The goal of establishing a church is obviously not a building, but a congregation of Christians in a certain locale. The universal church of all redeemed believers today, or of any period, is the church. But in this study, church means the followers of Jesus Christ—believers called out from all that is not of God, to gather together in a Muslim city in his Name.

The simplest "form" is found in Matthew 18:20, "where two or three come together in my name, there am I with them." Evans rightly encourages us to rejoice for each one of the multiple demonstrations in Muslim countries of God's church, in the two or three coming together in embryonic form. Still, the whole tenor of the New Testament would insist that the goals we set as church planting teams go beyond the embryo to the form and functioning entity that we expect to develop from the embryo.

"In describing this entity, we are seeking to avoid both the vagueness of concept, which would paralyze progress toward a goal, and a structural rigidity that would prevent the diversity of expression in autonomous local churches from being in harmony with their ethnic and cultural identity," says Evans. The church, then, is believers gathered under the lordship of Christ in a new relationship, not solely between them and God, but also between them and their brothers and sisters in Christ. "It is the corporate manifestation of this relationship involving privileges and duties which is commonly called 'the local church'" (pp. 1, 3).

It is this corporate, visible, indigenous, social entity that we are seeking to help come into being as church planters in Muslim cities. "A local church is a grouping of members of the universal church with sufficient structure to demonstrate its corporate identity within its social and cultural context and to carry out its corporate functions of worship, edification and outreach" (p. 1).

Arab World Ministries agreed that in order to call a group of believers an autonomous functioning local church, the group ought to have at least five essential elements:

- Baptized believers
- Christian families
- Scripturally qualified and locally recognized national (citizen) shepherds

- Meeting place(s) independent of the expatriate church planter
- Assumption of responsibility for finances and ministry by the local group

The serious student of church planting will want to absorb the works of Roland Allen, A. R. Hay, and John L. Nevius, as well as more modern writers on generic church planting, including David Hesselgrave's *Planting Churches Cross-Culturally* (1980). The vital question must be answered: What needs to exist before the team can say, "We've done our job, let's get out of here"? It is foundational that a church planting team determine the answers in measurable terms, agree on them, and consciously keep them as a guide by which all activities can be evaluated.

Then when a team member gets a job in Istanbul as a civil engineer that entails a two-hour commute, the entire team can evaluate it in terms of whether or not it is conducive to their corporate church planting ministry. In Frontiers, bivocational missionaries claim that everything they do must contribute to church planting. All activities must be demonstrably subservient and complementary to their church planting goals, otherwise they must be abandoned as soon as possible.

Are Arab World Ministries' essential components of a church biblically defensible? Do you agree that these are the essentials?

Baptized Believers

Is not this the clarion call of the Great Commission? "Therefore go and make disciples . . . *baptizing* them . . . " (Matt. 28:19). The vast majority of Christendom has always recognized a physical baptism with water as the initiation rite and mark of corporate identity with God's church.

Interestingly, in most of the Arab world, there is not a great deal of opposition for Muslims who want to visit missionaries or even participate in occasional Bible studies—but when a Muslim is baptized! It seems the Muslims generally realize that baptism is the watershed—the mark of apostasy, the crystal clear step that says the Muslim is defecting to a new community. In fact, the reaction has historically been so harsh that Charles Kraft and Phil Parshall have been tempted to wonder out loud whether we should consider some initiation rite other than baptism, which is so obviously offensive in a Muslim context.

Parshall challenges the change agent to reflect on what the Christian rite of baptism, as practiced within an Islamic country, conveys to the onlooking Muslims. Speaking of a face to face rural community, Parshall's experience is that Muslims perceive these newly baptized Muslims as having openly declared themselves traitors to Islamic social structures, political and legal systems, economic patterns, and worst of all, the religion of their fathers has been profaned and desecrated. He has now become a worshipper of three gods, a follower of a corrupted religious book, an eater of pork, a drinker of wine, and a member of an alien society of warmongers and adulterers.

Unfortunately, as Parshall points out, individual baptism of Muslim converts has also almost always led to exclusion from the Muslim's extended family and society, and inclusion in a foreign-influenced Christian community. Parshall, surveying ministry in different Muslim countries, has discovered that "baptism is one of the largest problems confronted in evangelism among Muslims. In each Muslim country the true biblical meaning of baptism has not been properly understood. Invariably it has led to alienation and is viewed as a change in identity or even treason" (1980:190–91).

Because of these explosive reactions, most Christian workers among Muslims sanction secret baptism with only a few fellow believers present. The Ethiopian eunuch is sometimes cited as a New Testament precedent. In Algeria, the believers commonly perform their baptisms at either remote ponds in the woods, or during a beach party on the coast. Unrelated Muslims on the beach watching assume that one going under the water was the subject of horse play.

Parshall agrees with Kenneth Cragg, who after a lifetime in the Middle East, proposes a delay in the baptism of converts until such time as a large number from one area can be baptized together. Cragg apparently feels that it would be helpful for new believers in Christ to live with an intermediate status for a while where they could be known as Muslim "lovers of Jesus." Cragg is convinced that Muslim converts need their own fellowship, under some designation other than Christian, that would be a type of prep school while they get used to the idea of what their new commitment calls for, and while Christians from a non-Muslim background get accustomed to them.

There are those who would suggest that Christian workers to Muslims might want to examine the rites of passage in Islam, in the city where one works, and redesign a baptismal service after the Islamic initiation rites, as a functional substitute. Parshall's eventual conclusion, however, is that baptism in another form, which still communicates changing communities, will bring the same hostile reactions from the Muslims. So what is the point of innovating a new form? Perhaps more controversial is the question of household salvation, baptizing the whole family together, including children. Although most missionaries do not come from a background of covenant/reformed theology, they must understand that baptizing the children of a believing household leader (or a believing mother, 1 Cor. 7:14b) is exactly the reading of Scripture that seems most natural to Muslims and other eastern peoples. It is likely that westerners tend to interpret the Bible through the grid of teachers nurtured in the "one man—one vote—go your own way" cultures developed by pioneers seeking freedom from oppressive state churches.

It is probably safe to assume, however, that in Philippi, both the Philippian jailer's and Lydia's household included children, and probably infants. Since in most Muslim cultures family decisions are made together, why should baptism be an exception? Is "family baptism" not again a way of saying to the world, "But as for me and my household we will serve the Lord" (Josh. 24:15)?

Christian Families

It is more problematic to require that the fellowship have married people before it can be called a local church. Yet a church composed entirely of single young people is foreign to scriptural practice, and can hardly be taken seriously by Muslim cultures. Evans says, "Worshipping groups in North Africa have historically been composed primarily of single young people. Experience indicates, however, that only Christian families can provide the necessary stability, maturity, and ability to understand and minister to all the members" (ibid.).

The Christian home is an indispensable place for fellowship, prayer, study of the Word, and counseling. Believers who are single are often isolated in a hostile environment at home, school, or work. These young people need a haven in the atmosphere of a home away from home. The access of young single believers to such a home in Algiers is perhaps the greatest single reason for a functioning, indigenous group in that city today. Prayer, counseling, encouragement, and vision were always available in an older lady's house, even though her husband was not a believer.

Twenty-five years of experience in North Africa has convinced Evans that the foreign missionary's family cannot fill this gap. As soon as possible, national families must provide the nurturing atmosphere necessary for a church to develop. Single people in Muslim societies are considered nonadults, and are not to be taken seriously. When one marries, he or she settles down and becomes responsible. Thus, until the church has families, it is not clear that it will continue.

Elders

Arguing from failure, Evans delineates three problems he has experienced when foreign missionaries have sought to make groups function as churches without scripturally qualified national leaders clearly in charge.

First, the church group never made the transition to local leadership. "A long-standing Muslim convert of the worshipping group in Casablanca, Morocco once said to me, 'The church in this city will never function without the missionaries.' The expectation of an indigenous church, if ever fostered, had apparently died," wrote Evans in 1982.

Second, a democratic congregational "one-man, one-vote" form of government in Casablanca has led to all the believers having equal authority. This has resulted in no one having authority, and when someone would rise up to champion a cause or take initiative, they were prevented from doing so because their initiative was seen as having negative motives. This has led in turn to even qualified individuals being unwilling to function as an elder. Evans tells of a young believer who defected from the evangelical group in Casablanca to the Seventh-Day Adventists, giving as his justification, "At least we know who is in charge over there" (ibid.).

Third, in other cases, nationals have been appointed who recognized and therefore did not have the support of the other believers. This resulted in that elder-appointee being ridiculed, criticized, and disgraced until he stepped down. Opponents simply refused to cooperate and the meeting ceased. The lesson should be obvious: qualified leaders must be identified and facilitated into leadership with the recognition (not necessarily unanimous), and thereby loyalty of the overall group. True leaders are those who lead, are followed, and are held in respect by the community as shepherds. First Timothy 3 is clear about the appointing of men who will not shrink from assuming responsibility as an overseer for the fellowship.

Nevius, in his classic text *The Planting and Development of Missionary Churches* (1899), emphasizes that elders must be "appointed in every city" (Titus 1:5), but points out how the practices by early Presbyterian missionaries in Korea unwittingly put their reasonings before the explicit instructions of Scripture.

If we cannot get men for elders as well qualified as we should like, we must take the best men we can find and hope that they develop in character and ability to fulfill the duties of elders, by having the duties and responsibilities of this office laid upon them. With these views and expectations, several churches were formally and constitutionally organized. It was found, however, that in most cases the elders did not or could not perform their official duties, and were an obstruction to anyone else attempting to do so. They were injurious to themselves and the churches. Some were hardly able to sustain the character of an ordinary church member, and some were excommunicated in the course of a few years.

Nevius propounded, "This duty [to appoint elders] is enforced in Scripture both by precept and example. However, while elders should be ordained as soon as practical, we should not forget that the qualifications of elders are minutely laid down in the Scriptures, and to choose and ordain men to this office without the requisite qualifications is in fact going contrary to rather than obeying the Scriptures" (p. 60).

A Meeting Place

Housing is a critical problem in most overpopulated Muslim cities. The missionaries usually have more money and therefore can rent a place that has a room big enough for a meeting. Also, they do not have the problem of hostile Muslim relatives living within the same walls. In the past, converts have most often been young singles, or even wives, who have no authority to designate their home as a meeting place.

In not a few subcultures, even when a young couple is married they live in the home of the groom's father. Thus, there are many reasons why the church often meets in the missionary's home. Yet Evans would unreservedly object. "It has proved an effective deterrent to national leaders truly making and carrying out their own decisions. The group must meet in some place for which they themselves, not the expatriate church planter, are responsible" (p. 4). Evans' way of solving the problem in Casablanca—converting his garage into "their" meeting place— has been criticized as a social blunder. It appeared to some that the missionary was simply trying to get the "natives" out of his house, so he gave them the garage! Understandably, the gathering did not last.

The need for meeting places for new converts reinforces the premise that priority must be given to evangelizing household leaders who have charge over their homes, so that after conversion they can authorize their house being used as a meeting place. The church in Corinth met in the house of Gaius (Rom. 16:23). In fact, it is common in Paul's writings to read of the church in a leading believer's house (Rom. 16:5; 1 Cor. 16:19; Col. 4:15; Philemon 2).

Interestingly, Evans mentions Aquilla and Priscilla to back up his argument that the gathering of converts should be in a national's home; it could be argued that Aquilla and Priscilla, in fact, were part of an expatriate church planting team imported from Rome via Corinth to Ephesus. Were they not outsiders setting up house to give the new believers a place to meet in the first stage of church planting in Ephesus (1 Cor. 16:19)? Priscilla, being one of the few wives mentioned in the Scriptures, was probably a strong leader-organizer of the new converts, like Lydia (who was likely a widowed business-woman). Aquilla and Priscilla may have used their home for the investigative Bible studies until the believers meetings could be transferred to the home of an Ephesian family.

Self-supporting/Organizing Activities

Nevius believed that the church will be strong in proportion to what the members do with what they have. She will be weak in proportion to what they do with what the foreign worker provides. The extension of the church must depend mainly on the godly lives and voluntary activities of its members. There is no indication that the early Christians ever complained to the apostles that they could not carry out the Lord's work because they were not being sufficiently financed. "I can find," Nevius wrote, "no authority from the Scriptures, either in specific teaching or apostolic example, to the practice so common nowadays of seeking out and employing paid agents as preachers" (p. 59).

In most Muslim cities very few converts aspire to the office of elder. Most Muslim converts, probably taking their cue from the missionaries, cannot conceive of a functioning congregation with leadership, programs, and finances. "Why bring unnecessary persecution on ourselves?" seems to be a common, though unspoken, doctrine of both the expatriate missionaries and the converts. How then can we assist potential national leaders to see that establishing a congregation is God's priority?

Ecclesiology

Christian workers have diverse convictions on the nature of the church. What forms of church structure, government, and activity are best suited for hostile Muslim cities? Some, unashamedly, sense conviction from God to establish a branch or synod of their own denomination in a particular area of a Muslim city. Today, the most common sentiment would rather see almost any type of church among their adopted Muslim people than none at all.

Can or should the missionary church planter decide how the new Muslim believers will read the Scriptures? An interesting turn of events occurred in Tunis, Tunisia, some years ago. The missionaries who were instrumental in establishing a church of about 10 believers basically taught the Scriptures as they understood them, which in this case happened to be mostly according to the dispensational school of theology. There was no particular problem (except little growth) until an Egyptian missionary from the Assemblies of God moved to Tunis. His concern was to teach "the full counsel of God" (Acts 20:27 KJV) as he understood it, which was classical Pentecostal doctrine. It seems that a number of the believers were fortified by this "new" emphasis. Some reacted in anger toward the older noncharismatic missionaries: "Why have you held this truth back from us? You just wanted to keep all the power for yourselves so that you could keep control over us," some mistakenly surmised.

It seems that the noncharismatic missionaries were naive in assuming that, in this "global village," the disciples in Tunis would not be hearing of other views of sanctification sooner or later.

Another illustration of the difficulty in establishing one's concept of a "pure New Testament church" also comes from Tunis. It seems that the missionaries had decided that a house church with a plurality of unpaid elders was the most practical (and scriptural) form of church government for the embryo group there in Tunisia's capital. However, one of the Tunisian believers visited Marseilles, France, where the missionaries invited him to help out at their radio-correspondence course center, and to enjoy the fellowship of the French Christians. When the Tunisian believer was taken to a French church, he immediately noticed a man up front in a special clergy uniform who was obviously in charge. It was explained to him that this was the salaried pastor. Upon returning to Tunisia, the brother presented a wonderful new idea: Why not make him the pastor of the new church, salaried by the missionaries? When they declined, he was hurt, felt devalued, and concluded that missionaries did not want the Arabs to have full-fledged churches with pastors as it is obviously done in the West.

Despite these and many other discouragements, after over a hundred years of mission in North Africa, Arab World Ministries' leaders have ventured some guidelines for establishing church life. Let the reader wrestle with them and improve them if possible.

1. Principles and procedures will be drawn from and tested by the New Testament. We will not introduce practices contrary to it even when such might be sanctioned by church history.
2. We will seek to be as flexible (no more, no less) than the New Testament. Where it is absolute, we will be dogmatic. In matters where it is not specific, we will encourage liberty within the parameters of clearly understood New Testament principles (Evans 1982:4).

Evans concludes that the New Testament gives broad parameters of how a church should be organized and how it should function. Within these parameters there is ample scope for pragmatic variation in the details of government, order, and function.

Church structure and definition is one thing—congregational life is another. God's purpose for his earthly communities is a people gathered as citizens of his Kingdom, demonstrating the reality that the living head of the church, Jesus Christ, can inculcate into lives individually, as families, and as a volunteer association par excellence. The church, wherever it is in the world, is to be a people who identify as God's family, who supernaturally care for one another seven days a week, or in the words of Scripture, who "devoted themselves to the apostles' teaching and to the fellowship, to the breaking of bread and to prayer. . . . All the believers were together and had everything in common . . . and much grace was upon them all. There were no needy persons among them . . . they gave to anyone as he had need. Every day they continued to meet together in the temple . . . broke bread in their homes and ate together with glad and sincere hearts, praising God and enjoying the favor of all the people. And the Lord added to their number daily those who were being saved" (Acts 2:42–47; 4:33–34).

If the passage above is taken as the essence of biblical church life, what would it look like in the context of a Muslim city? Parshall points out that the new Muslim believers have three options: to stay in the mosque as some kind of Jesus Muslim; to follow the well-established tradition to leave the mosque, be repudiated by their family, leave their community, and identify with the non-Muslim convert congregation (if it will accept them); or to stay in their community as part of a homogeneous house church with other Muslim converts.

I am empathetic of those Muslim followers of Jesus who seek to stay within the mosque as salt and light. Some have ventured that Muslim believers in Isa ought to be able to exist as an Islamic sect much as the early Christians were perceived as a Jewish sect. Parshall, however, gives four reasons why such a tactic has not yet proven to be possible: All Muslims exalt Mohammad (and some Ali) as the primary messenger (and often mediator) between God and man. Muslims devalue the Bible as corrupted beyond usability and therefore will not allow it to be read alongside the Koran. Muslims typically are very paranoid about spies in their midst with ulterior motives. Typically they react with great hostility when they discover believers in Christ in their midst who are representing themselves as Muslims (but are actually believers in Jesus as God). Muslims continuously and emphatically deny that there is any need for a Savior, an atonement, or even that their sin is much more than universal human weakness.

On the other end of the spectrum, the strategy to incorporate more than a few Muslim converts into churches of people with non-Muslim backgrounds has been singularly unsuccessful for well over a century throughout the Muslim world. Although there are certainly exceptions, Christians of non-Muslim background purposely or inadvertently insist that the Muslim converts become like them to be acceptable Christians. Unwittingly, this means changing cultures, vocabulary, adopting a new set of taboos, and, for the most part, holding that former Muslim in suspicion to the extent that non-Muslim Christians are unwilling to allow him to marry one of their daughters.

While ministering in Beirut, Lebanon, I attempted several times to bring a Muslim inquirer to one of the evangelical churches. Each time, my Muslim friend was taken aside by a church leader and chided, "What are you doing here? You know this is not your place. You're just here to see our women." Understandably, I was not able to bring them a second time.

My Pakistani colleague, Jonah, in Karachi, told us about a Muslim convert he knows who had been faithful to the Lord and the church for perhaps ten years. Last year, as he was waiting in line to take communion in a church of Pakistan, one of the elders forced him to get out of the queue and sit down, on the grounds that "it isn't for him—he's a Muslim," even though he protested that he had suffered for the Lord Jesus for years!

Because of many such instances, and the other reasons illustrated in this book, those of us influenced by the church growth school, with its emphasis on homogeneous units, would argue for the type of house church that has demonstrated itself to be fruitful in the hostile societies of China and the Soviet Union. When there is a plurality of shepherds or elders, hostile governments cannot easily dismantle the congregation by simply arresting the pastor.

Avoiding paid clergy, the believers circumvent the common Muslim accusation that they have been bribed to become Christians. To advocate a plurality of elders is not to demand that the church cannot follow leadership paradigms of its culture. On the contrary, the Muslim convert church is likely, if untampered with, to drift toward the known, and desire leadership that reminds them of the role of an Iman, a pir, or another kind of religious leader they have appreciated.

The change agent cannot, and should not, hinder the leadership already in the culture from coming to the front. However, just as an English WEC missionary discipled the revered Indian leader, Bahkt Singh, who presides over the strongest indigenous congregations in India, today's pioneer would hope to disciple the emerging leadership until it would:

- Memorize and teach the Scriptures with a hermeneutic that would cause the Bible passages to impact the congregation in a similar way as when it was first spoken.
- Take pastoral responsibility for the people, be "given to hospitality," and be available to be called on in time of need, including praying for the sick and oppressed.
- Meet the "righteousness" standards of the community as well as the Bible's, so the elders are perceived as men who walk with God and behave toward other people within biblical absolutes, yet free from lifeless legalism.
- Have a lifestyle on the level of the most exemplary local Muslim leaders, either entirely dependent on their own congregation for their livelihood, or fully or partially self-supported. Parshall warns from experience of the counterproductiveness of church leaders accepting foreign money. Perhaps the most that should be done with foreign funds is for them to be utilized to underwrite a nationally owned and operated enterprise that might possibly employ some of the church leaders, or better yet, help set them up in their own businesses that employ church members.

These Muslim convert churches should understand from the beginning the doctrine of the priesthood of the believer. They are all gifted to minister in at least one of the six missions of the church. All recognized leaders should be able to baptize, serve the sacraments, teach the Word, and give pastoral care.

The missionary enterprise has assumed in the last two hundred years that church leaders must have the opportunity to go to a theological institution to train for the ministry. With the advent of theological and biblical education by extension, a new mentality has arisen that sees something intrinsically wrong with the notion that people must leave their community in order to get prepared to minister in it. Therefore, many creative training modules are being developed that can keep the church leaders involved in their church and community while upgrading their knowledge and skills. Extension courses, tutoring, workshops, and one on one mentoring can be integrated into the natural working schedule of the target people so that their family, work, and community life is not disrupted unnecessarily or unnaturally.

To be serious about people movements is to plan on God bringing to himself some persons of higher learning, including some (not unlike Saul of Tarsus) who may come out of the Islamic religious colleges and Muslim courts. The church planting teams will want to continually ask God to raise up men of the stature of an Augustine, an Athenasius, or an Apollos, so that most of the decisions and even the teaching will be taken out of the foreigners' hands fairly quickly. Some of the expatriot team members can then serve the local church leadership to fill gaps. One brother in Istanbul specializes in helping the converts write their own spiritual songs, and others will move on with some of the new believers to pioneer that church's effort to start a sister church in a new sector of the city, or even in a new unreached city or nearby village.

The church must become a people like the Bereans, who "search the Scriptures to see if these things be so" (Acts 17:11). Disciples must understand the Scriptures to be their authority—the last and final word on their beliefs and behavior. This assumes that they have at least a complete and readable New Testament, if not the entire Bible. Where this is not the case, there will be a need in the interim period to utilize gifted bilingual converts to put portions of the Scriptures on cassettes, and to continually translate significant portions that the believers can chant, memorize, read responsively, and exposit while the Bible is being translated.

Unfortunately, as far as taking the Bible utterly seriously on face value, westerners may not be the best models to Muslim converts. Worship and religious practice by eastern people ought to be eastern. Phil Parshall says that we have much to learn from the enjoyment Muslims have in memorizing, chanting, and quoting the Koran. He perceives that the Muslim's love affair with the Koran is paralleled only rarely among evangelical Christians with our Bible.

Muslims have continually insisted that the internal proof that the Koran is the word of God is its literary majesty. "If you could just understand it, and hear it being chanted in Arabic, you would know it is the truth," they commonly insist.

Tragically, it seems that the vast majority of Muslim converts, rather than imitating devout Muslims' constant quoting of the Koran, tend to imitate western practice, which mainly relegates attention on the Bible to Sunday. Bahkt Singh's disciples in India, in contrast, have Bible verses posted and painted on every available space around their church compounds and houses.

I mentioned how Mazhar introduced chanting the Scriptures into house meetings in Cairo. It is natural for those Muslim converts who were faithful in the mosque to include in their church gatherings sessions of chanting, memorizing, and reciting the Scriptures. Putting Scripture to local music may be helpful, except among Muslims who consider music worldly and therefore unsuitable for holy revelation.

Westerners who have been in churches in Africa and Asia have often been startled by the contrast in enthusiasm when the believers were encouraged to utilize their own indigenous music and instruments, as opposed to singing translations of western hymns with western music. Recently, I heard a tape of a group of Albanian Muslim converts singing their own Scripture songs that they adapted to Albanian Muslim tunes. Their joy and laughter indicted a reality of worship not often seen among former Muslim followers of Christ.

Prayer should feel like prayer to the one praying. How can a Muslim, whose sense of reverence is connected with prostration, take seriously Christians who pray while slouched in chairs? Hopefully, new Muslim converts will not have observed western-type services, and therefore will pray in ways that are natural to them, which may mean standing with the prayer leader, everyone praying out loud at the same time, or holding out cupped hands in prayer positions they knew as Muslims.

Some converts from Islam have advocated the development of an Anglican-type prayer book, where Bible verses are recited or chanted antiphonally during prayer.

Above all, Muslim converts, like all believers everywhere, need to have a sense of the presence of God. They must sense that they are indeed in communication with their Heavenly Father; to worship God "in Spirit and in Truth." They need to be taught and shown the difference between prayer that is adoration, prayer that is thanksgiving, and that which is confession, or intercession. The Bugi, Uygur, or Kazakh needs to become more, not less, a man or woman of prayer, having come to know and love the Lord Jesus. In their prayer life, they need to understand the difference between prayer that is focused on God, that which is focused on themselves, and that which is focused on others.

Christianity, especially in the West, has moved away from its heritage of fasting. It may be our brothers and sisters from Islam who will bring it back into the church to a greater degree. Did not the Lord Jesus say that his disciples would fast when the Bridegroom was away? (Mark 2:20). Therefore, it may be the western Christians who need to adapt in this area more than the Muslim converts. New believers should be taught that fasting is not an act of merit, but it is to accompany a deep longing and hunger for God, and a way to spend more time with God during a time of crisis. Schisms should be avoided among Muslim converts through teaching that emphasizes their freedom to keep the tradition of fasting for a month, Muslim-style, or not to do so.

Missionaries may feel led to keep the Ramadan fast fully or partly, as identification with their Muslim friends (or in an effort not to be a stumbling block), thus patterning principles for the Muslim converts.

The New Testament account of the believers meeting for communion is probably culturally closer to most Muslims than modern westerners. Regular communion is basic to keeping the followers of Christ conscious and thankful, both cognitively and emotionally, of God's sacrifice. It would appear that the Lord established the communion liturgy as a typical Eastern way to keep his followers focused on the primary truth.

Seldom have Muslim converts transferred their primary loyalty from their blood relatives to their brothers and sisters in Christ. Perhaps this is because few have experienced biblical fellowship as described in Acts 2 and 4. If, however, the house church becomes a community that bears one another's burdens and confesses their faults one to another, taking responsibility for one another's welfare, it could, because of the electrifying contrast to their Muslim society, have the effect of "enjoying the favor of all the people," and seeing the Lord adding "to their number daily those who were being saved" (Acts 2:47). Biblical church life is evangelism. The reality of 1 Corinthians 14:24–25 is the goal. Unbelievers come into the gatherings, are convinced by all that they need the Savior, and "fall down and worship God exclaiming, 'God is really among you.'" Until the fellowship of a church in a Muslim city is at least as intimate and mutually caring as the 12-step program of Alcoholics Anonymous, it is unlikely that church growth will occur.

Forms such as covered heads, uncovered feet, standing or prostrate prayer positions must be chosen by the new believers themselves. You can encourage them to experiment until they have a serendipity of "worshipping in Spirit and in truth" (John 4:24). Westernized urban dwellers who have hardly ever attended a mosque are likely to choose forms quite different from rural conservative Muslims who are living in another area of the city.

To what degree should the Muslim convert church follow the Christian church calendar with its special days celebrated around the world? Parshall would advocate adapting at least Christmas, Good Friday, and Easter Sunday into culturally appropriate celebration days. Other biblical events could be celebrated, such as Pentecost, the call of Abraham, and the Passover of God's people from Egypt, if the church so desired, especially if they could parallel or be integrated into some of the Muslim festivals such as Al-Adha (the Feast of Sacrifice), which falls on the 10th day of the last month of the Muslim year. Al-Adha is celebrated in remembrance of Abraham's willingness to sacrifice his own son. In the past, a male goat, lamb, cow, or camel was butchered and eaten during a religious ceremony. Today in the cities, Muslims tend to buy their meat already butchered, not unlike an American's Thanksgiving turkey. In any case, believers from a Muslim background should be encouraged to transform Muslim holidays into remembrances of biblical events with modes of celebration or solemnity parallel to a local feast day: to meet their own needs, to identify with their Muslim neighbors, and as an opportunity for teaching biblical truth. Has not the church historically done this, baptizing some Greek and Roman festivals with Christian content?

Can the Muslim convert participate in Muslim festivals? Parshall claims that the Muslim *ids* are religious in nature, but usually not demonic or injurious to the Christian, and more often than not, simply a social celebration. The believer in Christ, Parshall feels, can enter into these with his Muslim family and friends as a show of solidarity, not unlike how nominal Christians, with great zest, celebrate Christmas.

In fact, it is almost impossible for a new convert from Islam not to participate to some measure in these celebrations, since they are so family oriented. To avoid them and dismiss them as wrong would be to create much offense and cut off natural bridges to the Muslim community.

The Muslim convert church will need to develop birth, baptism, marriage, and funeral customs that both honor Christ as preeminent, and have a positive effect on the Muslim community. Obviously, the cultural traditions that are not antibiblical can be preserved, while nonbiblical Koranic readings and other practices may need to be quietly deleted from ceremonies. It is important for some from the team to attend a number of such ceremonies in their adopted Muslim city, so that they can better assist the Muslim converts in designing contextualized ceremonies that will honor Christ and the Bible as opposed to Mohommad and the Koran. Keep what can be kept and exchange what must be exchanged. Funeral ceremonies should communicate high respect for the family and for the dead when they are for an unsaved family member, and, of course, great joy and celebration when for the believers demonstrating their conviction that the dead in Christ are not "dead" at all! Such genuine faith that "death has lost its sting" is a powerfully practical witness to the difference between Christianity and Islam.

In summary then, the churches established should be committed to reducing every unnecessary hindrance, both sociological and theological, to the Muslim becoming a follower of Christ and enjoying church life, while realizing that the world will be no friend to God's people, and that suffering is inevitable. The apostle Peter sums up our goals for the churches in Muslim cities: "As you come to him, the living Stone—

rejected by men but chosen by God and precious to him—you also, like living stones, are being built into a spiritual house to be a holy priesthood, offering spiritual sacrifices acceptable to God through Jesus Christ. . . . you are a chosen people, a royal priesthood, a holy nation, a people belonging to God, that you may declare the praises of him who called you out of darkness into his wonderful light . . . [You] are the people of God . . . . [as] foreigners and strangers in the world. . . . [live] such good lives among the [Muslims] that, though they accuse you of doing wrong, they may see your good deeds and glorify God on the day he visits us" (1 Pet. 2:4–6, 9–12).

9

Two Case Studies

Algiers, Algeria

A Muslim convert church has been established in Algiers, an Arab Muslim city of over two million people. Up to ninety believers meet in three different homes. The majority are baptized. The recognized leaders (with no title) are married Algerian men with believing wives. There are several Christian families in the congregation. The believers meet regularly to study the Bible and pray. The church has assumed responsibility for its own activities, including financial affairs, spiritual growth, and witness with no expatriate presence since 1981. The church is the result of over 25 years of labor on the part of missionaries, tent-makers, and faithful Algerians who have developed the fellowship. It is the largest of precious few assemblies of mature former Muslim Christians in all of North Africa and the Middle East, from Morocco, to Turkey, to Iraq.

Algiers' population includes both Arabs and Kabyles, the indigenous people of Berber descent who existed there before the Arabs settled. The Kabyle population consists of both Arabized and urbanized Berbers and mountain rural Berbers of different tribes. The Muslim government of Algeria assumes that every Algerian is a Muslim, though not necessarily religious. Though the government could be described as socialist, it has been an eclectic mixture of Islam, socialism, capitalism, and the charismatic personalities of the rulers. (Only as I write are the fundamentalists winning a free election and coming into power. Implications?)

Algeria has been independent from France since 1962. The French colonial influence explains why many of the educated Algerians over thirty speak mostly French, have had their education in French, and in many cases do not read Arabic well. Since independence the government has attempted to fully Arabize the country, but evidently it will still take years before Arabic becomes the dominant language of the educated. The urban segment of Algiers tends therefore to be western in their thinking and cannot be entirely unaffected by French culture with its pessimistic existentialism. University students, who may have no knowledge of the Sermon on the Mount may be quite familiar with Camus and Sarte.

The people of Algeria, and particularly those in the capital, Algiers, were not normally staunch Muslims—at least not when this church was established. A small percentage performed the daily prayers. Most have been caught up in eking out an existence, especially because of a critical job and housing shortage.

Although Christian missionaries have worked in Algeria for over a hundred years, they have never been there in great numbers. It may be that Algiers has never had as many as 25 missionaries at any given time. Christian work there, as in most Muslim cities, ebbs and flows. At one time there were a few Arab pastors in the country, salaried by the American Methodist Church, but now there are none.

Nevertheless, a steady stream of individual Muslims have responded to Christ in the last two decades. Today there are no expatriates with missionary visas in Algeria, but at any one time there continues to be at least four to ten bivocational missionaries spread around Algeria. Up until 1984, there were about 20 workers in the capital, some who had been there 20 years. It is not clear to what degree the continuity of the expatriate presence has enabled the church to take root.

In the last 4 to 5 years, a people movement in Bejaia, where the Kabyles live in the mountains, is growing faster than any urban church growth ever did anywhere in North Africa. Members of the Arab World Ministries tell that there may be more than 2000 believers in the mountain villages. And it happened without any expatriot workers being up there with them!

This movement is attributed to a couple of young Kabyle men who somehow got discipled by the church in the capital, and who were inspired to the obedience of proclamation by the example of some of the believers in Algiers.

The main growth of the missionary-taught believers in Algiers covered a 10 to 12 year period (1969–1981) with three expatriate men serving as the first elders of the church from 1974–1978. Present church leaders were high school age when first contacted through a reading room and Bible correspondence courses. Obviously, if they had been converted when older (20 to 30 years old), they would have reached leadership in a shorter time.

Each of these missionaries arrived in Algeria with a good working knowledge of French and some Arabic learned while there. Nearly all had university degrees. Two American couples, a French professor of science and his wife, and two single women seem to have been the major facilitators in seeing this church planted.

These expatriates befriended students through a reading room near the university (which before independence had been a Christian bookstore), out of which came an investigative Bible study. These Bible studies led to conversions and the establishing of a believers' Bible study. A worship meeting was started, led by the expatriates, but was dominated by single Algerians for several years.

However, as the believing students graduated, got jobs, and married, the group organized as a church with their own form of elders and membership. As they grew to 100 believers, they were less able to meet in one place, especially as police harassment intimidated some. When last heard, they were meeting in one, two, or three homes depending on circumstances. Periodically the leaders organize family camp retreats around holidays, which enable the believers to have a sustained time of fellowship in a larger group.

Most of the believers are between 25 and 40 years old, with perhaps half of them baptized. One or two older persons have provided some credibility and stability to the group. A large percentage of the converts have come out of the university or technical colleges, thus the congregation is well educated. Perhaps 65 percent of the congregation is Kabyle in background. One hypothesis is that Kabyles, not wanting to be dominated by the Arabs, may be more open to becoming Christians.

The church was hesitant to choose the young university students as elders until they were married. The three "elders" are married now and have been in that role since 1984. One of the older believers, the wife of a pilgrim (*hajji*) to Mecca, was able to rear her daughters in the Lord, and they became the wives of the men who became the leaders. Prayer meetings have been a relevant time of dealing with felt needs among believers. It has also provided an occasion for the salvation of searching Muslims, who have been brought there by the Muslim convert church members (see 1 Cor. 14:24–25).

Today, of the hundred known believers in Algiers, perhaps half are committed to the church and its purposes. The leaders organize the services, the style being somewhat similar to the Plymouth Brethren format, that is, a participatory service with no full-time pastor. Expatriates during the 1970s provided Bible training for six to eight Muslim converts at a time. These Theological Education by Extension (TEE) classes met mostly in the homes of the bivocational missionaries. It is believed that Algerians now in turn are training newer believers. Algerians, like other Arabs and Berbers, do not normally commit themselves to people outside their own family. Many still fear or find little motivation to identify themselves with the church and will only visit other believers in twos or threes. Yet, for several years, there has been a reasonably good body life, supportive relationships, and a fairly high trust level (for the Muslim world), all of which make the congregation attractive. As Arabs and Kabyles are able to meet together as Christ-loving Muslims (probably easier because they pursued higher education together), the credibility of Christ is greatly enhanced. The testimonies of the Algerian believers are the primary means of communicating the gospel.

The believers are under constant surveillance, personally, as well as their mail and phones. Although the police have interrupted the meetings only twice since 1981, those who fear repercussions tend to be frequently absent. Most of the believers who have been interrogated have stood firm before the police, but predictably, while some have grown in their courage as a result, others have gone underground.

A number of the believers have not revealed to their families that they are followers of Christ, and some marriages were done by Muslims, in Muslim forms and content, even though both the bride and groom were believers. Baptism leads to such great alienation that the believers have decided for the most part to allow their baptism to be discovered slowly. Although the leaders have been warned about possible consequences, there has not been a sustained effort to keep the believers from meeting.

Believers' groups outside the capital have suffered greater harassment by the police, indicating the more liberal policies of Algiers. Some of the believers are called in for interrogation periodically, but it seems mainly to be the routine practice to determine whether the unauthorized group has any political intentions.

Most Algerians have grown up thinking that Christianity and western lifestyle are synonymous, and therefore, Christianity is the inferior and dirty French Catholic religion. Because Islam and politics are inseparable, it is assumed by most Muslims that western politics and Christianity are one. For this reason, rejection of western political domination tends to automatically bring rejection of any serious consideration of Christianity. It is a new idea for many that one can be a follower of Christ and a loyal Algerian.

The church has shown a burden for outreach to others in Algeria. One young man, converted in France through Young Life, returned to the university in Algiers and, through holding evangelistic Bible studies, was able to bring several new students to the congregation. He started a Young Life type club that had as many as 40 attending. Some of the young people attending, particularly girls, found themselves in trouble with the police and therefore their parents. For this reason, the meetings at the University were intermittently halted and restarted, and finally ceased.

Expatriates enter Algeria initially as tourists. Some enter into Arabic study for which they can sometimes get a one-year resident visa. Other expatriates make the contacts to eventually secure a job. An approved work visa is usually granted for only one year at a time, so the expatriate worker is often back on the streets after two years looking for a new *raison d'etre*. Algeria, like most countries, understandably wants to replace every foreigner with an Algerian in their job market as quickly as possible.

Many Algerians have heard Christian radio programs from France, and not a few have enrolled in Bible correspondence courses. Some want to visit or be visited by an expatriate to further check out Christianity. A number of the present believers in the church were initially contacted through radio and Bible correspondence courses. Web evangelism, in which believers witness to friends and relatives, is the most common type of evangelism now.

The bivocational missionaries in Algeria have taken jobs in other cities that are without churches, leaving the national believers in Algiers to govern and teach themselves. The Algerians started new house groups in three other cities where bivocational missionaries had led Muslims to Christ.

One of the leaders from the capital city church is seen as an evangelist church planter and is helped financially by the church to visit isolated believers holding house meetings in their own homes. Nevertheless, both Algerians and expatriates acknowledge the need for gifted expatriates who can pioneer efforts in Algeria's 15 cities, each with populations of over 100,000.

The major reason why a church in Algiers emerged in the midst of many hardships was the ability of its pivotal people, that is, three or four Algerians and three or four bivocational missionaries, who kept the goal of an indigenous church before them. It was constantly taught that the church is God's idea and desire, so those who accepted Christ's lordship also made a commitment to the establishing church. Perhaps because of higher education, the believers have not been as paralyzed by social disapproval and government opposition as have less educated believers in other Muslim countries. Since they did not win heads of households initially, the missionaries had to provide a stability and continuity while the teenage converts matured, without which the church could not have emerged.

The church in Algiers does provide a model for what could happen in other cities of North Africa and the Middle East. Factors, then, that have contributed to the successful establishment of a vital congregation in Algiers are:

- The indigenous Kabyle people seem to be more responsive because of a reaction to Arab domination.
- Though the missionaries were few, they had continuity in relationships and could communicate well with university and high school students, in French and often in Arabic.
- The "tent-makers" held university degrees that allowed them to hold teaching positions and gain respect in the society.
- The missionaries were committed to a long-term discipling process. They were able to recognize leadership gifts among the Algerians, and instilled among some the vision to shepherd a congregation.
- Change agents effectively followed up inquiries from radio and correspondence course invitations, to identify true seekers.
- Sufficient time and effort were given to assisting male Muslim students to find empathetic converted wives, which led to Algerian families becoming the core of the congregation.
- Worship and prayer meetings utilized forms that enabled the believers to deal with felt needs, which in turn attracted more Algerians to Christ.

There are fine prospects for new missionaries and willing nationals to team up on compatible intellectual and spiritual levels for church planting in new cities as soon as expatriates who can speak French and/or Arabic are available, and can find a way to obtain a residence visa. Such missionaries, however, would need to be people who understand how to be a catalyst trainer, refraining from doing what the national brothers can already do themselves. And although the church is relatively strong in the capital, there are no meetings in several other cities such as Constantine.

Algiers demonstrates how progress in planting a new church is very slow until there is a critical mass of enough believers to make Christianity a viable alternative in the minds of the seekers. It may be that Muslim converts from other Muslim cities could visit the church in Algiers to gain a vision of how they could plant an indigenous church in their own city.

Bandung, Java, Indonesia

This case study on the Indonesian Sundanese gives an opportunity to compare what is being done with what occurred between 1965 and 1971 among Javanese Muslims.

Java is the most important of 3,000 inhabited islands that constitute the world's largest archipelago—Indonesia. Although Java has less than 7 percent of the total land area of Indonesia, 64 percent of its population lives there. One thousand and forty kilometers long and 120 kilometers wide, Java has one of the most dense populations in the world for an area of its size, with over 470 people per square kilometer. Four major ethnic groups (not counting Jakarta, which has scattered representatives from everywhere), inhabit Java.

Javanese comprise 70 percent of the population, Sundanese about 15 percent, with the remainder being Madurese, Chinese, and immigrants from other islands. Seventy percent still live in traditional villages, subsisting on the wet rice cultivation system. Bandung, the largest city after Jakarta, is home for approximately two million Sundanese Muslims.

This case study focuses on three new congregations that have been established among the Sundanese in Bandung since 1986 by first-term, western, bivocational missionaries. Bivocational missionaries from three different interdenominational American agencies saw Avery Willis' study of Javanese church growth to be relevant to church planting work today among the Sundanese of West Java. They also picked up cues from the earlier Dutch missiologist Henrik Kraemer (1958) who had astute insight both for western and Indonesian church planters.

Kraemer saw the problem of the gospel's slow progress among the Sundanese in two parts: (1) within the missionary enterprise and their methodology, and (2) within the Sundanese world and its culture. The Bandung work also reflects a turning from "mass evangelism" to an insistence on the need for long-term, face-to-face relationships. Handing out tracts and broadcasting radio messages are not, in reality, fulfilling our obligation to proclaim the gospel to Muslims. Church planting in Bandung confirms that, normally, Muslims are only going to take truth from a significant other in their life with whom they have a trust relationship. The vast majority of former Muslims in Java invited Christ to be their Lord because a friend, relative, or caring western teacher pointed them to Christ. It was initially because of confidence in the messenger that the message was considered valid.

These particular three house churches of Sundanese Muslims illustrate the principles of this study. Though under the official sponsorship of non-Muslim denominations, or a specially set up cultural foundation (to ensure legality), these new Sundanese congregations are not merged with their sponsoring congregations. None are associated with the much older West Java Christian Church (Dutch Reformed) in Bandung, who do have Sundanese members—extracted from their culture two or three generations previously.

The existing Baptist, Alliance, and Christian Reformed Churches in Bandung, composed of almost entirely non-Sundanese members, have not opposed work among the Sundanese since their denominations gain membership from the church growth. These new house churches are held in Sundanese medium, as opposed to the common practice of worshipping in the national language, Indonesian. Chinese, Batak, and Javanese language churches also exist in Bandung.

This new effort had to demonstrate that there would be significant response to an exclusively Sundanese language and cultural approach. According to Roger Dixon (1984), earlier attempts to utilize some non-Sundanese Bible School students in Bandung failed, first because the Batak or Dyak Christian workers felt themselves socially apart from their urbanized Sundanese audience, and second, because those particular non-Sundanese Indonesian workers seemed to have neither gift nor experience in cross-cultural evangelism.

Dixon maintains that non-Sundanese Indonesians must also be trained in cross-cultural sensitivity to Sundanese if they are going to be effective. The best methodology then, is inadequate until there are appropriately prepared and gifted persons available to utilize that methodology.

Thus, until someone came from the outside (Indonesian or expatriate) and became a trusted insider to whom the Sundanese Muslims could relate, there was little reason to expect them to leave the house of Islam and pledge allegiance to the Lord Jesus Christ. Some mainstream denominational mission leaders like George Fry have written that western missionaries cannot be utilized any longer for such pioneer church planting. "No Westerner knows, or can even pretend to know, what the person and power of Jesus will mean for Muslims" (Fry 1980:138). Apparently, such pessimism is unwarranted. Kraemer shares Fry's awareness of failure yet believes that the expatriate can be effective.

> The missionaries are working in partial or total blindness, remaining altogether outside the Sundanese culture. It's not enough to bring a certain amount of knowledge of theology, Islam, language, medicine, and teaching techniques. These do not open the missionary's mind and eyes to the reality of the world he is entering. Too few missionaries lack the urge to stand inside their adopted world.

Kraemer observed:

> Language is learned, technically flawless, without it becoming a vehicle for the unraveling and inner understanding of the psychological and cultural reality of the Sundanese. The missionary must make a lifetime effort to assimilate Sundanese literature (written or oral) with its underlying philosophy of life. Most missionaries do not know what is popular with the Sundanese or why it is. Most are ignorant of the manner in which the Sundanese formulate their spiritual problems because he does not have close friends who are Sundanese. (1958)

Kraemer was so insightful in 1958, he bears further quoting:

> The forms in which Christianity is expressed in West Java are thoroughly Dutch, deprived of any oriental setting or atmosphere, unintentionally, yet perfectly designed not to respond to the feelings and needs of the oriental mind. The need for self-expression among Sundanese people has been totally unused, since northern Europeans are clumsy in expressing emotion, so we elevate our awkwardness to a principle. We have brought iso-

lation on the Sundanese Christian. Our initiative led them into their isolation, and our initiative will have to lead them out of it.

Thomas Sinulingga, an Indonesian, agrees: "The evangelist must understand the local situation extremely well and the important factors of local custom and tradition, lest he appear rude and hurt the feelings of his audience unintentionally" (1969). Sinulingga also agrees with the Bandung workers that the dialogue method Paul used with the Athenians, combined with local-type music and culturally sensitive literature, is effective with the Sundanese.

Although theories and practices are still being tried, tested, and modified by experience, westerners are being effective communicators to Sundanese. One missionary leader there stated that he teaches westerners to ask, "How would Jesus become flesh and minister among the Sundanese? How would he relate to their particular Islamic culture? How can they better model genuine Sundanese Christianity?"

The Bandung work suggests that at least some of the change agents become increasingly effective by attempting to:

- Live with a Sundanese family and adopt customs and dress as a participant-observer.
- Take a Sundanese name.
- Switch diets, hairstyles, and grow long fingernails.
- Learn *pencak silat*, a traditional Sundanese dance and martial art. One American, after observing that a Muslim prayer leader was also an expert in martial art, recruited the man to be his teacher. They have since grown in a close friendship.
- Participate in numerous cultural events and religious rituals.
- Partially or fully keep the Ramadan fast to the degree that the target segment of people do.

All agree that there are biblical lifestyle parameters, and syncretism must be avoided. However, workers were guided not to reject everything in the culture by importing symbols and forms from the West. They attempted to carefully preserve biblical doctrine and standards. They have attempted to supplement existing religious concepts, slowly deleting nonbiblical ideas and substituting Christian content, while rein-

terpreting concepts and rituals that are usable but not sufficiently biblical.

The church planters in Bandung, without censure, openly discuss
with new believers their old practices for each occasion, seeking to discern the felt meaning so that old beliefs are not merely subjugated to
arise later. Group discussion takes place where a person presents an old
story, myth, and so forth, and then a wise Sundanese moderator leads a
discussion on how it agrees or is different from God's Word.

The new believers debate as long as necessary until the group has
reached consensus on how they are going to express their new beliefs.
In the process, they may decide what is unusable because it is too closely
associated with anti-Christian beliefs, what is usable without modifica-
tion, and what is usable if modified or explained with new meaning. In
this way, continuity with the past is kept.

Responding to criticism that these western change agents are deceiving Muslims, one bivocational missionary maintains that messengers
must clearly communicate that they are followers of Christ. Furthermore, he emphasizes that he is a learner and wants to understand the
Sundanese culture and religion, adopting an accept/respect model of
interpersonal relationships.

Sinulingga illustrates this methodology with an example of a pastor
who dialogued with Rafik Burhanuddin, a well-educated, devout Muslim who, after he came to Christ, wrote a book *Isa Didalam Al Quran*
(Jesus and the Koran). Rafik was won through the pastor's friendship,
sensitive dialogue, and clear testimony. Sinulingga has encouraged the
teams among the Sundanese to concentrate on influential individuals,
because such men are less intimidated and more able to teach others, as
was the case with Rafik.

The workers in Bandung attempt to combine a focus on discipling
an influential household leader with a wide proclamation of the Gospel.
One medium being so utilized is the Sundanese *wayang* (puppet the-
ater), which has been a primary medium of teaching morals. One expatriate has written a pamphlet in Indonesian advocating that wayang be
utilized to teach the Scriptures. Opponents say that there is little demand
today for wayang, or even traditional dance with flute, drum, and xylo-
phone—especially in the cities.

But Dixon, who has given years to the Sundanese, sees a place for the immensely popular wayang, which are based on Hindu epics with *gamelan* (native orchestra) in the life of a contextualized church. The problem has been to find Indonesians who are gifted and motivated to develop these plays with biblical content.

While in Bandung, I watched a wayang. It was mainly about wars between ancient kings. It would seem quite possible to adapt the many battles of the Old Testament and the spiritual warfare message of the New Testament into such puppet plays. Such a performance done well at a neutral location would draw a crowd and leave a deep impression. The audience then could be graciously invited to tea where more information about the message of the Holy *Injil* would be presented.

But communication is not enough. Veteran workers Roger Dixon, of Pioneers, and Neil Grindheim, of the Navigators, in Bandung, shared their conviction with me that ability to overrule demonic powers has been essential for their work among the Sundanese. The morning after our discussion in 1987, Grindheim was leaving with a Chinese doctor to visit a Muslim convert, who was reported to have suddenly been reduced to a prostrate position, without the ability to even raise his hand. No fever or other signs of illness were evident. This state was attributed to demonic activity. Three Sundanese believers were reported to be praying over the brother.

It is easier to apply a bandage than to rebuke a demonic presence. Phil Parshall reasons that if Paul needed signs and wonders to confirm his ministry, those in Muslim ministry need them as much, if not more. Since Muslims refuse to take the Bible seriously, such meeting of felt needs is considered by many of the missionaries to the Sundanese to be a key to unlocking hearts that have been deeply influenced against the message of the New Testament. Even though he has not worked in Indonesia, Parshall argues that if the teachings of the apostles needed authenticating in the first century, the apostle's doctrine needs it again in Java, where Muslims are taught that the Bible has been corrupted and is therefore irrelevant (1985:212). Still, I do not see that it has been direct power over the demonic that has brought the fruit either in Bangladesh or Java. This subject needs more examination.

Sundanese give great importance to the ritual feasts. Some workers in Bandung baptize such feasts with Christian meaning and celebration. Rick Love held a *selamatan* to dedicate the birth of his daughter Tessa, giving her a Sundanese name—Sisti. The Bible was read in place of the Koran, but the traditional *silat* dancing was performed by the change agent's Muslim silat teacher.

Silat is a form of martial arts, which has both a fighting and dancing element. Sundanese believers disagree about utilizing silat dancing. Dixon was advised against it by some Sundanese, who are now clergy in older established denominations.

Appropriate indigenous music is being used to draw the Sundanese to reflect on Christian truth. An Islamic teacher friend of Tessa's father reflectively and wistfully admitted that, of all the religions, Christians sing the most. Thus new and creative thought is being done to create these three new Isa communities in Bandung. They still wrestle with how to get the majority of Muslim inquirers to the place where they will see their need for a Savior, actually repent, and switch allegiance to the Lord Jesus Christ. Often the problem is not so much getting the Sundanese to be positive about Isa, but to get them to perceive that they are lost without reliance on the living Christ.

Presenting the Lord Jesus in a culturally sensitive manner appeals to the folk-Muslim among the Sundanese, and perhaps causes some to revere Jesus, but that is already true among many Sufis. How can missionaries see to it that Muslims internalize Jesus as "the way, the truth, and the life," the only mediator between God and man, realizing that they are eternally lost unless they reach out to the atoning, redeeming, incarnate Emmanuel?

If these new house churches can maintain a critical mass of believers who clearly declare, "Once I was blind but now I see" (John 9:25), then church growth seems likely. The goal is to see heads of families recognize that they are in the kingdom of darkness, and then lead their entire family to the Kingdom of Christ Jesus. A caring *umma* (community) of homogeneous believers with continuity will attract friends and relatives.

Dixon confirms that the problem is in establishing a long-term community of converts that is respected by outsiders. "The real problem," wrote Dixon, "is not evangelism, but creating the sense of identity in

Christ—the oneness of the Christian umma—that beckons Sundanese to fellowship without losing their ethnic identity. Islam has that in West Java, Christianity does not."

Chris Marintika believes that the best way to evangelize Indonesia is through establishing congregations of people who know they have been rescued. The proliferation of house churches throughout China seems to give his position validity.

Church formation and growth by people movements is what God had in mind in the Great Commission. It is not enough to reach people. We must see Sundanese and other Muslims gathered into a community that demonstrates the reality of Acts 2:46–47—a community that whets the appetite of the non-Christian because of the love within its fellowship, which is the greatest and final apologetic (John 17:21).

What can be concluded, then, concerning a team approach to church planting from these recent efforts among the Sundanese?

The missionaries have blended an emphasis on supernatural intervention with the principles of contextualization delineated in this book. This is to demonstrate the power of the living Christ to peoples who, below the surface, are animistic. As Kraemer advocated, to the best of their ability the workers in Bandung look, smell, and feel "Sundanese." At the same time, they whet the appetite of the Sundanese Muslim to become acquainted with a personal God who, through prayer to Jesus, can help them with their daily problems.

They have worked within the political boundaries of the Indonesian government by not asking for a missionary visa, and have satisfied the existing churches by submitting to church leadership. Their church planting efforts are joint ventures blessed by the existing denominations.

They walk Sundanese converts and other Indonesian brethren through the steps of "thinking church," what it takes to actually establish a congregation of converted Sundanese Muslims. Their method has been show and tell, as opposed to simply hiring nationals for jobs that are too difficult because they cannot envision the steps, and have not developed cross-cultural evangelistic skills.

They have not worked with marginal people, but have placed themselves where they could meet, befriend, and disciple mainly male heads of households who are able to command a following.

They have not taken visible leadership in conducting the congregational meetings, but have coached the potential elders privately, thus saving the face of the new believers who might be embarrassed to be attending a meeting led by a western Christian. The Sundanese observe their own neighbors as the leaders of these three new house churches.

10

A Proposed
Urban Church Planting Strategy

This chapter presents a hypothetical game plan for a team church planting effort in Baghdad, Iraq. (Note: this scenario was written before the Gulf War of 1991. For the purposes of illustration, let us assume that diplomatic relations are good enough for us to proceed.)

The purpose of this exercise is to illustrate the principles discussed in earlier chapters. Although it is theoretical, it is also a *composite* of techniques and activities that have been utilized at some time by missionaries laboring among Muslims.

Before Going Overseas

Let us assume that my wife, Sally, and I have come to a solid conviction (after investigation and confirmation from two sending churches) that we should take a church planting team to Baghdad, Iraq. Our goal is to establish the first Muslim convert congregation in that city, which David Barrett claims will be the eighteenth largest city in the world, with 11 million inhabitants by the year 2000. Ten million of Baghdad's population are Muslims, perhaps 30,000 will be expatriates from other countries, and the rest are Assyrian and Armenian Christians, roughly equivalent to Greek Orthodox in their orientation.

Before leaving for Baghdad, we will need to find sponsoring churches who want to establish a sister church in Baghdad; develop an entry/residence strategy that will provide residence visas conducive for ministry; find a mission agency that has as its mandate the facilitation of church planting teams to unreached people groups in restricted access countries (it would be particularly helpful if the agency has workers in similar Muslim cities so we can be well supervised, cross-pollinate ideas, and possibly exchange or share personnel with its other church planting teams); and develop a church planting team of at least eight appropriately gifted adults to join us.

These four activities would likely go on simultaneously.

Our first task is to probe every likely source to identify potential co-workers, additional partnership churches, and an appropriate agency under which to serve. Then we assign someone to contact service organizations or foundations that show a desire to help bivocational missionaries get projects or businesses started in a country where missionary visas are not granted.

We would also meet with agencies like Global Opportunities, Cooperative Services International, Strategic Ventures Network, and the Navigators, who service bivocational missionaries by helping them get residence in so-called closed countries. We will not attempt to get "missionary visas," since Iraq no longer has such a category.

People want to join an effort that is reasonably likely to succeed. Mission agencies, sending churches, and potential co-workers are all asking, "Who is going to lead this?" and "Do they have a workable plan?" Therefore, a written proposal must be prepared that not only clearly delineates the goals, but also gives some idea of how we are going to achieve them. A bank will loan money to an entrepreneur businessman if they think his business plan has a sufficiently high probability of succeeding. Sponsoring churches and potential co-workers are not going to take the risk of investing time and money either, unless they have confidence in both the leadership and the plan of operation.

Would-be co-workers also ask important questions about the character of the leadership and their walk with God. What is their track record? Is there any evidence in their past that they will be able to accomplish their goals? What is their leadership style? Is it controlling and authoritative? Too inattentive to people or details? Who has worked with them in the past and how can they be evaluated as leaders?

Knowing that the church planting plan will get revised several times, it is wise to designate it "First draft (date)," then "Second draft (date)," and so forth, as new information, obstacles, or answered prayers alter our course.

Although Baghdad may have had dynamic churches in the first four centuries of church history, by the time it was conquered by the Muslims in the seventh century, the churches had waned as biblical salt and light. Since Muslim conquest, the 8 to 10 percent of the population that are Armenian or Assyrian Christian gradually lost a biblical testimony. Today, they are tragically despised by the Muslim majority. Over time the Christians became preoccupied with their own survival, and are not particularly interested in being a witness to their Muslim neighbors.

Baghdad is known to have one Protestant church, a group of 40 to 50 persons with a Presbyterian pastor from Egypt. These church members are the children of Protestants who came out of the Catholic or Orthodox churches of Iraq, Egypt, Lebanon, or Palestine in the past. Due to hostile reaction, and sometimes oppression, in the last two decades, none of these believers feel that it is wise to confront Muslims with the claims of Christ. They justify their nonwitness stance with the common understanding that proselytizing Muslims is considered against the law in this police state.

Indeed, Iraq is ruled by Saddam Hussein and his small group of inter-related Muslims of the small Islamic Awalawi sect who are paranoid about a possible political coup attempt. Therefore it is important that the expatriate team make it abundantly clear to all parties that we are not interested in Iraq's politics or government affairs, except in how we might aid government agencies in certain social projects. We have decided as a team to fight "injustice," not directly, but by establishing communities of "new creatures" who will be "leaven in the lump" of Baghdad society. These "new men," a "holy nation" we hope to see established will let men so see their good works, that Iraqi Muslims (and their leaders) will praise their Father Who is in Heaven (Matt. 5:16).

As the team leader, I need to set aside at least three weeks to concentrate on finding people in North America who have contacts within Iraq. A good place to start would be Washington, D.C. Let us assume that the Iraqi government is eager to improve relationships with the United States. They must have someone in Washington whose job it is to accomplish that goal. I can go to Washington and, through evangelicals there, get leads on who can introduce me to the Iraqi government officials who can help us carve out a niche for ourselves in Baghdad. Second, through evangelical groups at universities, team members and the staff of our agency seek out students from Iraq across North America, the United Kingdom, Australia, and Europe. Some of these students will be a bridge, leading families into Baghdad.

The next step is to find out how we can minister to felt needs. What does Iraq want from other countries? Their infrastructure is severely damaged due to eight years of war with Iran and Kuwait. What services are needed now? We would emphasize that we are a team that provides services and expertise, not capital or goods. For example, we might explore the need to set up a clinic to design and fit artificial limbs for wounded soldiers. Or with the mass migration into Baghdad as a primary city, due to the wars and the insurrection of the Kurdish population, could our team help solve urban growth problems?

A potential team might have members trained in urban planning, civil engineering, hydrology, sewage disposal, mass transportation, or the like. Or we might pull together a team of engineers and administrators who could get contracts to repair nonfunctioning elevators, escalators, and X-ray machines at the airports and other large machines that they have bought from other nations, but which, for lack of maintenance, are not operational. Since it is common for such things to be out of order for months, there would be little pressure to get them fixed immediately. Such a team then would have plenty of time for social intercourse with officials and other businessmen whom they would meet in the natural course of work.

Choosing an Entry Strategy

It is important to find a task that will not put the team into competition with powerful Iraqi families. Therefore we emphasize service and information instead of manufacturing or selling. What the business/project will eventually be depends on whom God raises up to be part of the church planting team, and what is within their ability and experience. For the sake of this scenario, we will assume that the above projects came to naught, but through my friend at the Iraqi Consulate in Washington, I was able to meet the Minister of Education, who in turn has given me permission to set up an English-Arabic medium prep school that will facilitate Iraqi students getting entrance into western universities.

Let us say that God has "raised up" four couples, three single women, and a single man to join the church planting team. Our revised plan is to establish the *American-Iraqi University Preparation Institute*. The Institute will do the following:

- Teach English classes with the aim of assisting students to acquire the certificate in English proficiency required for British, Canadian, Australian, New Zealand, or American University entrance.
- Maintain an extensive collection of catalogs, brochures, and application papers from universities in the West.
- Provide educational and career counselling for Iraqi students.
- Help them with the applications and correspondence involved in getting entrance into a western university.

What does this have to do with church planting? Our strategy is twofold. We are working with students who want to study in the West. This may be a problematic approach since it will tend to screen out Muslim fundamentalists and other antiwestern families. Those who may have the most prejudice against Christians might be key to reaching certain segments of Iraq that could contain the most sincere God seekers. Second, since a student going to the West is a family affair, the students are ushering us into natural contact with their parents, grandparents, and entire extended family. Even after the students go to the West, we can continue to visit their families to show interest in their son or daughter's welfare and continue to offer liaison assistance.

While holding orientation, both at our Institute and in the homes of the student applicants, we will have one section of orientation that explains Christianity and how it is practiced in the West, since it is the dominant religion. We will also include a New Testament in the orientation packet, as well as a book on the life and customs of the country where the Iraqi will be studying.

The Institute will also offer housing services. It will be important to Iraqi families that their son or daughter is met by someone at the airport in Chicago, Toronto, Sydney, or London, and that they have a place to stay when they arrive. Our Institute will arrange accommodation through churches in the West that have a program of hospitality for international students. Thus, while we are establishing a significant relationship with the student's family in Baghdad, we arrange to have born-again Christians loving their son or daughter into the Kingdom while he or she is in the West!

Depending on what the Iraqi laws call for, we may need to have some Iraqis on the Board of our Institute. This gives us an opportunity to practice Matthew 10 and look for men who are "worthy," to whom we can attach ourselves. Backed by continuous prayer, we will be searching for open, liberal, noble men of character who have a good reputation in the community, and whose concern will be for the godliness and character of these Iraqi students going to the West.

We will be quite open about our abhorrence of irreligious behavior both in Iraq and the West, and thus be looking for "co-belligerents," or allies against atheism and immorality, who also believe it is important for their young men and women to experience the highest moral influences while they are at University. This gives us one more reason to explain why we are religious Christians committed to the high ideals of the Injil, and why we try to find homes for the Iraqi students in the West among the same kind of lofty minded, God-fearing people.

Gathering the Team

Those who are interested in church planting among Muslims tend to find each other. Utilizing our agency, we send our proposal to people concerned about Muslims and especially Arabs. We and some people in our churches pray daily to the Lord of the harvest to raise up laborers for this team. We are first of all concerned to find people who have a strong vision for the task, and who are ready to be set aside for pioneer apostolic church planting by their local church. They need to have experience in the area of ministry that they are to exercise in Baghdad. Letters, telephone calls, and weekend meetings with prospects will be used to increasingly discern whom God is assigning to this church planting team. As team leader, I will draft a memo of understanding (M.O.U.), which outlines the goals, strategy, and policies of the team. In the policy section we would include:

- Financial policies
- Missiological and doctrinal assumptions
- Lifestyle issues, both as individuals and as a team
- How the team functions in ministry, including decision-making and accountability

It would be important for the members of the first team to have consensus over the memo of understanding. Have we ascertained the Lord's mind in creating this document? All need to sign it without reservations, including our doctrinal statement, for how can "two walk together unless they have agreed to do so" (Amos 3:3)?

We need more than ideas and strategy. We also need gifted, anointed people because progress is made when appropriately gifted people are in the right place doing the right thing. Taking our cue from Ephesians 4:11, we pray that our 10 to 12 adults will include (besides the team leader/apostle) the following:

- Two with evangelistic gifts. They have seen a number of persons in their own culture come to Christ through personal friendship and ministry.
- A teacher with a practical understanding of missiology, anthropology, and theology. This might be one of our two or three seminary graduates.
- An older pastor/prophet. This man (and his wife) have taken early retirement from the pastorate after 27 years of boldly proclaiming the Word of God. They organized an effort that shut down

both an abortion clinic and pornography shop in Chicago, and organized two hunger programs, one for an area of inner city Chicago and one for a famine in Sudan. Because they are gray-haired and over 55 years old, we trust that they will be able to speak prophetically (even if they are limited to English) to Muslim family leaders about righteousness and the judgment to come. The wife actually is more gifted in hospitality, and can help the younger women through the trauma of giving birth and rearing a young child in a foreign land.

List of Team Members and Roles

Team Member	Ministry Emphasis	Task at Institute
Husband #1	Team Leader/Apostle	Director of public relations
Husband #2	Pastor/Prophet	Director of Admissions and Iraqi family liaison
Husband #3	Teacher/Theologian	Teacher of orientation
Husband #4	Evangelist	English teacher
Wife #1	Counselor	Counselor of women students—visa via husband
Wife #2	Evangelist	Part-time Librarian—visa via husband
Wife #3	Hospitality	Arranges social events and visits
Wife #4	Hospitality	None—two small children
Single woman #1	Administration	Deputy Director of Institute
Single woman #2	Evangelist	Secretary
Single woman #3	Pastor/Discipler	English Teacher
Single man #1	Disciple-maker	Arranges transportation and housing, in the west and in Iraq

Five sending churches have decided to make establishing a sister church in Baghdad a priority in their missions program. One gives the team $15,000 for launching the project. The team leader, his wife, and one of the single women come from Christ Community Church in

Pasadena, California. The pastor, his wife, and the second single woman come from Barton Road Evangelical Church, Canterbury, England. Each of the other team members come from a church that has owned the goal of sending them as part of a church planting team to Iraq, and has designated a member of their congregation to be the liaison person between the team and their church. Thus, through the team of 12, nine churches are involved, praying and supporting this church planting effort as sending churches. Team members receive prayer and financial support from another 20 churches and 86 individuals. The single man on the team has in his ministry job description the task of sending an update with prayer requests to these churches and prayer partners roughly every two weeks, depending on couriers or our opportunity to use a diplomatic mail pouch. Some communication is done via electronic E-mail. The Institute we are setting up has a Fax machine, to enhance communications between us and western universities. It is hoped that missions-minded Christians in each of the universities where we send Iraqis will be closely tied to the church planting effort. They will, therefore, receive information and pass it on to church people from time to time.

Because of the need to arrange admissions and housing, the Iraqi government will understand that open communication must flow by fax, modem, and telephone, as well as letters. Because the Institute is staffed by Christians with goals to help people, it is natural and not particularly damaging when a church bulletin from First Baptist, or a Bible study booklet from the Back to God Hour arrives in the Institute's post office box.

Ministry Strategy

In fact, it is the policy of the team to be quite open about our lifestyle as serious evangelical Christians. We believe that the Iraqis will respect religious people with high morals, if we practice and share our faith in a culturally appropriate way. Sharing biblical truths will go hand in hand with establishing rapport, and becoming trusted, significant persons to our Iraqi friends and clients.

As long as we are providing a desired service, the Iraqi government will not mind us being Christians, particularly since Iraq has an 8 percent Christian minority, and is not known for its Islamic piety. Baghdad is one of the Arab cities where nightclubs abound!

Having gathered and prepared the team and the sending churches, and established our entry/residence strategy for our Institute, we invite to the Institute Board a magazine editor, the Assistant Minister of Education, the director of the Red Crescent, and a well-known Iraqi poet. Now we are ready to embark on our church planting path.

Although the students who are our clients will be upgrading their English at the Institute, they are not our main ministry targets. We must learn both the spoken Iraqi Arabic, and the modern written Arabic of literature, to be at home in Baghdad. Since we already have an English school, we will hire someone to teach Arabic to foreigners in the school as well. The money we make teaching Arabic to the foreign community in Baghdad will pay the salary for the two Arabic teachers. Hopefully our lifestyle, natural walk with the Lord, and proclamation will influence these Iraqi teachers into the Kingdom.

Among our Iraqi staff, our board members, and government officials, we should be getting many invitations to social affairs, weddings, funerals, and be well on our way to establishing relationships as we are busy with language acquisition and socialization. In fact, we will have it in our contract that we will not open the school for the first year, but utilize that time to learn Arabic and connect the Institute to the universities, both in Iraq and in western countries. Since this is a business enterprise from the West, we will have no trouble receiving funds from our parent company (our agency) in Phoenix, Arizona. Church support goes to the mission agency that sends it on to the Institute's American Bank account at Chase, Manhattan in New York, or Barclays in London or Sydney.

As the team leader, I visit Baghdad at least twice before the other team members arrive. On one of those visits I do a study of the city with Steve Hawthorne, a missiologist we have chosen to be one of our main "coaches," to help me discern which segment of the society we should initially penetrate. We would then opt to rent apartments in buildings that house the kind of people (or segment of society) we want to reach. It will be easier for us to meet people in the apartment building than if we live in separate villas, which are also much more expensive. Later, we may rent one villa if we need more privacy to follow up "Nicodemus" type inquirers. From our Iraqi Board we will receive guidelines on how and where the single women should live so that they are perceived as good women. If possible, we will try to find Muslim families under whose protection and honor they can reside. Thus, when someone in a shop asks who that foreign woman is, the gossip will let it be known that she is a teacher and a friend of the Abu Nasri family, which will signal the community to treat her with respect, or they will have that family to deal with!

In fact, all of the team members will seek to practice the principles of Matthew 10, by finding "sponsors" both in their residence area and in the business world. We want to be connected to families of high moral reputation as well as influence. This is why, from the day we meet with the officials at the Iraqi Embassy in Washington, we will continually sort out Iraqi personages, seeking to discern with whom we should align ourselves.

In Iraq and the rest of the Arab Gulf, men of culture or political clout often sponsor a men's evening, called a *Diwanniye*, at their house once a week. This get-together is by invitation only, and one's status is often measured by whose Diwanniye he attends. It is common to have a robust evening of discussion about politics, religion, current events, and the problems of rearing families. Videos are constantly being shown in the background, not to mention countless cups of coffee and tea. Some women also have a version of Diwanniye, although it is not so common.

While visiting in the early stages, I inquire about the possibility of attending a Diwanniye, where men like to discuss the important things of life. As in other matters, through prayer God can open a door to a Diwanniye of a highly respected man truly concerned about ultimate issues. Because these meetings are weekly, one can become very close to the other men in his group by something that is perhaps akin to a western support group, or a tightly-knit social club. Early attempts to break into the right networks will often fail, but we must persevere until we find those that will be bridges for bringing household leaders to redemption in Christ Jesus.

One of the things we could do at the Diwanniye, once we have acquired the language, is to imitate the tack Jesus took (Matt. 5:21, 27,

33, 38, 43). "You have heard that it was said to the people long ago," then rehearse the common value system and worldview of your target group . . . "but the prophet Isa in the *Injil* said . . . ," and so begin to introduce the radical teachings of Jesus that would touch the felt needs of our Diwanniye comrades. This would need to be at the appropriate time, as related earlier in Don Larson's process of being a learner, trader, story teller.

Conversations will tend to be dominated by politics. So we might want to introduce a story Jesus told that is recorded in the *Injil* by the messenger Matthew (18:23–35). After I receive permission, I have one of them read the story in Arabic of how the Kingdom of heaven is like a king who wanted to settle accounts with his servants. After the Muslim finishes the reading, I start a discussion on what each thinks the prophet Isa is trying to teach through this story.

When my turn comes, I can make the contrast that, even though people have done unjust things toward each of us, we are much more guilty because of our offenses toward God. Since mistrust, enmity, and lack of forgiveness are prevalent in Arab culture, the Lord's teaching here is quite radical. Hopefully the discussion will eventually lead to how God can give power to "forgive your brother from your heart" (Matt. 18:35), something which is humanly impossible to do.

As we meet dozens, and eventually several hundred people, the task will be to get God's direction as to who we should concentrate on. Taking a cue from the Apostle Paul (Acts 19:8), we see that he debated in his Diwanniye, arguing persuasively about the Kingdom of God. As Paul experienced, we in Baghdad will find many obstinate people, and some who will seek to discredit both us and the teachings of Christ. The biblical pattern is to quietly change arenas, arranging to meet with those who show a hunger for more.

Paul found a setting, a time, and a place that was appropriate for religious discussions. He scheduled daily discussions for those who wanted to dialogue more. Our task in Baghdad is to find an appropriate setting and time for discussing the claims of Christ that fit with the context and are not alarming to the government because we have permission to teach. We also count on our "covering" from appropriate people of influence, as Tyrannus must have been for Paul (Acts 19:9).

We will need to discern whether these teaching times with the hungry can best be done in one of our homes, at the Institute office, in the home of one of our most influential inquirers, or in a public place. I maintain that in every city and subculture there are a time and a place where people speak together about the ultimates of life. In London it might be at the neighborhood pub, in Cairo among the lower middle class it tends to be certain coffee houses. Where and when does our target group meet for such interchange?

So while we are gaining a reputation for being people who are reliable, trustworthy, interesting to be with, and who care deeply for people, we will be praying daily for divine appointments. Over the years, my prayer has been, "Father, there's no point wasting your time and mine. Lead me to those faithful men who will be able to teach others."

Daily, as we go about our tasks, we are to be before God, fully relying on him to bring us into contact with those who will be the first elders of the church. We must be careful to avoid "getting entangled in the affairs of this world" (2 Tim. 2:4, KJV), like survival issues and family existence. It is our goal to spend at least 30 hours a week of quality time with Iraqi Muslims. The one person we are not requiring to spend that much time developing relationships is our single woman administrator, whom we realize must spend 50 hours a week keeping the Institute functioning well. We consider her the full-time *facilitator* of the team. She has no pressure for ministry beyond her Institute responsibilities.

We are not going to get disciples gathering as a church if we do not get people "searching the Scriptures to see if these things be so" (Acts 17:11). Hopefully, among the team members we will be able to establish three or four evangelistic bible studies or at least get Koran/Bible discovery groups going in Iraqi homes. In at least one of these, we might experiment by having a Muslim teacher give the Koran part of the study, meeting under the theme "Seeking God's Ways for Twentieth Century Man." During the first two years, one of these studies could probably start in English, possibly even at the Institute, but preferably in a Muslim's home, and as soon as possible in Arabic.

Everyone, including the mothers with small children, will be able to learn at least the conversational Iraqi Baghdad Arabic dialect. To do this, we will find ways to periodically put ourselves in an immersion situation where we must speak Arabic all day to function. Most of our Iraqi friends will have relatives in villages. They can arrange for different ones of us to reside there for two weeks at a time. Hopefully in the village only one or two persons speak English. Though difficult, such excursions will greatly accelerate our acquisition of Arabic.

Again, because we are sponsored, there should be little negative inquiry as to our presence in the village. Also in the village, people have a lot more time to sit around and talk, unlike the fast moving city, so there will be plenty of people with whom we can practice Arabic.

Most of us will want to become involved in social projects in the city as we associate with wealthy Muslims who are members of the Rotary club, the Red Crescent (Red Cross), and others. We would not go into direct social work as foreigners, but team up with Muslims who can take care of all the government arrangements, as well as communicate to the poor who we foreigners are.

Through such a project, we might be able to indirectly help another church planting team come into the city, which would work with the Kurds, for example, or help facilitate a third team that would concentrate on medical work. We might also be able to help other bivocational missionaries gain residency in the country because we have the needed government and business contacts.

Members of other missions might teach at the university, or work in the oil business. Whomever God would engineer into that city, whether they be from Korea, Ghana, Buenos Aires, or Zurich, we would consider to be on God's team. God expects us to be co-workers with his other soldiers, whether we arranged for them to be there or not. All the bivocational missionaries can meet weekly in an English worship service at the Anglican Church or perhaps as an English service Sunday mornings at the Intercontinental Hotel.

In order to facilitate distribution of Bibles and Christian literature, we may want to use our contacts to help reopen the Bible Society Book Shop, or help some bivocational missionary open up an English Book Shop near the university, which could also have a stock of Arabic Christian books and Bibles. A number of Muslim cities have such a shop now.

One of our projects with the Bible Society, in cooperation with Iraqi university professors, might be to get the New Testament translated into

Iraqi, Muslim-spoken Arabic, such as has been done in Bangladesh. It is a tragedy that existing Arabic Bibles use so much Christian church language that they are often experienced as foreign books by the Muslims.

A ministry principle I will push as team leader is that each of us should work with "five baskets," that is, five family heads (the women relating to their wives and daughters) whom we have identified as seekers. As we work to move them toward Christ, or get introduced by them to someone in the family who is even more the decision-maker, we will continually lessen our time with the less interested and thereby add a new basket, while dropping off one of the others.

The point of this is to use our time with those who are most seriously seeking, or who have the most potential to "be reliable men (women) who will also be qualified to teach others" (2 Tim. 2:2). As we discover that a particular seeker is marginal to his own society or family, or his motives are only to befriend a westerner to get an immigration or student visa to the West, we will gently disassociate so that we can concentrate on those most likely to give leadership to the emerging church in Baghdad.

Because we all work at the Institute and know each other, it will not be strange if one of us introduces one of the others to our seeking friend. I might take the brother of the director of the Red Crescent as far as I can go, but my co-worker with the prophetic gift may be able to break through this man's defenses and self-righteousness. Or a particular Iraqi might be less defensive to my friend's wife (since "she's merely a woman") who, because of her gift as an evangelist, might be able to directly confront him at a dinner party with his need for a Savior, more easily than the rest of us could. Thus we are seeking to utilize and pool our different gifts in a team effort.

Fear is a constant problem. Anyone who has worked in a hostile Muslim country knows this. The last mission effort by Christians in Baghdad ended with the Bible Society man being hung as an Israeli spy! Those on our team gifted in pastoral care will need to minister to oppression and depression problems that arise—problems triggered by every source, from insecurity about child rearing (and from one's own childhood traumas), to homesickness, to varying kinds of demonic activity. Thus we will need to stay in close contact with one another's needs, and be sure that all are being ministered to if we are going to be able to continually give ourselves to Iraqi Muslims, as well as model New Testament church life.

To many, pioneering a Muslim convert church from scratch seems comparable to taking a rocket ship to Mars. It is an interesting idea, but who has ever done it? A temptation will be for the team members to set their sights on seeing their Muslim friend become a follower of Christ, but no further. As we have stated in this book, however, it is vital that from day one, each team member and each new believer from Islam "think church."

In a culture where all the loyalty and affinity goes to blood relatives, we must emphasize the will of God as articulated by the Lord Jesus (Matt. 12:48–50). The new believers have a new family. Jesus, as an easterner, startled his listeners: "Who is my mother, and who are my brothers?" Pointing to his disciples he said, "Here are my mother and my brothers. For whoever does the will of my Father in heaven is my brother and sister and mother." Repeatedly, until the new believers internalize it, we must reiterate that commitment to Christ, our head, is not genuine without accompanying commitment to Christ's body, the other followers of Christ, as our brothers and sisters.

We will need to find creative ways to emphasize to the emerging converts that we must as quickly as possible become a critical mass, a support group related by the blood of Jesus, who are totally responsible for one another's welfare in the household of God (Eph. 2:19).

When the second and third Baghdad Muslims come to Christ, we will need to find creative ways to go on trips to Babylon or to the seaside together, to help these new believers build a trust relationship and bond with one another. Showing up for a weekly study will not be enough. Our first aim, of course, will be to engage in web evangelism, whereby we will ask the first convert to think and pray about whom he knows (and trusts well), who might also be interested in the Lord Jesus Christ. If his cousin comes to Christ, and then his cousin's uncle, and that uncle's best friend, we are well on our way to establishing a group of people who can trust one another because they already have a basis for relationship.

At the same time, it will be vital to help them understand the biblical truths of spiritual warfare. They have been granted not only to believe but also to suffer for him (Phil. 1:29). Conversations and studies (perhaps a booklet) about great saints (especially Middle Easterners) who have suffered after following Christ can inspire and arm the new believer to do likewise. Testimonies on video from other Arab lands or non-Arab Muslims could be helpful in this regard.

At some point the whole issue of baptism needs to be faced, and these believers realize it is not an option, but a command. We can teach them, and pray together that God will show them how, when, and with whom to take the step together.

It would be an aim of the team to recruit the new believers into the social projects we are doing under leading Muslims, until the church becomes strong and recognized enough to sponsor its own social projects. The aim would be to have followers of Christ become known as the most caring people in the country! Second, it gives a good reason for the Muslim convert to be seen in public with an expatriate. What better instructions do we have to pass on to the new believers than, "If you love those who love you, what reward will you get? Are not even the tax collectors doing that? And if you greet only your brothers, what are you doing more than others? Do not even pagans do that? Be perfect, therefore, as your heavenly Father is perfect" (Matt. 5:46–48). You are the light of the world . . . [let] your light shine before men, that they may see your good deeds and praise your Father in heaven (Matt. 5:14, 16).

The Umma

Umma means community in Arabic. It is a word taken from the root *um* (mother). What should the umma or *ekklēsia* (assembly of called out ones) look like in Baghdad? The Assyrian Christians have their crumbling cathedral, the Presbyterians meet in a service reminiscent of a similar Presbyterian Church in Philadelphia in the 1940s. How do we see our four or five believers grow into a functioning church that reflects what God has in mind?

The new brothers and sisters can memorize Ephesians 4:11. Since we as a team have been basing our ministry upon these different ministry gifts, we have been modelling it for the emerging church in Baghdad. We will continually teach the new believers that, as in churches across the world, God has six missions he wants them to be involved in: the apostolic mission, the prophetic mission, the evangelistic mission, the pastoral mission, the teaching mission, and the mission of worship. Our goal is to help the converts get excited about being co-workers (1 Cor. 3:9) with the living God, comparable to the believers in Thessalonica, who were spoken about in 1 Thessalonians 1: "You became imitators of us and of the Lord; in spite of severe suffering . . . you became a model to all the believers in Macedonia and Achaia [in] . . . how you turned to God from idols to serve the living and true God, and to wait for his Son from heaven, whom he raised from the dead—Jesus, who rescues us from the coming wrath" (1 Thess. 1:6–10).

As has occurred in at least one new Muslim convert church in Bangladesh, the believers would discuss these various gifts and recognize them in one another, then appoint men to give leadership to these six areas of church life. They will come to understand that they have been gifted by God in these areas, and will be judged on how faithful they have been as good stewards of these gifts in serving the living God.

Hopefully, in answer to prayer, we will find someone who can begin to put Arabic Scripture into chants, in a way that the group would consider conducive to true worship. Another Iraqi with teaching gifts will emerge and take increasing responsibility for leading Bible studies, with practical application to Iraqi felt needs. The Arab "prophets" in our midst would need to deal with the purity questions, particularly giving attention to morality, honesty, and staying reconciled with one another, keeping short accounts according to Matthew 5 and Matthew 18. Doubtless, the believers will get offended by each other. The key will be to see them be different from their fellow Iraqi Muslims, in that they will know how to get restored to one another, and apply the forgiveness of Christ liberally. This will be where satanic attacks come most viciously. No doubt all the principalities and powers know that if a group of Iraqis actually cared for one another, and lived in harmony and trust, their testimony would be so powerful that the Lord would be adding "to their number daily those who were being saved" (Acts 2:47).

The key will be God raising up committed, upbeat, full of faith leaders with motivational gifts who are unintimidated by all the powers of Hell, fearing not him who is able to kill the body, but only him who is able to kill the body and soul. With such umbrella protective leadership, the church (the majority of which will always be the "weak, the maimed, the blind and fearful"), will be able to stand and grow. This church planting account, unlike those in Chapter 11, is an untested dream that attempts to articulate what a possible urban church planting strategy could look like. It is not meant to be a blueprint, but a catalyst in your mind—to get you dreaming about what kind of a team, entry strategy, and methods of disciple-making church planting you might attempt. I am convinced by observing whom God has used over the years that he will give you a plan—a dream—and he will accomplish it through you and your teammates . . . if you all want it badly enough!

11

Finishing the Task

In a paraphrase of the writer of Hebrews, "What more shall I say for time [and space] fail me to speak of . . . so many issues, so many questions" (Heb. 11:32). A team approach to church planting in Muslim cities is a complex, intricate enterprise which, like space travel, is still in its infancy stages.

This study has been an attempt to describe how a team of expatriates can establish a Muslim convert church in a Muslim city. I have reviewed the history of church growth in the Muslim world, noting how few congregations with their own national elders from the Muslim populations exist, especially in the cities. I have reviewed attitudes and presuppositions of the last twenty-five years, and then sought to contrast that with what I believe it will take to see vital Muslim convert congregations become a reality in the years ahead.

I have defined the type of church planting team I believe will be effective in a Muslim urban context, enumerating its characteristics as a whole, and what is needed in each contributing member. I have stated and illustrated the attitudes, principles, and skills that must be utilized, including examples, two case studies, and a theoretical step-by-step approach in Baghdad, Iraq.

I have sought to enable the reader to visualize what a house church in an urban setting could look like, in an effort to delineate essentials from western church cultural patterns that may not be most conducive to church growth in the Muslim cities of North Africa, the Middle East, and Asia. Finally, I have sought to be realistic concerning the obstacles to be faced including persecution, historical enmity between peoples, and insufficiently questioned, seemingly nonbiblical, presuppositions of both expatriate and national Christians.

In many ways, the 44 dominantly Muslim countries are reminiscent of the context in which the early Christians found themselves—a tiny minority in a sea of hostile forces. Few Christian churches of former Muslims exist in the Muslim dominated cities—first, because they are not wanted, any more than one wants to find bacteria spoiling leftover food. To the Muslim masses, a Christian presence is a negative invasion to be cut or thrown out. Is it any wonder, then, that Christian citizens from non-Muslim backgrounds do not feel led to evangelize, and thereby agitate the Muslims, who can make life so unpleasant and difficult for them? Neither should we be surprised that expatriate change agents find it difficult to persevere at the church planting task, often crippled by fears of expulsion, prison, or failure.

How is the church planting team to overcome these overarching problems? For overcoming the obstacles, we must think in terms of a critical mass. Tertullian's declaration that "the blood of the martyrs is the seed of the church" is only true if there are a sufficient number of believers in protective fellowship when persecution comes. We have seen in the past in Muslim areas that the blood of the martyrs is often the extinction of the church.

Therefore, throughout this study, we have sought to point out that the pioneer church planting team must find ways to gather a group of believers together under an unintimidated national shepherd, perhaps seeing several baptized at the same time, and thereby creating a critical mass. The bivocational missionary in these Muslim cities could be likened to a camper in the forest on a wet, rainy night. The camper seeks to start a fire, but the wind and rain keep putting out his matches or his burning paper and twigs. However, if he can protect the twigs with a slightly larger stick until they are sufficiently burning, the fire can get to the point where the wind becomes its ally, causing it to burn better.

Thus the pioneer church planting team must put its concentration into bringing the first believers to the point where they "think church," are determined to follow in the steps of those who have suffered greatly for the Lord, and give priority to church growth, until their congregation is a reality with its own national elders in place.

One of the reasons why church planting among Muslims has occurred so infrequently is the mentality that assumes Christians are not supposed to go and make disciples in a city whose government has not granted a special visa to do missionary work. In my lifetime such areas have been dismissed as *closed countries*. Such a mentality would seem strange to Christians who sought to carry out the Great Commission for 1,800 years before European colonial regimes invented the missionary visa. The missionary visa is a product of European conquest. It was nonexistent in the past. Today, the Christian church faces the normal situation once again. We must carry out the Great Commission with or without missionary visas.

In Chapter 7 we considered the ethical question of being merchants, teachers, or students with missionary intentions. There are critics of pioneer church planting who maintain that no one should go to a Muslim city and seek to make disciples if it is considered illegal by the reigning government. We must ask such persons what they think of the position of the apostles Peter and John who, when clearly instructed by ruling authorities not to speak in the name of Jesus or spread his teachings in Jerusalem, replied, "We must obey God rather than men" (Acts 5:29). They were ready to take the consequences and were imprisoned, beaten, but never concluded that they were to discontinue their proselytizing.

Many fail to carefully consider the fact that government officials who do not allow expatriates to spread their religion are sometimes in their own mind trying to protect their young people from a stereotype of Christianity (or Christian civilization) that is portrayed in American television and films, or which some Muslims experienced while in the West. Therefore, Christians, whether expatriate or national, have a duty to get close enough to the Muslims and their rulers to dissolve the negative stereotypes. Our goal is to enable Muslims to understand the biblical Christ as opposed to the "American Jesus" or the history of the Roman Catholic Church. The most loving action is to go where we are not initially wanted and to persevere until officials realize that the living Christ can empower their citizens to be noble and help them to accomplish worthy national aspirations.

Our new brothers and sisters from Muslim background therefore need to be fortified until they have a clear vision of church history, beginning with the first disciples as recorded in the New Testament. Pertinent Scriptures should be memorized, chanted, or posted in calligraphy in places where they can be imbibed daily. In the classic summation passage on church planting (Acts 14:21–23), we note the following:

- As a team, they proclaimed the message so that it was heard as good news.
- They won a large number of persons (disciples) who switched their allegiance to Jesus Christ.
- They encouraged and strengthened the disciples who would be tempted to reevaluate their commitment to Christ during the post-decision days.
- They clearly taught that "many hardships" were normative to those who were entering the Kingdom of God. (Cf. "Think it not strange, brothren . . ." [1 Pet. 4:12].)
- The change agents appointed elders or shepherds for the new believers in each church.
- Expecting a demonically inspired counterattack, Paul and Barnabas modeled the antidote by leading the new believers through sessions of prayer and fasting, demonstrating to them how they could resist the Devil (cf. 1 Pet. 5:7–9 and James 5:7). Then the missionaries left, but continued to send communications to the house churches, often holding up as examples believers in different places who were modelling what it meant to follow Christ. "You know how we lived among you for your sake. You became imitators of us and of the Lord in spite of severe suffering . . . you became a model to all the believers in Macedonia and Acacia" (1 Thess. 1:5–7).

The church planting team must make strong disciples. A disciple knows his Bible, knows how to pray, and knows how to exercise power and authority over the invisible world. If you are serious about being fruitful in the Muslim world, you must get to the place where you have credibility, as an example to the new Muslim disciples, filling their minds with the Scriptures on suffering, following Christ by "taking up his cross," and motivating them to follow the early Christians who stood against all kinds of hostility.

Many Muslims will not fully follow Christ because of their fear of losing their possessions and inheritance. But there will be no full-fledged "lighthouse type" churches until, through our careful persevering discipling, appropriately gifted nationals (who can influence others), determine that they will seek first the Kingdom of God, his righteousness, and his church. Those on the team who have shown an ability to implant such a vision into others in their own culture should have their time protected, so that they can give themselves to discipling potential leaders for the new house church. Without such spiritual reproduction, the highest value of converted Muslims will most likely be not establishing a church, but their own social, economic, and upward mobility.

We have noted how the church in Korea has become 40 percent of the population today because at the turn of the century missionaries were willing to be drowned as the Buddhist forces sunk their ships. The earliest Korean converts were massacred willingly because "they sought a better country" (Heb. 11:14). Four Turkish Uygur believers in Urumchi, China, having become aware of the price that the Chinese (whom Uygurs despise) have paid to follow Christ, have become much more courageous, holding house church meetings themselves (Phil. 1:12).

But the Muslim converts will never become "overcomers" until the expatriot workers do! The Christian worker can foster a spirit of fear, or a spirit of courage. If the church planters are fearful and are of a mindset to avoid difficulties (including leaving the Muslim city as soon as they have family or economic difficulties), then the new Muslim believers' only model is to go into hiding, or to become "secret believers" when facing difficulties and obstacles.

Expatriate workers need to overcome four primary fears.

- Fear of failure
- Fear of not being adequate parents

- Fear of rejection or expulsion
- Fear of being inadequate or fruitless

This study maintains that these very rational fears can best be overcome within a team environment. When the team leader is adequately supervising, seeing to it that vision, motivation, biblical pastoral care, and good administration are being imported, individual team members will be able to avoid a sense of isolation and be buoyed by the faith of whoever is strong at any given moment. A sense of inadequacy can be overcome when each one on the team realizes that he or she does not need to be able to do everything! What they accomplish will be done as a team.

Bivocational missionaries must realize that because they are serving God, it is ultimately God's responsibility to get them in, keep them in, and enable them to become effective. If in the providence of God they are expelled, they must realize that God has the last say in these matters. Their duty is simply to make themselves available for God's next assignment.

Although we must be prepared for prison and even death in following the one who went through both, it is more common that would-be missionaries are ignored by the officials of a Muslim city because they are making little significant impact upon the citizens. If they are going to worry, they should worry more about the latter than the former.

Those who are going to be fruitful in establishing churches among Muslims in an urban context will be those who are most determined. Overcomers will find the appropriate resources to face every natural and supernatural obstacle until they see what they sense God sent them out to do become a reality. Thus, both the expatriate and the national believer must be walking closely together, encouraging one another with the truth that it is possible to establish Muslim convert churches in Muslim cities through a team, even where missionary visas are not available. The obstacles, though formidable, can be overcome!

Establishing viable congregations with their own national leadership among Muslims in the urban context of the Muslim world is a do-able task. A biblical attitude and mindset will be determinative factors. Teams with the appropriate components of skills and experience are vital. If a much greater quantity of the right people are doing the right things, synchronized with the purposes of God in history, we can be reasonably sure that the prototypes, theories, and techniques propounded in this study will, in the years ahead, produce significant numbers of viable con-gregations of former Muslims loyal to the Lord Jesus Christ in many Muslim cities of the world, from Nouchoutt, Mauritania, to Zamboanga, Philippines.

Appendix  A

Interview Questions
Put to Church Planters in Muslim Cities

The goal of these interviews was to delineate some of the contributing factors that led to the establishment of existing Muslim convert congregations.

1. How long and how often have these former Muslims been associating as a group?
2. What do you believe are the primary reasons they come to these meetings? (What felt needs are being met?)
3. Which ones come of their own initiative and who is coming because of the authority of another?
4. How are decisions to attend such a meeting made?
5. What do those attending perceive their relationship to be to one another? How would you compare it to their loyalty or commitment to blood relatives?
6. To what degree have those attending had to resist opposition to come to these meetings?

7. Are there levels of belonging or acceptance in the group with which you are working, for example, members vs. observers?
8. What is required to become a fully integrated "member"?
9. How would you describe the turnover rate?
10. To what would you attribute the turnover? What factors contribute to absenteeism?
11. What felt needs would motivate a person to stop identifying with the group?
12. Where fear is perceived as being a major factor in preventing a believer from congregating with the group, what do you ascertain are the primary fears?
13. What would it take on a human level to see a cluster of congregations of former Muslims become a reality in this city?
14. What theory or applications do you feel must be applied by the existing change agents in this location?
15. What do you think is the most effective activity being practiced by church planters among Muslims anywhere?

Appendix B

Steps to Conversion

My close friend, Nate Mirza, an Iranian who supervises the Navigators' international student ministries, graciously allowed me to present his excellent summary of the evangelistic process with Muslims.

I. Tilling (Identification—Lev. 19:18, 33–34)
   Goal: To communicate a quality of relationship characterized by the love of God.
   A. Is a relationship underway? This is true when:
      1. A meeting has occurred
      2. Basic information about each other has been exchanged
      3. Formal or informal plans of seeing each other again have been made
   B. Is there acceptance? A satisfactory degree of acceptance is being established when there is:
      1. No threat from their differentness (religion, culture, personality, habits, tastes, and values)
      2. Respect for their differentness
      3. Openness—an attitude of learning from them

     4. Sincerity—attentive listening and remembering shared information

     5. Frankness—saying what you feel without fear of the relationship being threatened

  C. Is there freedom in the relationship? A satisfactory degree of freedom is established where there is:

     1. No struggle with making conversation

     2. Initiative taken by both

     3. Fun and laughter

  D. Is there trust? A satisfactory degree of trust is being established where there is:

     1. Sharing and keeping of confidential information

     2. Speaking well of each other to others

     3. Asking each other for favors and advice

     4. An active awareness of each other's needs

     5. The entrusting of responsibility

II. Sowing (Exposure—Matt. 5:16; Mark 5:19)

Goal: To develop a clear understanding of what it means to be a Christian by highlighting a life changed through conversion to Christ.

Has the concept "Christian" been clarified?

     1. Do they identify me as a committed Christian rather than a cultural one?

     2. Have I introduced them to other practicing Christians?

     3. Have they heard my testimony of conversion, including what Christ means to me today?

     4. Are they aware that I have a personal and community relationship with Christ?

     5. Have they heard or read other testimonies to reinforce mine?

     6. Are they aware of the meaning and necessity of "conversion" in the life of a committed Christian?

III. Sowing & Watering (Investigation—Acts 8:26–40; 17:11)

  A. Has the Bible been discussed?

     Goal: To establish that the Bible is the basis of our message

     1. Do they have a portion of the Bible? Do they read it?

       2. Do they ever discuss what they read with me?

       3. Have they ever attended any Christian events, like a church service, where the Bible is taught? Was it discussed afterward?

       4. Have they ever been in an evangelistic Bible study series?

  B. Has a sufficiently accurate picture of Jesus been conveyed?
    Goal: To present Jesus accurately and let him attract them

       1. Do they have a biographical knowledge of Jesus?

       2. Is their information based on the Bible or hearsay?

       3. Have they seen a visual portrayal of Jesus—films or plays?

  C. Has the gospel message been explained and understood?
    Goal: To establish understanding of the message as the basis of response

       1. Do they know the irreducible core of the gospel that must be believed in order to be saved?

       2. Have they verbalized a clear understanding of the gospel to someone?

       3. Have they been introduced to books or booklets for seekers?

  D. Has the key to responsiveness been identified?
    Goal: To identify the area of responsiveness

       1. What motivates them?

       2. What disturbs them?

       3. What is their aim in life?

IV. Reaping (Commitment—Acts 8:36–40; 16:30–34)
Goal: To communicate the necessity of personal response, and to help them make it

  A. Has a personal decision been faced?

       1. Are they clearly aware that the next step is theirs to take?

       2. Do they know that a personal decision is required?

       3. Have they been asked to make a commitment?

       4. Have they considered what it may cost them to follow Christ?

       5. Do they believe I will remain their friend no matter what they decide?

  B. Has a personal decision been made?

If "yes":
1. Was it made privately, or together with someone?
2. Have they verbalized their decision before me?
3. Have they been helped with the assurance of salvation?

If "no":
1. How tentative is their rejection? Will they keep seeking?
2. Where is the stumbling block?

Nate Mirza. 1987. Reprinted by permission.

Bibliography

Abd al Ati, Hammudah
  1977   *The Family Structure in Islam.* Indianapolis, Ind.: American Trust.
Abdulaziz, Y. Saqqaf, ed.
  1987   *The Middle East City.* New York: Paragon.
Abu-Lughod, Janet
  1976   *Cairo—A Thousand Years.* Princeton, N.J.: University Press.
  1980   *Rabat: Urban Apartheid in Morocco.* Princeton, N.J.: University Press.
Abu-Sulaiman, Amad
  1981   Enter the Tentmaker. *Impact International* 9:203.
Accad, Fuad
  1976   The Quran: A Bridge to Christian Faith. *Missiology* 4:331–342.
  1980   *Theological Principles in the Towrah, the Zabur, the Injil and the Koran.*
         Limassol, Cyprus: Navigators.
Adeney, David H.
  1981   "A Two Stage Approach to Church Planting in a Muslim Context."
         In *Perspectives on the World Christian Movement.* Ralph Winter and
         Steve Hawthorne, eds., 722–728. Pasadena, Calif.: William Carey.
  1985   *China: The Church's Long March.* Ventura, Calif.: Regal. al Munir.
Aldridge, Joseph
  1981   *Life-Style Evangelism.* Portland, Oreg.: Multnomah.
Ali, A. Yusuf
  1983   *The Holy Koran.* Brentwood, Md.: Amana.
Allen, Roland
  1927   *The Spontaneous Expansion of the Church.* London: World Dominion.
  1960   *Missionary Methods: St. Paul's or Ours?* London: World Dominion.
  1964   *Missionary Principles.* Grand Rapids, Mich.: Eerdmans.
And, Metin
  1978   *Magic in Istanbul.* Calgary, Alta: Micky Hades International.

Atiyah, Edward
    1955   *The Arabs.* Middlesex, United Kingdom: Penguin.
Badeau, John
    1968   *The American Approach to the Arab World.* New York: Harper.
Bailey, Kenneth E.
    1987   *Peasant and Through Peasant Eyes.* Grand Rapids, Mich.: Eerdmans.
Baird, William
    1964   *The Corinthian Church—A Biblical Approach to Urban Culture.* Nashville, Tenn.: Abingdon.
Bakke, Raymond
    1986   The Challenge of World Urbanization To Mission Thinking and Strategy. *Urban Mission* 4:6–17.
    1987   *The Urban Christian.* Downers Grove, Ill.: InterVarsity.
Banton, Michael
    1968   *The Social Anthropology of Complex Societies.* London: Cambridge University Press.
Barclay, Harold B.
    1963   Muslim Religious Practice in a Village Suburb of Khartoum. *Muslim World* 53:205–211.
Barna, George.
    1991   *What Americans Believe.* Ventura, Calif.: Regal.
Barrett, David
    1986   *World-Class Cities and World Evangelization.* Birmingham, Ala.: New Hope.
Barrett, David, and James Reapsome
    1988   *Seven Hundred Plans to Evangelize the World.* Birmingham, Ala.: New Hope.
Barth, Philip
    1982   "Practices and Institutions of Moroccan Saint Veneration: Implications for Missions." Fuller Theological Seminary.
Bavinck, J. H.
    1966   *The Church Between the Temple and Mosque.* Grand Rapids, Mich.: Eerdmans.
    1969   *Introduction to the Science of Missions.* David Hugh Freeman, trans. Phillipsburg, N.J.: Presbyterian and Reformed.
Beals, Paul A.
    1985   *A People for His Name: A Church-Based Mission Strategy.* Pasadena, Calif.: William Carey Library.

Beaver, R. Pierce

1967 *To Advance the Gospel.* Grand Rapids, Mich.: Eerdmans.

1977 *American Missions in Bicentennial Perspective.* Pasadena, Calif.: William Carey Library.

Beck, Lois

1980 "The Religious Lives of Muslim Women." In *Women in Contemporary Muslim Societies.* Jane I. Smith, ed., 27–60. Lewisburg, Pa.: Bucknell University Press.

Beekman, John, and J. Callow

1984 *Translating the Word of God.* Dallas, Tex.: SIL.

Bell, William

1974 Muslim World Still Looks Like Impregnable Fortress. *Evangelical Missions Quarterly* 10:75–79.

Bellah, Robert

1958 Religious Aspects of Modernization in Turkey and Japan. *American Journal of Sociology* 64:1–5.

Bello, Iysa Ade

1981 The Society of Muslim Brethren: An Ideological Study. *Islamic Studies* 20:111–127.

Benet, Francisco

1963 The Ideology of Islamic Urbanization. *International Journal of Comparative Sociology* 4:211–226.

Ben-Shemesh, A., trans.

1979 *The Noble Koran.* Tel Aviv: Massada.

Bentley-Taylor, David

1967 *The Weather Cock's Reward.* London: Overseas Missionary Fellowship.

Berger, Monroe

1970 *Islam in Egypt Today: Social and Political Aspects of Popular Religion.* New York: Cambridge University Press.

Bijl, Andrew v.d.

1985 *Is Life So Dear?* Nashville, Tenn.: Nelson.

Blair, Colin

1983a "Communicating to Hindus and Muslims in India." M.A. thesis, Fuller Theological Seminary.

1983b Tentmaking: A Contextualized Approach to Islam. *Missiology* 11:217–227.

Blauw, Johannes
   1961   *The Missionary Nature of the Church.* Geneva, Switzerland: World Council of Churches.

Bolton, Robert J.
   1976   *Treasure Island: Church Growth Among Taiwan's Urban Minnan Chinese.* Pasadena, Calif.: William Carey Library.

Bong, Rim Ro
   1989a   *Christian Suffering in Asia.* Taichung, Taiwan: Asia Theological Association.
   1989b   *Urban Ministry in Asia.* Taichung, Taiwan: Asia Theological Association

Bonhoeffer, Dietrich
   1954   *Life Together.* New York: Harper.
   1973   *The Cost of Discipleship.* New York: Macmillan.

Borthwick, Bruce M.
   1967   The Islamic Sermon as a Channel of Political Communication. *Middle East Journal* 21:299–313.

Bowen, Barbara M.
   1944   *Strange Scriptures that Perplex the Western Mind.* Grand Rapids, Mich.: Eerdmans.

Braun, Neil
   1971   *Laity Mobilized.* Grand Rapids, Mich.: Eerdmans.

Brewster, E. Thomas, and Elizabeth Brewster
   1976   *Language Acquisition Made Practical.* Colorado Springs, Colo.: Lingua House.
   1984   *Bonding and the Missionary Task.* Colorado Springs, Colo.: Lingua House.

Brock, Charles
   1981   *Principles and Practices of Indigenous Church Planting.* New York: Broadman.

Bromiley, Geoffrey W.
   1978   *Historical Theology: An Introduction.* Grand Rapids, Mich.: Eerdmans.

Brown, Kenneth
   1976   *People of Sale: Tradition and Change in a Moroccan City 1830–1930.* Cambridge, Mass.: Harvard University.
   1985   "The Discrediting of a Sufi Movement in Tunisia." In *Islamic Dilemmas: Reformers, Nationalists and Industrialization,* Ernest Gellner, ed., 146–168. New York: Mouton.

Bruce, Alexander B.
 1979 *The Training of the Twelve.* 1st ed. T. and T. Clark 1871. New Canaan, Conn.: Keets.
Bruce, F. F.
 1977 *First Century Faith.* Leicester, England: InterVarsity.
Bruce, F. F., and William Barclay
 1962 *Paul and His Converts.* New York: Butterworth.
Bryant, David
 1984 *In the Gap: What It Means to be a World Christian.* Ventura, Calif.: Regal.
Burke, Todd, and DeAnn Burke
 1973 *Anointed for Burial.* Plainfield, N.J.: Logos.
Cable, Mildred, and Francesca French
 1935 *Ambassadors for Christ.* London: Hodder and Stoughton.
Carpanzano, Vincent
 1975 Saints, Jinn and Dreams: An Essay in Moroccan Ethnopsychology. *Psychiatry* 38:145–159.
Castillo, Metrosalem
 1976 "The Church in Thy House (Philippines)." M.A. thesis, Fuller Theological Seminary.
Chandy, Verghese
 1981 "The Discipling of Muslims in Sri Lanka." M.A. thesis, Fuller Theological Seminary.
Chastain, Warren
 1981 "Establishing a Church in an Unreached Muslim Area." In *Perspectives on the World Christian Movement.* Ralph Winter and Steve Hawthorne, eds., 688–694. Pasadena, Calif.: William Carey Library.
Christiansen, Jens
 1977 *The Practical Approach to the Muslim.* Upper Darby, Pa.: North Africa Mission.
Chun, Chaeok
 1977 "An Exploration of the Community Model for Muslim Missionary Outreach by Asian Women." M.A. thesis, Fuller Theological Seminary.
Clark, Charles Allen
 1930 *The Korean Church and the Nevius Methods.* New York: Revell.
 1937 *The Nevius Plan for Mission Work.* Seoul, Korea: Christian Literature Society.

Coggins, Wade, and E. L. Frizen, Jr.
    1979   *Christ and Caesar in Christian Missions.* Pasadena, Calif.: William
            Carey Library.
Coleman, Robert E.
    1963   *The Master Plan of Evangelism.* Old Tappan, N.J.: Revell.
Committee of Evangelical Missionaries to Islam
    1968   *Report of Fourth Bi-Annual Conference.* Hackensack, N.J.: Interde-
            nominational Foreign Missions Association.
Conn, Harvie
    1978   Urbanization and Muslim Evangelism: Obstacle or Opportunity?
            LCWE, Paper presented at the Lausanne Committee for World
            Evangelization, Zeist, Holland, June 27–July 4.
    1982   *Evangelism—Doing Justice and Preaching Grace.* Grand Rapids,
            Mich.: Zondervan.
    1984   *Eternal Word and Changing Worlds: Theology, Anthropology, and Mis-
            sion in Trialogue.* Grand Rapids, Mich.: Zondervan.
    1987a   Urban Church Planting and Growth. Unpublished syllabus,
            Alliance Theological Seminary, Nyack, N.Y.
    1987b   *A Clarified Vision for Urban Mission.* Grand Rapids, Mich.:
            Zondervan.
Cook, Guillermo
    1985   *The Expectation of the Poor.* Maryknoll, N.Y.: Orbis.
Cooley, Frank L.
    1968   *Indonesian Church and Society.* New York: Friendship Press.
Cooley, John K.
    1965   *Baal, Christ and Mohammed.* New York: Holt, Rinehart and
            Winston.
Costas, Orlando E.
    1974   *The Church and Its Mission.* Wheaton, Ill.: Tyndale.
Costello, V. F.
    1977   *Urbanization in the Middle East.* London: Cambridge University
            Press.
Cowley, Deborah
    1984   *Cairo.* Cairo: American University.
Cragg, Kenneth
    1956   *The Call of the Minaret.* Maryknoll, N.Y.: Orbis.
    1959   *Sandals at the Mosque.* New York: Oxford University Press.
    1979   "Islamic Theology: Limits and Bridges." In *The Gospel and Islam.*
            Donald M. McCurry, ed., 196–207. Monrovia, Calif.: MARC.
    1984   *Mohammad and the Christian.* Maryknoll, N.Y.: Orbis.

1985 *Jesus and the Muslim.* London: George Allen & Unwin.

Crossley, John

1960 *Explaining the Gospel to Muslims.* London: Lutterworth.

Danker, William J.

1971 *Profit for the Lord: Economic Activities in Moravian Missions and the Basel Mission Training Company.* Grand Rapids, Mich.: Eerdmans.

Dawson, John

1989 *Taking Our Cities For God.* Lake Mary, Fla.: Creation House.

Dayton, Edward R.

1978 *Planning Strategies for Evangelism—A Workbook.* Monrovia, Calif.: MARC.

1979 *That Everyone May Hear: Reaching the Unreached.* Monrovia, Calif.: MARC.

Dayton, Edward R., and Sam Wilson

1982 *Unreached Peoples '82, Focus: Urban Peoples.* Elgin, Ill.: David C. Cook.

Dehgani-Tafti, Hassan

1963 *Design of My World.* London: Lutterworth.

Deshmukh, Ibrahimkhan O.

1982 *The Gospel and Islam.* Bombay: GLS.

DeVries, Anne

1967 "Pauline Concept of Identification in the Missionary Task." M.A. thesis, Wheaton College.

Dixon, Roger

1984 "A Strategy for Sundanese Evangelism and Church Planting." Unpublished manuscript.

Dodd, Carley H.

1982 *Dynamics of Intercultural Communication.* Dubuque, Iowa: William Brown.

Dollar, Harold

1980 "A Cross Cultural Theology of Healing." M.A. thesis, Fuller Theological Seminary.

Dom, Mohammed

1979 *Malay Superstitions and Beliefs.* Kuala Lumpur, Malaysia: Federal Publications.

Donovan, Vincent J.

1978 *Christianity Rediscovered: An Epistle from the Masai.* Maryknoll, N.Y.: Orbis/Claretian.

Douglas, Robert
  1977   "Strategic Components in a Proposed Experimental Approach
         to Evangelization of Muslims." M.A. thesis, Fuller Theological
         Seminary.
Draine, Cathie, and Barbara Hall
  1986   *Indonesia Culture Shock.* Singapore: Times Books International.
Dretke, James P.
  1979   *A Christian Approach to Muslims: Reflections from West Africa.*
         Pasadena, Calif.: William Carey Library.
Drewery, Mary
  1978   *William Carey.* Grand Rapids, Mich.: Zondervan.
DuBose, Francis M.
  1978   *How Churches Grow in an Urban World.* Nashville, Tenn.: Broadman.
Dwyer, Daisy
  1978   "Women, Sufism and Decision-making in Moroccan Islam." In
         Women in the Muslim World. L. Beck and N. Keddie, eds., 585–598.
         Cambridge, Mass.: Harvard University Press.
Dwyer, Kevin
  1982   *Moroccan Dialogues.* Baltimore, Md.: Johns Hopkins University.
Eames, Edwin, and Julius Goode
  1977   *Anthropology of the City.* Englewood Cliffs, N.J.: Prentice Hall.
Eims, Leroy
  1978   *The Lost Art of Disciplemaking.* Grand Rapids, Mich.: Zondervan.
Eisenstadt, S. N., and L. Roniger
  1984   *Patrons, Clients and Friends.* London: Cambridge University Press.
Ellison, Craig
  1974   *The Urban Mission.* Grand Rapids, Mich.: Eerdmans.
  1987   Addressing Felt Needs of City Dwellers. *Urban Mission* 4:26–41.
Engel, James
  1975   *What's Gone Wrong with the Harvest?* Grand Rapids, Mich.:
         Zondervan.
  1988   *How to Communicate the Gospel Effectively.* Achimota, Ghana: Africa
         Christian.
Evans, Wendell
  1977   Guidelines for Preparation and Appointment of Church Elders.
         Available from Arab World Media, 240 Montolivet, Marseille,
         France.
  1982   Church Planting in the Arab-Muslim World. Available from Arab
         World Media, 240 Montolivet, Marseille, France.

Farnham, Bruce (Denis Alexander)
  1986   *The Way of Jesus.* Bellville, Mich.: Lion.
Fernando, Ajith
  1987   *The Christian's Attitude Toward World Religions.* Wheaton, Ill.: Tyndale.
Fernea, Elizabeth
  1980   *A Street in Marrakech.* Garden City, N.Y.: Anchor.
Fernea, Elizabeth, and Qattan Bezirgan Basima
  1977   *Middle Eastern Women Speak.* Austin, Tex.: University of Texas.
Finley, Allen, and Larry Lutz
  1981   *The Family Tie.* Nashville, Tenn.: Nelson.
Foster, George M.
  1962   *Traditional Cultures and the Impact of Technological Change.* New York: Harper and Row.
Foster, George M., and R. V. Kemper, eds.
  1974   *Anthropologists in Cities.* Boston: Little and Brown.
Foxe, John
  1926   *Foxe's Book of Martyrs.* 1st ed. John Day 1563. Philadelphia: Winston.
Foyle, Marjory
  1987   *Honorably Wounded.* London: Evangelical Missionary Alliance.
Fraser, David A.
  1979   "An 'Engel Scale' for Muslim Work?" In *Gospel and Islam.* Donald M. McCurry, ed., 164–181. Monrovia, Calif.: MARC.
Friedman, Thomas L.
  1989   *From Beirut to Jerusalem.* New York: Farrar Straus Giroux.
Fry, George, and James King
  1980   *Islam: A Survey of the Muslim Faith.* Grand Rapids, Mich.: Baker.
Geertz, Clifford
  1968   *Islam Observed.* New Haven, Conn.: Yale University Press.
  1979   *Meaning and Order in Moroccan Society.* New York: Cambridge University Press.
Gellner, Ernest
  1977   *Patrons and Clients in Mediterranean Societies.* London: Duckworth.
Gerstner, John
  1980   *Heaven and Hell.* Grand Rapids, Mich.: Baker.
Gibb, H. A. R., and J. H. Kramers
  1965   *Shorter Encyclopedia of Islam.* Ithaca, N.Y.: Cornell University Press.

Gibbs, S., A. Lorenz, and L. Schmida
   1987   *Teaching Opportunities in the Middle East and North Africa*. Washington, D.C.: Amid East.
Gilchrist, John
   1988   *The Christian Witness to the Muslim*. Benoni, South Africa: Jesus to the Muslims.
Gilliland, Dean S.
   1983   *Pauline Theology and Mission Practice*. Grand Rapids, Mich.: Baker.
Ginder, Glenn
   1987   *Interaction Among Malay Communities of Kuala Lumpur*. Unpublished manuscript. Mesa, Ariz.: Frontiers.
Glasser, Arthur F.
   1979   "Power Encounter in Conversion from Islam." In *The Gospel and Islam*. Donald M. McCurry, ed., 129–142. Monrovia, Calif.: MARC.
Glasser, Arthur F., and Donald A. McGavran
   1982   *Contemporary Theologies of Mission*. Grand Rapids, Mich.: Baker.
Goble, Philip E.
   1974   *Everything You Need to Grow a Messianic Synagogue*. Pasadena, Calif.: William Carey Library.
   1989   "Everything You Need to Grow a Jesus Mosque." Unpublished manuscript.
Goble, Philip E., and Salim Munayer
   1985   "The New Creation Book for Muslims." Unpublished manuscript.
Goldsmith, Martin
   1976   Community and Controversy: Key Cases of Muslim Response. *Missiology* 4:317–323.
   1980   Parabolic Preaching in the Context of Islam. *Evangelical Review of Theology* 4:218–222.
   1991   *What in the World Is God Doing?* Eastbourne, United Kingdom: MARC.
Goodall, Norman
   1957   Some Reflections on the Near and Middle East. *International Review of Missions* 6:5–10.
Green, Denis J.
   1985   "Strategy for Evangelizing Kejawen Muslims." Unpublished manuscript, Fuller Theological Seminary.
Green, Michael
   1970   *Evangelism and the Early Church*. Grand Rapids, Mich.: Eerdmans.

Greenway, Roger
 1973 *An Urban Strategy for Latin America.* Grand Rapids, Mich.: Baker.
 1976 *Guidelines for Urban Church Planting.* Grand Rapids, Mich.: Baker.
 1978 *Apostles to the City.* Grand Rapids, Mich.: Baker.
 1979 *Discipling the City: Theological Reflections on Urban Mission.* Grand Rapids, Mich.: Baker.
Griffiths, Michael
 1970 *Give Up Your Small Ambitions.* London: InterVarsity.
 1972 *Who Really Sends the Missionary?* Chicago: Moody.
Grigg, Viv
 1984 *Companion to the Poor.* Sutherland, N.S.W., Australia: Albatross.
Groseclose, L. Davi
 1986 "A Plan for Discipling a Believer of Israeli-Muslim Arab Background." M.A. thesis, Fuller Theological Seminary.
Grunlan, Stephen A., and Marvin K. Myers
 1979 *Christian Anthropology.* Grand Rapids, Mich.: Zondervan.
Guillamre, Alfred
 1966 *The Traditions of Islam.* Beirut: Khayats.
Gulick, John
 1989 *Humanity of Cities.* Granby, Mass.: Bergin and Garvey.
Gutierrez, Gustavo
 1973 *The Theology of Liberation.* Maryknoll, N.Y.: Orbis.
Haggoy, Willy N.
 1960 "Fifty Years of Evangelical Missionary Movement in North Africa, 1881–1931." Ph.D. dissertation, The Hartford Seminary Foundation.
Hahn, Ernest
 1980 *Understanding Some Muslim Misunderstandings.* Toronto: Fellowship of Faith for Muslims.
Haines, Byron, and Frank Cooley
 1987 *Christians and Muslims Together.* Philadelphia, Pa.: Geneva.
Haines, John
 1983 Worship: The Neglected Way to Reach Muslims. *Evangelical Missions Quarterly* 19:42–45.
 1984 Reaching Muslims in French Cities. *Urban Mission* 2:20–33.
Haleblian, Kricor
 1979 "Worldview and Evangelization: A Case Study on Arab People." M.A. thesis, Fuller Theological Seminary.

Hall, Edward T.

1959   *The Silent Language.* New York: Doubleday.

1969   *The Hidden Dimension.* New York: Doubleday.

1976   *Beyond Culture.* New York: Doubleday.

1979   Learning the Arab's Silent Language. *Psychology Today* 13:44–54.

Hamada, Louis Bahjat

1986   *God Loves the Arabs Too.* Nashville, Tenn.: WinstonDerek.

Hamady, Sania

1960   *Temperament and Character of the Arab.* New York: Twayne.

Hannakonda, K. Gikoe

1986   "A Balanced Growth Model for Lutheran Churches Ministering in the Urban Context of Jakarta." M.A. thesis, Fuller Theological Seminary.

Haqq, Akbar

1978   *Sharing the Lord Jesus Christ with Muslim Neighbors.* Minneapolis, Minn.: Billy Graham Association.

Harris, George K.

1949   *How to Lead Muslims to Christ.* Philadelphia, Pa.: CIM.

Harrison, Myron

1983   "Developing Multinational Teams." M.A. thesis, Trinity Evangelical Divinity School.

Harrison, Paul

1924   *The Arab at Home.* New York: Crowell.

Hassan, Madhat

1978   "Culture, Behavior, and Urban Form: A Study of Low Cost Housing with Special Reference to Cairo, Egypt." Ph.D. dissertation, Sheffield University.

Hawthorne, Steve

1987   "Envisioning Evangelism: A Missiology and a Model for Frontier Mission Research." Unpublished manuscript.

Hay, Alex Rattray

1947   *The New Testament Order for Church and Missionary.* Audubon, N.J.: New Testament Missionary Union.

Hay, Ian

1972   "The Emergence of a Missionary-Minded Church in Nigeria." In *Church/Mission Tensions Today.* Peter Wagner, ed., 193–214. Chicago: Moody.

Hedlund, Roger
    1987   Urbanization and Evangelization in South India. *Urban Mission* 4:16–31.

Hefley, James, and Marti Hefley
    1974   *Uncle Cam*. Milford, Mich.: Mott Media.

Hermassi, Elbaki
    1972   *Leadership and National Development in North Africa*. Berkeley, Calif.: University of California Press.

Hesselgrave, David J.
    1978   *Communicating Christ Cross-culturally: An Introduction to Missionary Communication*. Grand Rapids, Mich.: Zondervan.
    1980   *Planting Churches Cross-Culturally: A Guide for Home and Foreign Missions*. Grand Rapids, Mich.: Baker.

Hicks, Richard, Jr.
    1976   "An Annotated Bibliography of the Contribution of Sociology and Religion to Missiology." M.A. thesis, Fuller Theological Seminary.

Hiebert, Paul G.
    1978   Power Encounter and the Challenge of Folk Islam. Paper presented at the meeting of the Lausanne Committee for World Evangelization, Zeist, Holland, June 27–July 4.
    1982   The Flaw of the Excluded Middle. *Missiology* 10:35–47.
    1983   *Cultural Anthropology*. Grand Rapids, Mich.: Baker.
    1985   *Anthropological Insights for Missionaries*. Grand Rapids, Mich.: Baker.

Hinton, Keith
    1985   *Growing Churches Singapore Style: Ministry in an Urban Context*. Singapore: OMF.

Hodges, Melvin L.
    1978   *The Indigenous Church and the Missionary*. Pasadena, Calif.: William Carey Library.

Hostetter, Richard
    1976   Voluntary Associations in Urban African Churches. *Missiology* 4:427–430.

Howard, David
    1969   *The Costly Harvest*. Wheaton, Ill.: Tyndale House.
    1977   What Happened at Urbana: Its Meaning For Missions. *Evangelical Missions Quarterly* 13:141–147.

Huffard, Evertt
    1985   "Thematic Dissonance in the Muslim-Christian Encounter: Theology of Honor Versus Love." D.Miss. diss., Fuller Theological Seminary.
Hunt, Everett Nichols, Jr.
    1980   *Protestant Pioneers in Korea*. Maryknoll, N.Y.: Orbis.
Inch, Morris.
    1986   *Making the Good News Relevant*. Nashville, Tenn.: Nelson.
Inniger, Merlin W.
    1979   Getting to Know Their "Heart Hunger" Is a Key to Reaching Muslims. *Evangelical Missions Quarterly* 15:540.
Isais, Juan
    1966   *The Other Side of the Coin*. Grand Rapids, Mich.: Eerdmans.
    1985   "Success in Evangelism-in-Depth." Unpublished manuscript.
Israeli, Raphael
    1976   Muslims Versus Christians in China. *Asia Quarterly* 4:327–35.
    1977   Muslims in China: The Incompatibility Between Islam and the Chinese Order. *T'oung Pao* 63:296–323.
Jacobs, Jane
    1984   *Cities and the Wealth of Nations*. New York: Random House.
Jadid, Iskandar
    1970   *Did God Appear in the Flesh?* Basel, Switzerland: Centre for Young Adults.
Jain, S. P.
    1975   Caste Stratification among the Muslims. *Eastern Anthropology* 28:255–270.
Jansen, Frank K., ed.
    1989   *Target Earth*. Kailua-Kena, Hawaii: University of the Nations.
Jennings, George J.
    1977   "The Arab Ethos." Unpublished manuscript, Geneva College, Beaver Falls, Pa.
    1980   Is Islamic Theistic Socialism a Barrier to Christian Missions? *Missiology* 8:155–166.
Johnstone, P. J.
    1981   *Operation World: A Handbook for World Intercession*. Bromley, United Kingdom: Send the Light.
Johnes, L. Bevan
    1964   *Christianity Explained to Muslims*. Calcutta: Baptist Mission Press.

Joshua Project
    1984   Reaching the Muslim Peoples of Alexandria, Egypt. Available from Caleb Project, Littleton, Co.
    1985a The Baluch of Karachi, Pakistan. Available from Caleb Project, Littleton, Co.
    1985b Reaching the Peoples of Istanbul, Turkey. Available from Caleb Project, Littleton, Co.
    1988a Church Planting Among Delhi Muslims. Available from Caleb Project, Littleton, Co.
    1988b Reaching Bombay's Muslims. Available from Caleb Project, Littleton, Co.

Kahn, Margaret
    1980   *Children of the Jinn*. New York: Seaview.

Kateregge, Badru D., and David W. Shenk
    1980   *Islam and Christianity*. Grand Rapids, Mich.: Eerdmans.

Kelly, D. P.
    1982   Destroying the Barriers. Vernon, B.C., Canada: Laurel.

Keyes, Lawrence
    1982   *The Last Age of Missions: A Survey of Third World Missions*. Pasadena, Calif.: William Carey Library.

Keysser, Christian
    1980   *A People Reborn: Caring Communities, Their Birth and Their Development*. Pasadena, Calif.: William Carey Library.

Khan, Anwar M.
    1976   "Strategy to Evangelize Muslim Jats in Pakistan." M.A. thesis, Fuller Theological Seminary.

Kidron, Michael, and Ronald Segal
    1987   *The New State of the World Atlas*. New York: Simon & Schuster.

Kinnear, Angus
    1971   *Monsoon Daybreak*. London: Open Books.

Kraemer, Henrik
    1958   *From Mission Field to Independent Church*. London: SCM.

Kraft, Charles H.
    1979a *Christianity in Culture: A Study in Dynamic Biblical Theologizing in Cross-Cultural Perspective*. Maryknoll, N.Y.: Orbis.
    1979b "Dynamic Equivalents to Churches in Muslim Society." In *Gospel and Islam*. Donald M. McCurry, ed., 115–127. Monrovia, Calif.: MARC.

1980   *Communicating the Gospel God's Way.* Pasadena, Calif.: William
         Carey Library.

1983   *Communication Theory for Christian Witness.* Nashville, Tenn.:
         Abingdon.

1989   *Christianity With Power.* Ann Arbor, Mich.: Vine.

Kraft, Charles, and Tom Wisley

1979   *Readings in Dynamic Indigeneity.* Pasadena, Calif.: William Carey
         Library.

Kraft, Marguerite

1978   *Worldview and the Communication of the Gospel.* Pasadena, Calif.:
         William Carey Library.

Kritzinger, J. N. T.

1981   Islam as Rival of the Gospel in Africa. *Evangelical Review of The-
         ology* 5:232–252.

Kyle, John E.

1984   *The Unfinished Task.* Ventura, Calif.: Regal.

1987   *Should I Not Be Concerned?* Downers Grove, Ill.: Inter-Varsity.

Lapidus, Ira

1969   *Middle Eastern Cities.* Berkeley, Calif.: University of California Press.

Larson, Donald N.

1981   "The Viable Missionary." In *Perspectives on the World Christian
         Movement.* Ralph Winter and Steven Hawthorne, eds., 444–451.
         Pasadena, Calif.: William Carey Library.

1984   *Guidelines for Barefoot Language Learning.* St. Paul, Minn.: CMS.

Latourette, Kenneth Scott

1937–45 *A History of the Expansion of Christianity.* 7 vols. New York: Harper
         and Row.

Lausanne Committee for World Evangelization

1978   *Glen Eyrie Report.* Lausanne Occasional Papers, No. 4. Wheaton,
         Ill.: Author.

1980   *The Thailand Report on Muslims.* Lausanne Occasional Papers, No.
         13. Wheaton, Ill.: Author.

Lawrence, Carl

1985   *The Church in China: How It Survives and Prospers Under Commu-
         nism.* Minneapolis, Minn.: Bethany House.

LeBar, Lois E.

1958   *Education That Is Christian.* Westwood, N.J.: Revell.

Lenning, Larry

1980   *Blessing in Mosque and Mission.* Pasadena, Calif.: William Carey
         Library.

Lewis, Bernard
    1970   *Race and Color in Islam.* New York: Harper and Row.
Liao, David C. E.
    1979   *The Unresponsive: Resistant or Neglected?* Pasadena, Calif.: William Carey Library.
Lingenfelter, Sherwood G.
    1985   "Left Brain, Right Brain and Biblical Discourse Structure." Unpublished manuscript, Biola University, La Mirada, Calif.
    1986   "Formal Logic or Practical Logic." Unpublished manuscript, Biola University, La Mirada, Calif.
Lingenfelter, Sherwood G., and Marvin K. Mayers
    1986   *Ministering Cross-Culturally: An Incarnational Model for Personal Relationships.* Grand Rapids, Mich.: Baker.
Livingstone, Greg
    1968   "Utilizing Students to Amplify Established Missionary Endeavors." M.A. thesis, Wheaton Graduate School.
    1986a How Can We Reach Muslims By Working Together? *Evangelical Missions Quarterly* 22:246–251.
    1986b "The Sundanese: Today's Challenge in Indonesia." Unpublished manuscript.
Loewen, Jacob A.
    1983   *Culture and Human Values.* Pasadena, Calif.: William Carey Library.
Love, Richard D.
    1983   "Islam and Contextualization." Unpublished manuscript.
Luzbetak, Louis J.
    1976   *The Church and Cultures: Applied Anthropology for the Religious Worker.* Pasadena, Calif.: William Carey Library.
Mackay, Sandra
    1987   *The Saudis.* Boston: Houghton Mifflin.
Madany, Bassam M.
    1981   *Sharing God's Word with a Muslim.* Palos Heights, Ill.: Back to God Hour.
Magnuson, Douglas
    1987   "Pioneer Church Planting." Unpublished manuscript, Frontiers.
Maguire, Lambert
    1983   *Understanding Social Networks.* Beverly Hills, Calif.: Sage.
Mains, Karen
    1976   *Open Heart, Open Home.* Elgin, Ill.: David C. Cook.
Mansfield, Peter
    1976   *The Arabs.* London: Penguin.

Mardin, Serif
    1977   Religion in Modern Turkey. *International Social Science Journal*
            29:279–297.
Matheny, Tim
    1981   *Reaching the Arabs: A Felt Need Approach.* Pasadena, Calif.: William
            Carey Library.
Mathews, R. Arthur
    1978   *Born For Battle.* Robesonia, Pa.: OMF.
Mayers, Marvin K.
    1974   *Christianity Confronts Culture.* Grand Rapids, Mich.: Zondervan.
McAlpine, Thomas
    1991   *Facing the Powers.* Monrovia, Calif.: MARC.
McBurney, Louis
    1977   *Every Pastor Needs a Pastor.* Carbondale, Colo.: PMR.
McCurry, Donald M., ed.
    1979   *The Gospel and Islam.* Monrovia, Calif.: MARC.
    1982   *Sharing the Gospel with Iranians.* Altadena, Calif.: Zwemer Institute.
McGavran, Donald A.
    1955   *The Bridges of God.* New York: Friendship.
    1979   *Ethnic Realities and the Church: Lessons from India.* Pasadena, Calif.:
            William Carey Library.
    1980   *Understanding Church Growth.* Grand Rapids, Mich.: Eerdmans.
    1984   *Momentous Decisions in Missions Today.* Grand Rapids, Mich.: Baker.
McGavran, Donald A., et al.
    1973   *Church Growth and Group Conversion.* Pasadena, Calif.: William
            Carey Library.
McGinnis, Alan
    1979   *The Friendship Factor.* Minneapolis, Minn.: Augsburg.
McNee, Peter
    1976   *Crucial Issues in Bangladesh.* Pasadena, Calif.: William Carey Library.
McQuilkin, J. Robertson
    1974   *Measuring the Church Growth Movement.* Chicago: Moody.
Meeks, Wayne A.
    1983   *The First Urban Christians.* New Haven, Conn.: Yale University Press.
Mellis, Charles J.
    1976   *Committed Communities: Fresh Streams for World Missions.* Pasadena,
            Calif.: William Carey Library.
Mernissi, Fatima
    1975   *Beyond the Veil.* Cambridge, Mass.: Schenkman.

Miller, William McElwee
  1971   The Future Role of Western Missions to the Muslim World—
         Africa, India, and Asia. *Evangelical Missions Quarterly* 7:231.
  1989   *My Persian Pilgrimage.* Pasadena, Calif.: William Carey Library.
Mitchell, Richard
  1969   *The Society of the Muslim Brothers.* London: Oxford University
         Press.
Mokhzani, B. A. R.
  1974   The Malay Family and Religion. *East Asian Cultural Studies*
         13:37–50.
Molla, Clyde F.
  1966   Rising Tide. *Frontier* 9:261–265.
Monsma, Timothy
  1979   *An Urban Strategy for Africa.* Pasadena, Calif.: William Carey Library.
Monsma, Timothy, and Roger Greenway
  1989   *The Cities, Mission's New Frontier.* Grand Rapids, Mich.: Baker.
Morgan, Russ
  1983   "Strategy and Methods for Reaching Muslims: A Digest of the
         Major Evangelical Literature 1974–1982." M.A. thesis, Colum-
         bia Graduate School, Columbia, S.C.
Mott, John R.
  1924   *Conferences of Christian Workers Among Moslems.* New York: Inter-
         national Missionary Council.
Mumper, Sharon E.
  1986   An Indonesian Leader Speaks to the Church in the West. *Evan-
         gelical Missions Quarterly* 22:6–11.
Murphy, Edward
  1972   "Guidelines for Urban Church Planting." In *Crucial Issues in Mis-
         sions Tomorrow.* Donald McGavran, ed., 245–265. Chicago: Moody.
Musk, Bill
  1979a "Turkey: Towards a Harvest Strategy." M.A. thesis, Fuller Theo-
         logical Seminary.
  1979b "Popular Islam: The Hunger of the Heart." In *The Gospel and Islam.*
         Donald M. McCurry, ed., 208–224. Monrovia, Calif.: MARC.
  1989   *The Unseen Face of Islam.* Eastbourne, United Kingdom:
         MARC/EMA.
  1992   *Passionate Believing.* Tunbridge Wells, United Kingdom: Monarch.
Muzaffar, Chandra
  1987   *Islamic Resurgence in Malaysia.* Petaling Jaya: Penerbit Fajar Bakti.

Neander, Augustus
> 1844   *History of the Planting and Training of the Christian Church by the Apostles.* Trans. from 3rd ed. of the original German by J. E. Ryland. Philadelphia, Pa.: James M. Campbell.

Nehls, Gerhard
> 1988   *Christians Answer Muslims.* Bellville, South Africa: SIM International.
> 1989   *The Great Commission: You and the Muslims.* Claremont, South Africa: Life Challenge.

Neill, Stephen
> 1964   *A History of Christian Missions.* Baltimore, Md.: Penguin.

Nevius, John L.
> 1899   *Planting and Development of Missionary Churches.* Phillipsburg, N.J.: Presbyterian and Reformed.

Nida, Eugene
> 1954   *Customs and Cultures: Anthropology for Christian Missions.* Pasadena, Calif.: William Carey Library.
> 1960   *Message and Mission.* New York: Harper & Row.

Nida, Eugene, and William Reyburn
> 1981   *Meaning Across Cultures.* Maryknoll, N.Y.: Orbis.

Niklaus, Robert
> 1986   *All for Jesus.* Camp Hill, Pa.: Christian Publications.

Nizami, Khaliq Ahmad
> 1984   Impact of Sufi Saints in Indian Society and Culture. *Islamic Culture* 58:31–54.

North Africa Mission
> 1976   *Reaching Muslims Today.* Bromley, United Kingdom: Send the Light.

Obion, Frank
> 1974   *Building Bridges of Love.* San Bernardino, Calif.: Campus Crusade.
> 1978   Obstacles in the Way of Winning Muslims. *Evangelical Missionary Quarterly* 14:178–182.

Ortiz, Juan Carlos
> 1975   *Disciple.* Carol Stream, Ill.: Creation House.

Otero, George
> 1977   *Teaching About Perception: The Arabs.* Denver, Colo.: University of Denver Press.

Otis, George, Jr.
> 1991   *The Last of the Giants.* Tarrytown, N.Y.: Revell.

Otis, Gerald E.
> 1980   Power Encounter—The Way to Muslim Breakthrough. *Evangelical Missions Quarterly* 16:217–220.

Ozturk, Orhan M.
    1964   "Folk Treatment of Mental Illness in Turkey." In *Magic Faith and Healing*. Ari Kiev, ed., 343–363. New York: Free Press of Glencoe.

Palen, John
    1975   *The Urban World*. New York: McGraw Hill.

Parrinder, Geoffrey
    1977   *Jesus and the Quran*. New York: Oxford University Press.

Parshall, Phil
    1977   A Small Family Is a Happy Family. *Evangelical Missions Quarterly* 13:207–211.
    1979a Contextualized Baptism for Muslim Converts. *Missiology* 7:501–515.
    1979b God's Communicator In the 80's. *Evangelical Missions Quarterly* 15:215–221.
    1980   *New Paths in Muslim Evangelism*. Grand Rapids, Mich.: Baker.
    1982   Muslim Misconceptions About Missionaries. *Evangelical Missions Quarterly* 18:31–34.
    1983   *Bridges to Islam*. Grand Rapids, Mich.: Baker.
    1985a *Beyond the Mosque*. Grand Rapids, Mich.: Baker.
    1985b How to Change Medicine to Muslims. *Evangelical Missions Quarterly* 21:253–255.
    1987   How Spiritual Are Missionaries? *Evangelical Missions Quarterly* 23:10–16.
    1989   *The Dove and the Crescent*. Wheaton, Ill.: Tyndale.

Pastner, Stephen L.
    1978   Power and Pirs Among the Pakistani Baluch. *Journal of Asian and African Studies* 13:231–243.

Patai, Raphael
    1973   *The Arab Mind*. New York: Scribner & Sons.

Pate, Larry D.
    1989   *From Every People*. Monrovia, Calif.: MARC.

Pearson, Robert P.
    1985   *Through Middle Eastern Eyes*. New York: Center for International Training.

Peck, Scott
    1983   *People of the Lie*. New York: Simon & Schuster.

Peristiany, J. G.
    1976   *Mediterranean Family Structures*. London: Cambridge University Press.

Peters, George W.
   1981   *Theology of Church Growth*. Grand Rapids, Mich.: Zondervan.
Pfander, Carl G.
   1867   *The Balance of Truth*. R. H. Weakly, transl. London: Church Missionary House.
Pfautz, Harold
   1964   "A Case Study of an Urban Religious Movement: Christian Science." In *Contributions to Urban Sociology*. Ernest Berge, ed., 284–303. Chicago: University Press.
Phillips, H. E.
   1936   Should Moslem Converts Unite with the Church? *The Muslim World* 26:119–126.
Pickett, J. Waskom
   1956   *Church Growth and Group Conversion*. Lucknow, India: Lucknow Publishing House.
Piper, John
   1986   *Desiring God*. Portland, Oreg.: Multnomah.
   1991   *The Pleasures of God*. Portland, Oreg.: Multnomah.
Rahbar, Daud
   1965   Christian Apologetic to Muslims. *International Review of Missions* 54:353–359.
Rahman, Fazlur
   1966   The Status of the Individual in Islam. *Islamic Studies* 5:319–330.
Ream, W. G. B.
   1956   The Support of the Clergy in the First Five Centuries A.D. *International Review of Missions* 45:420–428.
Reed, Lyman E.
   1985   *Preparing Missionaries for Inter-cultural Communication*. Pasadena, Calif.: William Carey Library.
Register, Ray G., Jr.
   1979   *Dialogue and Interfaith Witness with Muslims*. Fort Washington, Pa.: WEC International.
Richardson, Don
   1974   *Peace Child*. Ventura, Calif.: Regal.
Richardson, Kenneth
   1968   *Garden of Miracles*. London: Africa Inland Mission.
Richter, Julius
   1910   *A History of Professional Missions in the Near East*. New York: Revell.

Rickards, Donald
   1978   North Africa: The Last Frontier. *Evangelical Missions Quarterly* 14:91–92.
Riggs, Henry
   1941   Shall We Try Unbeaten Paths in Working for Moslems? *The Muslim World* 31:116–126.
Ring, Jack
   1985   *Planting Churches in the Third World*. Bend, Oreg.: Shield of Faith.
Roberts, Vella
   1981   "The Urban Mission of the Church from Urban Anthropological Perspectives." M.A. thesis, Fuller Theological Seminary.
Rosen, Lawrence
   1984   *Bargaining for Reality*. Chicago: University Press.
Roslan, Samsuri
   1986   40,000 Malays Become Christian. Untitled manuscript. Kuala Lumpur, Malaysia.
Roy, Asim
   1973   The Social Factor in the Making of Bengali Islam. *South Asia* 3:23–25.
Roy, O.
   1983   Sufism in the Afghan Resistance. *Central Asian Survey* 4:61–79.
Rugh, Andrea B.
   1979   *Coping With Poverty in a Cairo Community*. Cairo: American University of Cairo Press.
   1985   *Family and Contemporary Egypt*. Cairo: American University of Cairo Press.
Samovar, Larry A., and Richard E. Porter
   1976   *Intercultural Communication: A Reader*. Belmont, Calif.: Wadsworth.
Samuel, George
   1973   "Growth Potential of Urban Churches (in Bombay)." M.A. thesis, Fuller Theological Seminary.
Saqqaf, Abdulaziz
   1987   *The Middle East City*. New York: Paragon.
Sargunan, Ezra
   1973   "Multiplying Churches in Urban India: An Experiment in Madras." M.A. thesis, Fuller Theological Seminary.
Schaeffer, Francis
   1970   *The Mark of a Christian*. Downers Grove, Ill.: InterVarsity.
   1971   *True Spirituality*. Wheaton, Ill.: Tyndale.

Schaller, Lyle E.
  1978   *The Change Agent.* Nashville, Tenn.: Abingdon.
Schanzlin, G. L.
  1940   Policies and Methods of Mission Work among Moslems. *The Moslem World* 30:144–150.
Schlorff, Samuel
  1980   The Hermeneutical Crisis in Muslim Evangelization. *Evangelical Missions Quarterly* 16:143–151.
  1981   *Discipleship in Islamic Society.* Marseilles, France: North Africa Mission.
Schreiber, Kent
  1987   "Friendship Evangelism in Istanbul." Unpublished manuscript.
Scott, Waldron
  1980   *Bring Forth Justice: A Contemporary Perspective on Mission.* Grand Rapids, Mich.: Eerdmans.
Seale, Morris S.
  1964   *Muslim Theology.* London: Luzac.
Shah, Indries
  1979   *The World of the Sufi: An Anthology of Writings About Sufis and Their Work.* London: Octagon.
Shearer, Roy
  1966   *Wildfire: Church Growth in Korea.* Grand Rapids, Mich.: Eerdmans.
Sinulingga, Thomas
  1969   "A Study of Factors Leading Muslims to Become Seventh Day Adventist Christians in Java 1960–1968." M.A. thesis, Philippines University College, Manila.
  1975   "An Adaptation of American Studies on Evangelism to the Need of Indonesia." Th.D. dissertation, Claremont School of Theology.
Smalley, William A., ed.
  1978   *Readings in Missionary Anthropology II.* Pasadena, Calif.: William Carey Library.
Smith, Clinton
  1970   "The Effect of Twentieth Century Arab Nationalism on The Christian Witness in The Near East." M.A. thesis, Wheaton Graduate School.
Smith, Ebbie C.
  1970   *God's Miracles: Indonesian Church Growth.* Pasadena, Calif.: William Carey Library.

Smith, Harold
1939   The Philosophy of Missions for North Africa. *The Muslim World* 29:13–30.

Snyder, Howard A.
1977   *The Community of the King.* Downers Grove, Ill.: Inter-Varsity.

Spradley, James P.
1979   *The Ethnographic Interview.* New York: Holt, Rinehart and Winston.

Stacey, Vivienne
1976   Toward a Current Strategy: Discerning God's Hand in Islam Today. *Missiology* 4:363–372.

Stanton, Weitbrecht
1969   *The Teaching of the Quran.* London: SPCK.

Stedman, Raymond C.
1972   *Body Life.* Glendale, Calif.: Regal.

Steele, Francis R.
1981   *Not in Vain: The Story of North Africa Mission.* Pasadena, Calif.: William Carey Library.

Stott, John
1975   *Christian Mission in the Modern World.* Downers Grove, Ill.: Inter-Varsity.

Stube, Edwin B.
1982   *According to the Pattern . . . A Manual for Church Planting.* Baltimore, Md.: Holy Way.

Tadros, Helmi
1978   *Rural Resettlement in Egypt.* Cairo: American University of Cairo Press.

Tertullian,
1937   "Apologeticus." In *Familiar Quotations.* John Bartlett, ed., 1012. Boston: Little and Brown.

Tillapaugh, Frank
1982   *Unleashing the Church.* Ventura, Calif.: Regal.

Tisdall, W. St. Clair
1980   *Christian Reply to Muslim Objections.* Villach, Austria: Light of Life. (Original 1904).

Tippett, Alan R.
1970   *Church Growth and the Word of God.* Grand Rapids, Mich.: Eerdmans.
1987   *Introduction to Missiology.* Pasadena, Calif.: William Carey Library.

Tomczak, Larry
  1984 *Apostolic Team Ministry.* Washington, D.C.: People of Destiny.
Tonna, Benjamin
  1985 *A Gospel for the Cities.* Maryknoll, N.Y.: Orbis.
Torjesen, Edvard P.
  1982 *Fredrik Franson: Model for Worldwide Frontier Evangelism.* Pasadena, Calif.: William Carey Library.
Tozer, A. W.
  1978 *Tragedy and the Church: The Missing Gifts.* Harrisburg, Pa.: Christian Publications.
  1985 *Whatever Happened to Worship?* Camphill, Pa.: Christian Publications.
Trimingham, J. Spencer
  1955 *The Christian Church and Islam in West Africa.* London: SCM.
Tucker, Ruth
  1983 *From Jerusalem to Irian Jaya: A Biographical History of Christian Missions.* Grand Rapids, Mich.: Zondervan.
Vander Werff, Lyle F.
  1977 *Christian Mission to Muslims.* Pasadena, Calif.: William Carey Library.
Van Ess, Dorothy F.
  1974 *Pioneers in the Arab World.* Grand Rapids, Mich.: Eerdmans.
Verwer, George
  1972 *Come, Live, Die.* Wheaton, Ill.: Tyndale.
Vincent, Eileen
  1988 *C. T. Studd and Priscilla.* Bromley, United Kingdom: Send the Light.
Von Grunebaum, G. E.
  1962 *Modern Islam: The Search for Cultural Identity.* Berkeley, Calif.: University of California Press.
Vos, Jan H.
  1986 *Video in the Middle East: A Survey of Preferences and Opportunities.* Arnhem, Netherlands: Holland Training Services.
Waddy, Chris
  1976 *The Muslim Mind.* New York: Longman.
Wagner, C. Peter
  1979 *Our Kind of People.* Atlanta, Ga.: John Knox Press.
  1983 *On the Crest of the Wave: Becoming a World Christian.* Ventura, Calif.: Regal.
  1991 *Territorial Spirits.* Chichester, United Kingdom: Sovereign World.
Wang, Thomas, ed.
  1989 *Countdown to AD 2000.* Pasadena, Calif.: William Carey Library.

Ward, Ted
    1984   *Living Overseas: A Book of Preparations.* New York: The Free Press.
Watson, David
    1981   *Discipleship.* London: Hodder & Stoughton.
Watt, W. Montgomery
    1970   *Bell's Introduction to the Koran.* Edinburgh: Edinburgh University Press.
Weekes, Richard V.
    1978   *Muslim Peoples: An World Ethnographic Survey.* London: Greenwood.
Weitz, Raanan
    1973   *Urbanization and the Developing Countries.* New York: Praeger.
Westgate, James
    1986   Emerging Church Planting Strategies for World Class Cities. *Urban Mission* 4:6–13.
White, John
    1976   *The Cost of Commitment.* Downers Grove, Ill.: InterVarsity.
Whitehouse, A.
    1981   *Topical Concordance to Koran.* Melbourne, Victoria, Australia: B.C.V.
Wiebe, Abe
    1978   *Cross and Crescent, Winter.* Upper Darby, Pa.: North African Mission.
Wikan, Unni
    1980   *Life Among the Poor in Cairo.* New York: Tavistock.
Wilder, John W.
    1977   Some Reflections on Possibilities for People Movements Among Muslims. *Missiology* 5:301–320.
Wilken, Robert L.
    1984   *The Christians as the Romans Saw Them.* New Haven, Conn.: Yale University Press.
Willis, Avery T., Jr.
    1977   *Indonesian Revival: Why Two Million Came to Christ.* Pasadena, Calif.: William Carey Library.
Wilson, J. Christy, Jr.
    1979   *Today's Tent Makers—Self-support: An Alternative Model for World-wide Witness.* Wheaton, Ill.: Tyndale.
    1981   *Afghanistan: The Forbidden Harvest.* Elgin, Ill.: David C. Cook.
Wilson, J. Christy, Sr.
    1952   *Apostle to Islam: A Biography of Samuel M. Zwemer.* Grand Rapids, Mich.: Baker.

Wimber, John
    1985   *Power Evangelism*. London: Hodder & Stoughton.
    1986   *Power Healing*. London: Hodder & Stoughton.
Winter, Ralph D.
    1970   *The Twenty-five Unbelievable Years: 1945–1969*. Pasadena, Calif.:
            William Carey Library.
    1978   *Penetrating the Last Frontiers*. Pasadena, Calif.: William Carey
            Library.
Winter, Ralph D., and Steven C. Hawthorne, eds.
    1981   *Perspectives on the World Christian Movement*. Pasadena, Calif.:
            William Carey Library.
Wirth, Lewis
    1979   *Urban Profile of the Middle East*. New York: St. Martins.
Woodbury, Dudley
    1989   *Muslims and Christians on the Emmaus Road*. Monrovia, Calif.:
            MARC.
Wootton, R. W. F.
    1982   *Jesus More Than a Prophet*. Bromley, United Kingdom: Send the
            Light.
World Vision (Producer) and Donald M. McCurry (Director)
    1980   *Unlocking the Door*. [Film]. Monrovia, Calif.: World Vision.
Yamamori, Tetsunao
    1987   *God's New Envoys*. Portland, Oreg.: Multnomah.
Yost, Jim
    1984   Development Work Can Hinder Church Growth. *Evangelical Mis-
            sions Quarterly* 20:352–360.
Youssef, Michael
    1978   "Theology and Methodology for Missionary Evangelism in
            Egypt." M.A. thesis, Fuller Theological Seminary.
Zwemer, Samuel
    1912   *The Moslem Christ*. New York: American Tract Society.
    1921   Sacrifice Among the Shias. *Moslem World* 11:389–394.
    1936   *Taking Hold of God*. Grand Rapids, Mich.: Zondervan.
    1941   *The Cross Above the Crescent*. Grand Rapids, Mich.: Zondervan.
    1946   Islam's Allah and the Christian God. *Muslim World* 36:19–26.

Index

Accountability, 100, 109–10
Adopt-A-People Clearing House, 71
Africa Inland Mission, 51
Agape Force, 50
Algiers, 189–96
Allen, Roland, 171
Amsterdam '86, 53
Apollos, 75
Aquilla, 75, 176
Arab World Ministries, 20, 46, 49,
    52, 169, 170–71, 178, 191
Arief, Rushi bin, 44

Bandung (Java, Indonesia), 196–204
Bangladesh, 56–57
Baptism, 171–73
Barnabas, 71, 113, 114, 153
Bell, William, 40–41
Bertuzzi, Federico, 53
Bethea, Ralph, 60
Brewster, Elizabeth, 118
Brewster, Thomas, 118
Brown, Don, 67
Burhanuddin, Rafik, 200
Bush, Louis, 53

Caldron, Carlos, 53
Caleb Project, 50
Calling
    confirmation of, 71
    discernment of, 74
    as stewardship, 74–75
    types of, 90–93
Campus Crusade for Christ, 49, 50,
    61–62
Carey, William, 95
Carillo, Pablo, 53
Change agent, role of, 65–86
Chastain, Warren, 45
Christian Life, 39
Christianity Today, 39
Christiansen, Jens, 20–21, 22, 67
Church calendar, 185–86
Church growth
    biological, 32
    conversion, 18, 32
    transfer, 18, 32
Church Growth Bulletin, 39
Church growth movement, 19
    presuppositions of, 33
Church planters
    calling of, 90–93
    characteristics of, 75–83
    definition of, 72–75
    marital status of, 83–86
Church planting team, 100–115
    components of, 101–8
    functioning of, 108–15
    gathering of, 210–13

Church planting
    activities in, 73
    challenge of, 25–62
    choices in, 87–115
    definition of, 72
    failure of, 35–41
    New Testament, 228
    premises of, 25–34
    prerequisites for, 65–165
    proposed strategy for, 205–23
    prospects of, 42–54
    task of, 169–231
CIM, 51
Citizen Christian, 15
Civil disobedience, 99
Colombia, missions in, 42
COMIBAM, 66
Communicology, 161–62
Contextualization, 46, 56
Conversion
    allegiance and, 13
    predisposing factors of, 146–50
    steps to, 235–38
Convert church, characteristics of,
    169–87
Cragg, Kenneth, 172
Critical mass, principle of, 14–15,
    226

DeVries, John, 60
Dixon, Roger, 30, 156, 157, 197,
    201, 202–3

Ecclesiology, 177–87
Eicher, Ray, 111
Elders, 174–75
Enculturation, 118–24
Erastus, 113
Eternity, 39
Ethics, 95–99
Evangelical Fellowship of Mission
    Agencies (EFMA), 49

Evangelical Missions Quarterly
    (*EMQ*), 39, 46
Evangelism, failure of, 35–41
Evangelists, 103–4
Evangelize Every Muslim, 66
Evans, Wendell, 21–22, 72, 122,
    169, 170, 173, 174, 175–76, 178
Excluded middle, principle of,
    27–28, 148

Facilitators, 106–8, 119
Families
    Christian, 173–74
    and mission work, 85–86
Fasting, 184
Fellowship of Singapore Christian
    Malays, 44–45
Fraser, David A., 145–46
Friend makers, 102, 128–32
From Every People, 66
Frontiers, 20, 49, 52, 69, 101, 171
Fry, George, 198
Fuller School of World Mission, 52

Glasser, Art, 38
Goldsmith, Martin, 54
Goodall, Norman, 39
Gospel Missionary Union, 52
Gospel, proclamation of, 73, 139–65
Great Commission, 11, 12, 33, 68,
    171
Green, Keith, 50, 74
Griffiths, Michael, 68, 94
Grigg, Viv, 89
Grindheim, Neil, 201

Haines, John, 47
Hall, Edward T., 124, 136–37
Harvest theology, 31, 46
Hawthorne, Steve, 161–63
Hay, A. R., 171
Hesselgrave, David, 171

Hiebert, Paul G., 27–28, 148
Home schooling, 85, 107
Homogeneous unit principle, 56, 67, 78, 101, 130
Hosts, 103
House churches, 16, 59, 60–61, 153–54, 178–79, 185
Howard, David, 49
Hunt, Everett, 42

Impact International, 44
Incarnational evangelism, 122
Inniger, Merle, 47
Inter-Varsity, 49
Interdenominational Foreign Missions Association (IFMA), 49, 84
International Christian Fellowship, 47, 52
International Missions, 20, 49
International Students, Inc., 70
International Teams, 52
Ishmaelite Salvation Association, 66
Islam
    diversity of, 17
    influence of, 9

Jennings, George, 139
John Mark, 113
Judson, Adoniram, 99

Kershaw, Max, 149
Koran, 56, 159, 179, 183
Korea, missions in, 42, 175, 229
Kraemer, Hendrik, 196, 198–99, 203
Kraft, Charles, 149, 179
Kraft, Marguerite, 85

Language, learning of, 72, 124–26
Larson, Donald N., 125
Latourette, Kenneth Scott, 29

Lausanne Committee for World Evangelization, 47
Lingenfelter, Sherwood, 122, 123–24
Love, Rick, 202
Lyth, David, 133

Magnuson, Douglas, 74, 80, 134–35
Mallouhi, Mazhar, 104
Marintika, Chris, 91, 157, 203
Martyn, Henry, 29
Mathew, Art, 36
Mayers, Marvin, 122
McCurry, Donald M., 158
McGavran, Donald, 19, 31–33, 56, 89, 92
McNee, Peter, 155
McQuilken, J. Robertson, 33
Meeting places, 175–76
Mentors, 128–32
Message systems, cultural, 124–25
Miller, William, 149
Missiology, 39
Mizra, Nate, 235
Molla, Clyde, 39
Mombasa (Kenya), 60–61
Moody Monthly, 39
Mueller, George, 69
Musk, William, 149
Muslim World, The, 55
Muslims
    intellectual approaches to, 139–41
    resistance to Christianity of, 13–14, 44
    view of religion, 96

NAM Associates. *See* Frontiers
National Student Mobilization Coalition, 50
Nationals, 66–68
Navigators, the, 49
Nee, Watchman, 99

Nevius, John L., 171, 175, 176–77
North Africa Mission (NAM). *See*
  Arab World Ministries
North American church
  involvement, 68–72

Olson, Viggo, 91
Operation Mobilization, 41, 50, 51
Otis, George, Jr., 36
Otis, Gerald, 47
Overseas Missionary Fellowship, 51

Parshall, Phil, 19–20, 37, 46, 47,
  55–57, 86, 88, 122, 149, 159, 171,
  172, 179–80, 181, 183, 185, 186,
  201
Pastors, 104
Patterson, George, 53
Paul (the apostle), 29, 71, 80, 90,
  113, 141, 162, 216
People group mentality, 31–32
People International, 52
People movements, 33, 160–65
Persaiuan Melaya-Kristian
  Singapura. *See* Fellowship of
  Singapore Christians Malays
Pfander, Carl Gottleib, 29
Pickett, Robert, 107
Pioneers, 52
Power evangelism, 26, 27
Prayer
  and the church planting team,
    112–13
  and Muslims, 183–84
  as witness, 123
Priscilla, 75, 176
Project Maghgreb, 53
Prophets, 104–5

Quieroz, Edison, 66

RBMU International, 51

Reconciliation, 112, 115
Relationships, establishment of,
  117–37
Richardson, Don, 162
Rickards, Don, 46–47
Riggs, Henry, 55
Rudvin, Arne, 20
Rushi bin Arief, 44

Schaeffer, Francis, 112
Schriber, Kent, 108
Seekers, identification of, 141–46
Servants Fellowship International,
  53
Siemens, Ruth, 49
Silas, 80
SIM International, 20, 47, 51, 52–53
Sinulingga, Thomas, 199, 200
Slimbach, Richard, 164
Smith, Oswald J., 36
Smith, Paul, 93
Southern Baptist Foreign Mission
  Board, 53
Stacey, Vivienne, 45–46
Steele, Frances, 36
Stott, John, 146
Student Missionary Advance, 50
Student Volunteer Movement, 49
Suffering, normativity of, 28

Tag-team evangelism, 113
Teachers, 105–6
Team leaders, 101–2, 114–15
Tent-making ministry, 49, 50, 93,
  227
Theological Students for Frontier
  Missions, 50
Thompson, Allan, 51
Timothy, 75, 80, 91, 113
Tippett, Alan, 25, 31
Titus, 80
Townsend, Cam, 130–31

Training programs, 52–53, 75, 79–80, 185, 192
Trust, 79, 132–37
Turkey, 61–62
Tyndale, William, 99

U.S. Center for World Mission (USCWM), 46, 71
Unlocking the Door, 46
Urbana Missionary Convention, 49

Values, learning of, 126–28
Van der Bijl, Andrew, 99
Verwer, George, 114
Vins, George, 99
Visas
    denial of, 76–77
    obtaining, 77–78, 97–99

Wagner, Peter, 19, 36
WEC International, 51

West Java, 30, 57–60, 156–57
Wiebe, Abe, 29
Wilder, John, 45
Willis, Avery, 57–60, 156, 196
Wilson, Christy, 49, 93
Wimber, John, 27
Winter, Ralph, 19, 43, 50, 93, 169
Woodbury, Dudley, 26, 93
World Evangelical Outreach. *See* Pioneers
World Home Bible League, 60
World Vision, 46, 48
Worldteam, 51, 52
Wycliffe Bible Translators, 53

Youth With a Mission (YWAM), 50, 54

Zwemer Institute for Muslim Studies, 47
Zwemer, Samuel, 55